THE LEGO® BOOK

LONDON, NEW YORK,
MELBOURNE, MUNICH, DELHI

For DK
Senior Editor Alastair Dougall
Senior Designer Lisa Sodeau
Designers Owen Bennett, Jon Hall, Mark Richards, and Clive Savage
Design Manager Ron Stobbart
Publishing Manager Catherine Saunders
Art Director Lisa Lanzarini
Publisher Simon Beecroft
Publishing Director Alex Allan
Pre-Production Producer Andy Hilliard
Producer Louise Daly
Senior Producer Melanie Mikellides

For the LEGO Group
Head of the LEGO Idea House Jette Orduna
Assistant Licensing Manager Randi Kirsten Sørensen

For Tall Tree
Editors Rob Colson and Jon Richards
Designers Malcolm Parchment, Ben Ruocco, and Ed Simkins

First published in Great Britain in 2009. This revised edition published in 2012 by Dorling Kindersley Limited
80 Strand, London WC2R ORL.
Penguin Group (UK)
10 9 8 7 6 5 4 3 2 1
001-185969-09/12

THE LEGO® BOOK

Written by
Daniel Lipkowitz

Contents

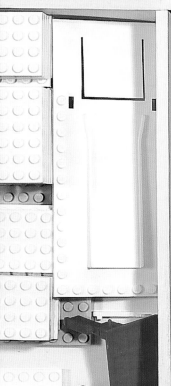

An inspirational leaflet from 1959 shows children some of the countless things they can build with their LEGO bricks.

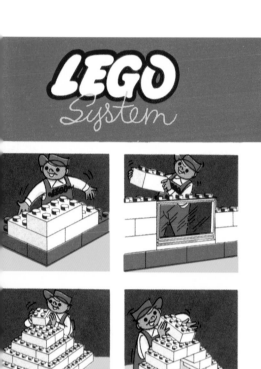

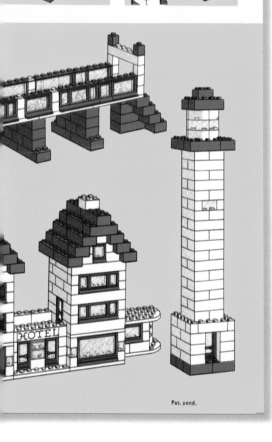

Pat. pend.

Foreword

Dear Reader,

On January 28, 1958, the LEGO Group patented the LEGO® brick with its now well-known tubes inside and studs on top. That day marked the beginning of an adventure that we are still on.

Although the LEGO brick is now more than 50 years old, it is as young as ever. We are often asked why the LEGO brick continues to inspire and excite children and adults all over the world. I can think of at least three reasons.

First of all, it's a new toy every day. The possibilities for play really are endless. With just six 2x4 LEGO bricks of the same color, you can build more than 915 million different creations. So LEGO play never stops. A police station today can become a space rocket tomorrow.

Secondly, it's more than a toy; the LEGO brick has educational applications. Of course, children don't deliberately look for a toy that will develop their skills and capabilities. They want a fun toy. But playing with a toy that gives you a real feeling of achievement and pride is fun. LEGO play gives you that feeling. And meanwhile you develop your motor, social, and creative skills—and your curiosity. You develop systematic creativity. That is what we call playful learning.

Thirdly, LEGO bricks foster collaboration and social skills. If you gather together children of different nationalities, who don't understand each other's language, and give them LEGO bricks to play with, they will instinctively begin to build and play with each other. The LEGO brick is a global language!

This book is packed with information about the company that invented the LEGO brick and all the fantastic creations that have so far come from it. There are many, many more creations to come.

What will *you* make next?

Happy reading.

Jørgen Vig Knudstorp
Chief Executive Officer of the LEGO Group

"Only the Best..."

"ONLY THE BEST IS GOOD ENOUGH."

That was the motto of LEGO Group founder Ole Kirk Kristiansen, and he believed in it so strongly that his son Godtfred Kirk Christiansen carved it on a sign and hung it on his father's carpentry workshop's wall. Ole Kirk believed that children deserved to have toys made with the highest quality materials and workmanship, and he was determined that the toys manufactured in his workshop would last and remain just as fun through years of play. Today, the words of the company's founder remain its driving force, and LEGO® products continue to be passed down from one generation to the next, sparking the creativity and imaginations of millions of children and adults all over the world ●

Carved in Danish as a reminder to his employees to never skimp on quality, Ole Kirk's motto has been a guiding principle for the LEGO Group for more than 75 years.

Workers pose for a photograph, taken in the late 1940s. Above their heads, Ole Kirk's motto is proudly displayed upon the workshop wall.

A Family Business

THROUGH THREE generations of family ownership and family management, the LEGO Group has grown from a small local company into one of the world´s leading providers of creative, developmental play products. Each generation has contributed to the LEGO® brand's expansion and continued success ●

Ole Kirk Kristiansen recreates the patterns for the wooden LEGO duck in 1943 after a fire the previous year destroyed the LEGO workshop and all of the company's designs.

AN IMAGE OF HOPE

The year 1932 was a difficult one for company founder Ole Kirk Kristiansen, combining Europe's economic depression, looming bankruptcy, and deep personal loss at the death of his wife. While bringing up four young sons on his own, Ole Kirk created a new business: making wooden toys. The years that followed were little easier, often forcing him to borrow money from his family to keep his workshop afloat and maintain his standards for creating the finest possible wooden toys.

This wooden plane is a reconstruction of the one on top of the ladder in the photograph on the left. Today, it symbolizes the company's ability to rise above adversity.

Workers pose with a range of the first wooden toys in 1932. "It was not until the day that I said to myself, you must choose between your carpentry and the toys that things started to make sense," Ole Kirk recalled.

CHILDREN DESERVE THE BEST

The company's toys needed to work and work well, even in the hands of the most enthusiastically active child. From the very start, Ole Kirk was dedicated to quality. He worked under the self-coined motto "Only the best is good enough," and his sons and employees were often reminded that "This is the way we do things" at the LEGO workshop. By choosing a name contracted from "LEg GOdt," or "Play Well" in Danish, Ole Kirk emphasized that the LEGO name needed to represent a standard of quality that would set the company apart from its competitors.

Ole Kirk and his son Godtfred examine a wooden LEGO farm in the late 1940s.

A SYSTEM OF PLAY

Godtfred Kirk Christiansen (GKC) continued his father's philosophy when, under his leadership, the company changed to concentrate on the new LEGO System of Play in 1955. The need to constantly improve product quality led him to develop the LEGO brick's unique "clutch" principle, and better materials and production technology maintained its precise shape. Godtfred Kirk was a firm believer in the LEGO code of "good play," and in 1963, he introduced the "10 important characteristics" for future LEGO product development.

GKC's Watchwords for the LEGO System

- Unlimited play possibilities
- For girls, for boys
- Enthusiasm for all ages
- Play all year round
- Healthy and quiet play
- Endless hours of play
- Imagination, creativity, development
- Each new product multiplies the play value of the rest
- Always topical
- Safety and quality

Ole Kirk Kristiansen, Godtfred Kirk Christiansen, and Kjeld Kirk Kristiansen at Ole Kirk's 60th birthday party in 1951. Three generations building on each other's achievements!

From early on, Kjeld Kirk Kristiansen realized the potential of LEGO bricks and built his own models, some of which became official sets. Here, Kjeld and his father discuss one of Kjeld's models in 1978.

> "Children mean everything to us. Children and their development. And this must pervade everything we do."
>
> Kjeld Kirk Kristiansen, 1996

FOCUS ON CHILDREN

Third-generation company owner Kjeld Kirk Kristiansen created a "system within the system" with his own model for product development, establishing a division to provide each age group of customers with the right toys at the right time in their lives. Kjeld Kirk Kristiansen believed strongly in the LEGO brand and became a driving force to change the consumer's perception of it from just a great construction toy to a world-recognized icon of quality, creativity, and learning. In 1996 he explained: "My grandfather's main drive was the perfection of quality craftsmanship. My father's main focus was on our unique product idea with all its inherent possibilities. I see myself as a more globally oriented leader, seeking to fully exploit our brand potential for further developing and broadening our product range and business concept, based upon our product idea and brand values."

Wooden Toys

Yo-yos (1932)

Launched in 1932 as one of the workshop's first wooden toys, the yo-yo enjoyed a brief period of great popularity. When the craze and sales declined, the remaining stock was recycled into wheels for other toys, like the pull-along pony and trap below.

Pony and Trap (1937)

THE STORY of one of the world's most successful toy companies began in 1916 when Danish master carpenter Ole Kirk Kristiansen bought a workshop in the little town of Billund and set up a business building houses and furniture. In 1932, with the worldwide Great Depression threatening to close his carpentry shop for good, Ole Kirk turned his skills to creating a range of toys for children. These beautifully made and painted playthings included yo-yos, wooden blocks, pull-along animals, and vehicles of all kinds ●

PULL-ALONG TOYS

During the 1930s and 1940s, the company had great success with its wide range of pull-along wooden toy animals for young children. Produced in several different color schemes, this rolling duck, painted to resemble a male mallard, was one of the most popular early LEGO toys.

WOODEN BLOCKS

Decorated with colorful painted letters and numbers, LEGO wooden blocks could be stacked and arranged into words to help young children learn the alphabet and spelling. Forerunners of the plastic brick (which appeared in 1949), these blocks date from 1946.

Duck (1935)

Beak opens and shuts as wheels turn

"Clumsy Hans" (1936)

"CLUMSY HANS"

From the popular "Klods-Hans" fairy tale by Danish writer and poet Hans Christian Andersen, Clumsy Hans bobs up and down on his billy goat as you pull this toy along.

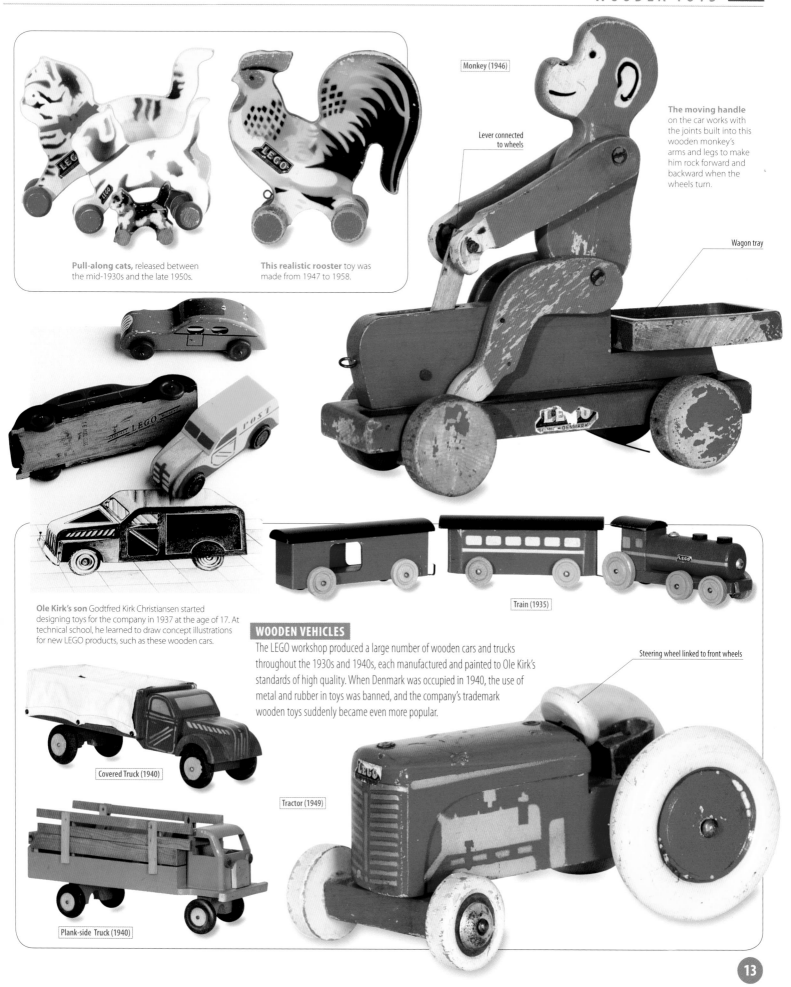

Pull-along cats, released between the mid-1930s and the late 1950s.

This realistic rooster toy was made from 1947 to 1958.

Monkey (1946)

Lever connected to wheels

The moving handle on the car works with the joints built into this wooden monkey's arms and legs to make him rock forward and backward when the wheels turn.

Wagon tray

Ole Kirk's son Godtfred Kirk Christiansen started designing toys for the company in 1937 at the age of 17. At technical school, he learned to draw concept illustrations for new LEGO products, such as these wooden cars.

Train (1935)

WOODEN VEHICLES

The LEGO workshop produced a large number of wooden cars and trucks throughout the 1930s and 1940s, each manufactured and painted to Ole Kirk's standards of high quality. When Denmark was occupied in 1940, the use of metal and rubber in toys was banned, and the company's trademark wooden toys suddenly became even more popular.

Covered Truck (1940)

Plank-side Truck (1940)

Tractor (1949)

Steering wheel linked to front wheels

13

Plastic Toys

IN 1947, Ole Kirk purchased a plastic injection-molding machine imported from Britain. One of the first in Denmark, the machine cost DKK 30,000, one-15th of the company's entire earnings for the year. Plastic toys were expensive to manufacture, but the risk paid off: by 1951, half of the company's toys were made from plastic ●

One of the company's first plastic toys was a baby's rattle shaped like a fish. Blending different plastic colors inside the molding machine gave it an eye-catching marbled appearance.

LEGO Mursten (1953)

The slits in the bricks enabled builders to insert windows and doors.

BIRTH OF A BRICK

The first LEGO® bricks were produced in 1949 under the name "Automatic Binding Bricks." At first, they were just a handful out of about 200 plastic and wooden toys the company manufactured. Made from cellulose acetate, they resembled today's bricks but had slits on their sides and were completely hollow underneath, without tubes to lock them together. In 1953, they were renamed LEGO Mursten ("LEGO Bricks").

The boy in the white shirt is Ole Kirk's grandson, Kjeld Kirk Kristiansen; the girl is his sister.

CARS AND TRUCKS

A new series of realistic plastic cars based on real auto models started in 1958 with the launch of the company-wide LEGO System of Play. Designed to complement the new Town Plan sets, many of the vehicles included bases and display containers with studs for attaching LEGO bricks.

262 Opel Rekord with Garage (1961)

This plastic car came in a transparent display case with an opening door and LEGO System studs on top.

260 VW Beetle (1958)

Produced in various colors and sizes between 1957 and 1967, the VW Beetle could also be purchased with a showcase box that included a LEGO brick VW logo plate.

CARS AND TRUCKS

With the new plastics technology came the ability to design and produce toys with much greater detail and accuracy than ever before. Colorful cars and trucks were a popular product among children, who could collect and play with all the latest models and styles.

Colorful artwork decorates the box of this 1950s Chevrolet truck collection.

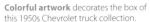

Many toys combined plastic with other materials. This Esso fuel truck had a plastic cab and a painted wooden trailer.

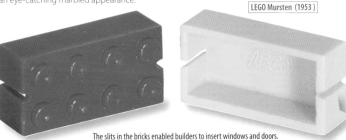

SAMLESÆT TIL *Ferguson* MODEL TRAKTOR

FREMSTILLET AF LEGO · DANMARK

The real Ferguson Model TE20 tractor (nicknamed the "Little Grey Fergie"), illustrated here on the toy's new 1953 packaging, was manufactured from 1946 to 1956.

Just like the real thing, the LEGO Ferguson Tractor was designed to pull a variety of farming attachments.

Originally sold fully assembled, the tractor was released again in 1953 with the option of putting it together yourself.

FERGUSON TRACTOR (1952)

One of the company's biggest early successes in plastic toys was the Ferguson Tractor. Its highly-detailed plastic-injection mold cost as much to make as the price of a real tractor, but with 75,000 pieces sold in its first year alone, the gamble quickly paid off. The increasing popularity of industrialized farming in Europe meant that the Ferguson Tractor arrived during a time when more and more farmers were switching from horses to tractors, making it a must-have toy for the 1950s child. The profits that the toy tractor earned made it possible for the company to invest in its still new and unproven plastic bricks.

Realistic color scheme

Ferguson logo

Front wheels connected to steering wheel

Detailed wheels and rubber tires

Work Hard, Play Well

THE LEGO GROUP has been making its famous bricks for over half a century, but its story doesn't begin there. Presented here is a timeline of the company's earliest days, from the birth of its founder, to its humble beginnings in a carpentry workshop in the Danish village of Billund, the move to producing wooden and then plastic toys, the birth of the first LEGO® bricks, and the dawn of the revolutionary LEGO System of Play ●

Ole Kirk aged 20 years old.

1891
● Ole Kirk, founder of the LEGO Group, is born at Omvrå near Filskov, not far from the village of Billund in Denmark.

Ole Kirk's 1936 motto for the company.

1935
● The business manufactures the first LEGO wooden duck, and markets "Kirk's Sandgame," its first construction toy.

1936
● Ole Kirk coins the company motto, "Only the best is good enough." His son Godtfred Kirk Christiansen carves Ole Kirk's motto and hangs it on the workshop wall.

1937
● Godtfred Kirk Christiansen begins designing models for the company at the age of 17.

1939
● The LEGO factory hires its 10th employee.

1942
● A fire destroys the factory and Ole Kirk's life's work. A new toy factory is built, and he remakes all of the lost designs himself.

1950
● On his 30th birthday, Godtfred Kirk Christiansen is appointed Junior Managing Director of the company.

1952
● The LEGO Ferguson tractor is released.
● A building base with 10 x 20 studs is sold for use with the interlocking bricks.

1952
● A new LEGO manufacturing plant is built at the cost of DKK 350,000.

1953
● "Automatic Binding Bricks" are renamed "LEGO Bricks" ("LEGO Mursten" in Danish). The LEGO name is molded onto every brick.

Some of Ole Kirk's tools.

1916
● Ole Kirk buys the Billund Joinery Manufacturing and Carpentry Workshop and sets up business as a self-employed carpenter and joiner.

1924
● Ole Kirk's three sons play with matches and the workshop burns down! He builds a larger one, renting out the remaining space.

1932
● Ole Kirk starts to manufacture and sell wooden toys.

1934
● Ole Kirk holds a competition among his employees to name the company, with a bottle of wine as the prize. He wins it himself with the name "LEGO," short for "LEg GOdt," or "Play Well" in Danish. Coincidentally, the word can also mean "I put together" in Latin.

Illustrations of animals and people added more possibilities.

AUTOMATIC BINDING BRICKS
The first bricks have no logo

1943
● The company gains its 43rd employee.

1946
● New LEGO products include wooden blocks with painted letters and numbers.

1947
● Ole Kirk imports a plastic injection-molding machine from the UK.
● The company produces its first plastic toys, including a ball for infants and Monopoli, an educational road safety game.

1948
● The firm now employs 50 people.
● New products include a pinball game.

1949
● "Automatic Binding Bricks," the company's first plastic interlocking bricks, are produced. The company now makes about 200 plastic and wooden toys, including a new plastic fish and sailor.

1954
● The name "LEGO" is officially registered in Denmark.
● The first brick-compatible LEGO window and door elements are produced.
● Godtfred Kirk Christiansen has the idea of creating a LEGO System of Play based around the amazingly versatile LEGO brick.

1955
● The System of Play is launched with the release of the Town Plan range of 28 construction sets and eight vehicles.

The LEGO® System of Play

The first LEGO System set was "Town Plan No. 1." Appearing on its packaging was young Kjeld Kirk Kristiansen, son of GKC and the grandson of company founder Ole Kirk Kristiansen.

1954 WAS A YEAR in which Godtfred Kirk Christiansen (GKC) did a lot of thinking about the future of the LEGO Group. Returning from a toy fair in Britain, he got talking to a colleague, who pointed out that there was no *system* in the toy industry. That was all the inspiration GKC needed. He decided to create a structured system of products. Reviewing all the toys made by the company, he saw that the LEGO® brick was the best choice for this project. The LEGO System of Play launched the following year with the Town Plan range of construction sets ●

Of the System of Play, GKC wrote: "Our idea is to create a toy that prepares the child for life, appeals to the imagination, and develops the creative urge and joy of creation that are the driving force in every human being."

Town Plan No.1 (1955)

Additional Town Plan boards were sold separately

A GROWING SYSTEM

The idea behind the LEGO System was that every element should connect to every other element; the more bricks, the more building possibilities. With Town Plan, children could make their towns bigger and better with each new set, and thanks to the included extra building ideas (pictured below left), they could make more than just what was pictured on the box.

Pre-assembled, realistic 1950s cars and trucks

HOTEL

TOWN PLAN

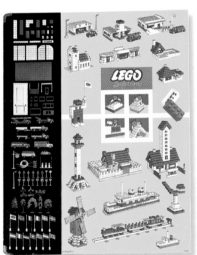

The original Town Plan No. 1 set included everything children needed to assemble their own realistic town centers, from a colorful street board to citizens, cars and trucks, and lots of red, white, and blue LEGO bricks. The first street boards were soft plastic; they were changed to wooden fiberboard in 1956.

A NEW TOWN PLAN

In 2008, the company celebrated the 50th anniversary of the patenting of the modern LEGO brick with a new version of the classic Town Plan set. The special-edition set let kids and collectors create a town center from the 1950s, with a movie theater, gas station, and town hall.

In honor of the LEGO brick's golden anniversary, the set included three metallic gold bricks built into the town's central fountain.

Kjeld Kirk Kristiansen, now the owner of the company, reprised his childhood starring role by appearing on the new Town Plan set's packaging.

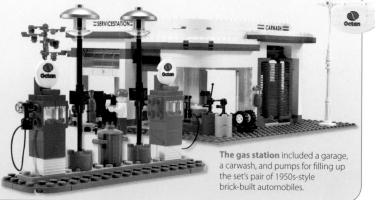

Built from 1,981 pieces, 10184 Town Plan (2008) included a newly-married minifigure bride and groom, elements in rare shapes and colors, and a letter from Kjeld Kirk Kristiansen. Its movie theater had a ticket booth, seats, a popcorn machine, and LEGO themed posters.

The gas station included a garage, a carwash, and pumps for filling up the set's pair of 1950s-style brick-built automobiles.

Detailed traffic signs

Painted crossing guards directed traffic

Esso gas station

TREES AND TRAFFIC SAFETY

Town Plan models came with pre-molded and painted trees, people, vehicles, and road signs. Produced in collaboration with the Danish Road Safety Council, the sets helped teach traffic safety to children in an era when automobile ownership was steeply on the rise.

A Worldwide System

THANKS TO THE NEW LEGO® System of Play, the company was no longer just another toy manufacturer. It now had a unique brand identity all its own, and a mission to bring its message of creative fun to the rest of the world. It wasn't easy to convince the first few international markets to gamble on importing plastic bricks, but by the end of the 1960s, the LEGO name was known in every household, with sets for preschoolers and even its very own theme park ●

1956
● The first foreign sales company, LEGO Spielwaren GmbH, is founded in Hohenweststedt in Germany.

Fire destroys the wooden toy stock.

Production concentrates on plastic products.

1958
● Ole Kirk passes away and Godtfred Kirk Christiansen becomes head of the company.
● The company now has 140 employees.
● The first sloping roof-tile bricks are produced.

1959
● The LEGO Futura department is established to conceive, plan, and oversee the design of new LEGO sets.
● LEGO divisions are founded in France, the UK, Belgium, and Sweden.
● New products include BILOfix wood and plastic construction toys.

1960
● A fire destroys the workshop where the company's wooden toys are made. A decision is made to stop making wooden toys and focus entirely on the LEGO System.
● LEGO divisions are established in Finland and the Netherlands. Approximately 400 employees now work at the company headquarters in Billund.

The 1966 version has a 4.5 volt motor

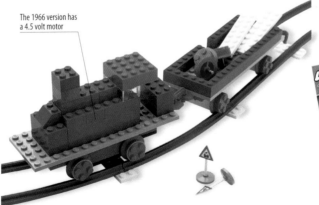

Just one of 1967's millions of LEGO sets.

1964
● LEGO model sets with building instructions are produced.
● LEGO products are sold in the Middle East.
● LEGO bricks are exhibited at the Danish pavilion of the New York World Fair.
● The Ole Kirk Foundation is established to help support the arts and other cultural activities.

1965
● LEGO product sales start in Spain.
● The company now has more than 600 employees.

1966
● The first battery-powered LEGO Train sets are launched.
● LEGO products are now sold in 42 countries.
● The first official LEGO Club begins in Canada.

1967
● More than 18 million LEGO sets are sold during the year.
● The LEGO® DUPLO® building system is patented in August.
● There are now 218 different LEGO element shapes.
● A LEGO Club is founded in Sweden.

The LEGO brick patent application.

The new interlocking brick

1957
- The LEGO Group celebrates its Silver Jubilee.
- New products include bricks with light-bulbs and VW Beetles in eight colors.

1957
- The LEGO brick is updated with a new stud-and-tube interlocking system that increases building possibilities and improves model stability.

1958
- The LEGO brick's interlocking principle is patented at 1:58 pm on January 28th.

The LEGO airplane at Billund Airstrip.

The launch of LEGO bricks in the US.

1961
- The design for a LEGO wheel is discovered in a product developer's drawer. Wheels are released the next year, letting children build rolling vehicles of all kinds.

1961
- Godtfred Kirk Christiansen buys a small airplane, and a landing field is built outside Billund.
- LEGO sales begin in the US and Canada through a license agreement with the Samsonite Corp. luggage company.
- The first LEGO preschool lines are launched: Terapi I, II, and III.
- LEGO Italy is established.

1962
- LEGO products are first sold in Singapore, Hong Kong, Australia, Morocco, and Japan.
- LEGO Australia is established.

1963
- ABS (acrylonitrile butadiene styrene) replaces cellulose acetate as the material used to make LEGO bricks. It is more color-fast and allows better molding.
- Billund airport officially opens.
- LEGO Austria is established.

LEGO DUPLO bricks were eight times the size of original bricks.

Tiny fingers. Big blocks. LEGO DUPLO from 18 months.

1968
- The first LEGOLAND® park opens in Billund on June 7th. 625,000 people visit in the first year.
- LEGO DUPLO bricks are test-marketed in Sweden.

1969
- The LEGO DUPLO range for children under five years old is launched internationally.
- A 12-volt motor is added to the LEGO Train series.

Bricks for Everyone

THE 1970s saw LEGO® products branch out in new ways. Creating construction toys that girls, boys, and experienced builders of all ages would enjoy became a key goal, and all of the company's products and brands were brought together under an iconic new logo. LEGO people appeared for the first time, leading up to the minifigures that LEGO fans know today, and the classic LEGO Play Themes were born ●

1970

● The company now has almost 1,000 employees in Billund.
● Small car sets are sold at pocket-money prices.

US Presidents Washington, Jefferson, Roosevelt, and Lincoln

1974

● The first LEGO people are released, with round heads, movable arms, and bodies built from bricks.
● The best-selling #200 LEGO Family set included a father, mother, son, daughter, and grandmother.

1974

● A brick replica of Mount Rushmore is constructed in LEGOLAND® Billund by Danish artist Bjørn Richter.
● The park receives its 5 millionth visitor.
● LEGO Spain is established.

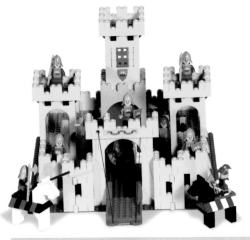

1978

● The first three LEGO Play Themes are introduced.
● The LEGO Castle theme features medieval knights and castles.

1978

● The first modern-style minifigures with printed faces and movable arms and legs appear.
● The LEGO Town theme lets children build modern buildings and vehicles.
● LEGO baseplates with road markings are produced.

1978

● The LEGO Space theme lets builders' imaginations run wild with outer space adventures.
● A LEGO Club is founded in the UK with a magazine titled *Bricks 'n' Pieces*.
● LEGO Japan is established.

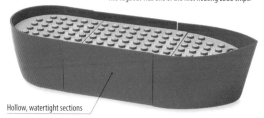

The tugboat was one of the first floating LEGO ships.

Hollow, watertight sections

1971
● LEGO sets for girls are launched, including dolls' houses and furniture.

1972
● 1.8 billion LEGO bricks and other elements have been produced.

1973
● A new LEGO logo unifies all of the company's products

1973
● The first LEGO ship designed to float is released.
● LEGO Systems Inc. USA and LEGO Portugal are established.

The Expert Series featured more realistic details for experienced builders.

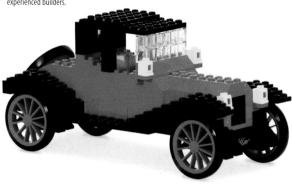

DUPLO figures came with different colors and faces.

1975
● The Expert Series of vintage car models is released.
● The LEGO Group now has 2,500 employees.
● LEGO USA moves from Brookfield, Connecticut, to its present location of Enfield, Connecticut.
● A new, smaller LEGO figure is launched with a blank face and non-moving arms and legs.

1977
● The LEGO Technic series of mechanical models is launched.

1977
● LEGO® DUPLO® sets with door, window, and figure elements are launched.

Nu kan hun lave sine egne smykker - igen og igen.

Scala

LEGO SCALA featured necklaces and bracelets that girls could build and customize.

The animal-headed characters of LEGO FABULAND sets had easy-to-construct buildings and vehicles.

1979
● Kjeld Kirk Kristiansen, Godtfred Kirk Christiansen's son and Ole Kirk's grandson, is appointed President and Chief Executive Officer of the company.

1979
● New products include the FABULAND™ series for young builders and LEGO® SCALA™ jewelry.

Building the Future

IN THE 1980s, the company invested heavily in technology, education, and the global community. It sponsored international events like building competitions and awards, developed durable new products for infants and toddlers, created special sets for school programs, and incorporated light and sound into many of its models. New products included buckets full of LEGO® pieces for creative building without instructions, the LEGO Maniac ruled the television screen, and the LEGO Pirates set sail ●

1980
- The LEGO Educational Products Department is established in Billund.
- The LEGO® DUPLO® rabbit logo is used for the first time.
- 70% of Western European families with children under 14 now have LEGO bricks in their home.

Posable arms and legs

1983
- The LEGO DUPLO Baby series is launched, along with new big DUPLO figures with movable arms and legs.
- The company now has 3,700 employees worldwide.

1984
- The first international LEGO building competition is held in Billund. Children from 11 countries take part.
- LEGO Brazil and LEGO Korea are established.
- LEGO Castle gains its first factions: the Black Falcons and Crusaders.

1985
- The LEGO Prize is founded as an international annual award for exceptional efforts on behalf of children anywhere in the world.
- The company has about 5,000 employees worldwide.

1986
- LEGO Technic Computer Control launches in schools.
- The LEGO Technic figure is created.
- The LEGO Group is granted the title "Purveyor to Her Majesty the Queen" on April 16, the birthday of Queen Margrethe of Denmark.

1987
- New products include the motorized LEGO Space Monorail Transport System
- *Brick Kicks*, the official LEGO Club magazine, is mailed to the homes of LEGO Club members across the US.

1988
- The first official LEGO World Cup building championships are held in Billund in August. 38 children from 14 countries take part.
- The "Art of LEGO" exhibition tours the United Kingdom.
- LEGO Canada is established.

1988
- The "LEGO Maniac" bursts on the scene in a series of TV commercials with a memorable tune, becoming a LEGO mascot for years to come.

1981
- The first LEGO World Show takes place in Denmark.

1982
- The LEGO Group celebrates its 50th anniversary.
- The LEGO DUPLO Mosaic and LEGO Technic I educational lines launch.
- LEGO South Africa is established.

NEW

Bricks in buckets.

Here they are: The big new LEGO® and DUPLO buckets.
A special offer for more elements. And much space to store a lot more.

1986
- Electronic Light & Sound kits are added to LEGO Town and LEGO Space.

1987
- The LEGO Club starts in Germany, Austria, Switzerland, France, and Norway.
- Buckets are sold containing basic LEGO and LEGO DUPLO elements.
- Launch of the Space sub-themes Blacktron and Futuron.

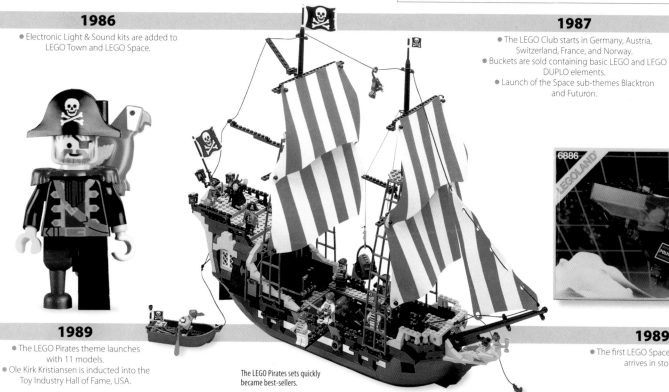

1989
- The LEGO Pirates theme launches with 11 models.
- Ole Kirk Kristiansen is inducted into the Toy Industry Hall of Fame, USA.

The LEGO Pirates sets quickly became best-sellers.

1989
- The first LEGO Space Police series arrives in stores.

LEGO® Catalogs

SINCE THE DEBUT of the LEGO® System of Play, the company's mission has been to let parents and children know about all of the different ways to play with LEGO bricks. For decades, colorful, informative, and fun-filled LEGO brand catalogs have displayed all of the very latest exciting LEGO sets and themes. Here is just a small selection of catalogs, all of which have inspired, or continue to inspire, LEGO fans around the world to new heights of creativity ●

1959

1974

1963

1981

1984

1969

1981

1993

1997

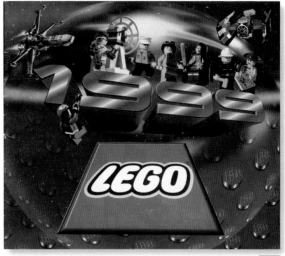

1999

2004

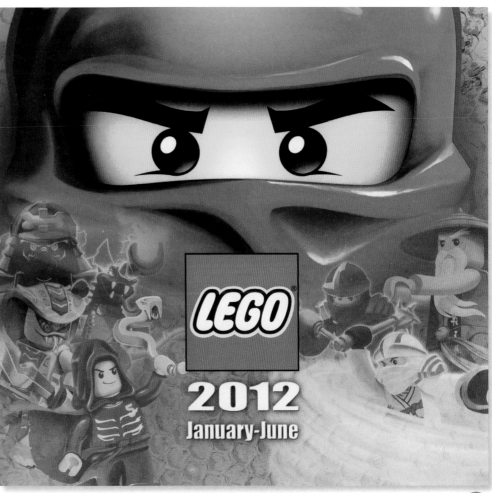

2012
January-June

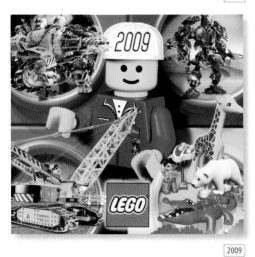

2009

2012

Full Speed Ahead!

THE 1990s were a time of big risks for a company that had become one of the world's largest toy manufacturers. The decade saw the opening of stores that sold only LEGO® products, a branded clothing shop, the first LEGO video games, the launch of the official LEGO website, the release of a high-tech building system for constructing programmable robots, and a leap into licensed themes with the record-smashing debut of LEGO® *Star Wars*™ ●

1990

- The LEGO Group is now one of the world's ten largest toy manufacturers, and the only one of the ten in Europe.
- LEGOLAND® Billund gets over 1 million visitors in a single year.
- LEGO Malaysia is established.
- The Model Team series and the LEGO® DUPLO® Zoo are launched.

DUPLO PRIMO figures

1993

- A LEGO building event takes place in Red Square in Moscow, Russia.
- LEGO Space travels to the Ice Planet 2002.

1994

- The United Nations Commission on Human Rights (UNCHR) uses LEGO minifigures as part of an awareness campaign.
- The LEGO® BELVILLE™ line of building sets for girls is released.
- LEGO Mexico is established.
- LEGO products are advertised on Chinese television for the first time.
- The company has 8,880 employees worldwide.
- *Brick Kicks* becomes *LEGO Mania* magazine.

1995

- Godtfred Kirk Christiansen passes away.
- Weekly LEGO programs air on TV in Latvia and Lithuania.
- LEGO events and exhibitions take place in Latvia, Peru, Hungary, Switzerland, Denmark, Greenland, the US, Canada, Italy, and Ecuador.
- LEGO Aquazone and DUPLO® PRIMO™ are launched.

1997

- More than 300,000 children take part in a LEGO building event at Kremlin Palace in Moscow, Russia.
- The LEGO Kids Wear shop opens in Oxford Street, London, UK.

1998

- The company adopts the slogan "Just Imagine…"
- Japanese Emperor Akihito and Empress Michiko visit LEGOLAND Billund.
- The LEGO® MINDSTORMS® and Znap lines launch.

1998

- The LEGO logo is updated.
- The LEGO Space Insectoids appear.
- The LEGO Adventurers explore Egypt.

1991

- The company now has 7,550 employees and 1,000 injection-molding machines at the five LEGO factories.
- New products include the LEGO Town Harbor sets, Technic flex-system elements, and transformer-controlled 9-volt trains.

1991

- The LEGO System Brick Vac helps pick bricks up off the floor.
- The LEGO Town Nautica series starts.

1992

- The first LEGO Imagination Center opens at the Mall of America in Bloomington, Minneapolis, USA.
- The world's largest LEGO Castle is built on Swedish television out of more than 400,000 bricks.
- The second LEGO World Cup Final in Billund features 32 children competing from 11 countries.
- Paradisa and Res-Q sets are released for LEGO Town.

Fort LEGOREDO, the wildest Wild West set of them all!

1996

- LEGOLAND® Windsor opens in the UK.
- The official LEGO website, www.LEGO.com, goes online.
- LEGOLAND Billund receives its 25-millionth visitor.

1996

- LEGO Western and LEGO Time Cruisers are launched.

1997

- The *LEGO Island* computer game is released.
- A new LEGO Imagination Center opens in Disney Village, Florida, USA.
- The first LEGO® MINDSTORMS® Learning Center opens at the Museum of Science and Industry in Chicago, Illinois, USA.

The first year's sets included models from the classic trilogy and the brand-new prequel movie.

1999

- LEGOLAND® California opens in Carlsbad, CA, USA.
- Fortune Magazine names the LEGO brick one of the "Products of the Century."
- The LEGO World Shop opens at www.LEGO.com.
- New LEGO themes include Rock Raiders, LEGO® DUPLO® Winnie the Pooh and Friends™, and one of the biggest ever: LEGO® *Star Wars*™.

New Worlds to Discover

LICENSES ABOUNDED during the first few years of the new millennium, as everything from super heroes to talking sponges moved from the big and small screens to the construction toy aisle. The first LEGO® figures based on real people were produced, changing the familiar yellow face of the minifigure forever. The company even created its own new worlds with original science fiction and fantasy themes complete with stories that were told through books, comics, and movies ●

2000
- The British Association of Toy Retailers names the LEGO brick "Toy of the Century."
- LEGO Studios launches, letting budding film-makers build and animate their own LEGO movies.
- The LEGO Sports theme launches with LEGO Soccer/Football.
- Disney's Baby Mickey™ sets are released.

2002
- LEGOLAND® Deutschland opens in Günzburg.
- "Play On" replaces "Just Imagine…" as the company slogan.
- LEGO® Spider-Man™ swings into action to accompany the new movie.

2002
- *LEGO Mania* magazine becomes *LEGO Magazine*.
- LEGO Spybotics sets invade homes.
- LEGO® DUPLO® becomes LEGO Explore and introduces LEGO® Bob the Builder™ sets.
- LEGO Brand Retail stores open in Germany, England, and Russia.

2002
- Galidor: Defenders of the Outer Dimension, based on the TV series, features action figures with swappable body parts.
- LEGO Island Xtreme Stunts sets based on the video game arrive.
- LEGO Racers teams compete in the Racing Drome, with an accompanying video game.

2003
- The LEGO minifigure celebrates its 25th birthday.
- LEGO Sports NBA Basketball and Hockey sets join the game.

2004
- LEGO EXPLORE is replaced by three building systems for the very young: LEGO DUPLO, BABY, and QUATRO.
- The US LEGO Club creates the premium LEGO BrickMaster program.

2004
- LEGO Factory lets builders create models online and buy the pieces to make them.
- The LEGO Group partners with Ferrari to create a line of licensed LEGO Racers sets.
- Several traditional LEGO brick colors are retired and new colors are introduced.
- LEGO Dora the Explorer sets explore the globe.

2005
- The LEGO System of Play celebrates its 50th anniversary.
- The LEGOLAND parks are sold to the Merlin Entertainments Group. The LEGO Group owners maintain a shareholding in Merlin Entertainments Group.
- The first LEGO® *Star Wars*™ videogame is released to rave reviews.
- The third BIONICLE movie, *Web of Shadows*, is released on DVD.
- LEGO World City is renamed LEGO City.
- LEGO Dino Attack and LEGO Dino 2010 roar to life.

2005
- LEGO DUPLO introduces Thomas and Friends™ building sets.
- The LEGO Vikings set sail.
- The LEGO Group sets up its LEGO Ambassador program to create closer ties between the company and adult LEGO fans.

2000

- The LEGO KNIGHTS' KINGDOM series launches.
- LEGO Writing office and school supplies are introduced.
- LEGO Mosaic lets you create your face in LEGO bricks.
- Action Wheelers brings racing action into younger hands.
- LEGO Arctic unleashes the first LEGO polar bear.
- The LEGO Adventurers travel to Dino Island.

2001

- The BIONICLE® line launches worldwide with a huge publicity campaign.
- The magic of LEGO® Harry Potter™ begins.
- Jack Stone rescues his city from natural disasters in a new "4 Plus" figure scale for younger builders.
- The LEGO Dinosaurs line is hatched.

2001

- LEGO® SERIOUS PLAY™ is founded to help businesses learn creative thinking through the use of LEGO bricks and building.
- Life on Mars takes LEGO Space to the Red Planet.

2001

- The LEGO Alpha Team battles to save the world from the evil Ogel.
- LEGO Racers starts its engine with a line of crashing mini-cars with alien drivers.

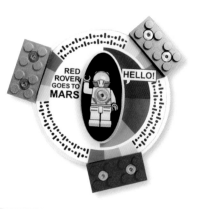

Kids could build a jungle for Dora and Diego to explore.

2003

- LEGO Discovery NASA sets based on modern space exploration are released. LEGO Minifigure astrobots Biff Starling and Sandy Moondust—or pictures of them, at least—become the first Earthlings to reach the planet Mars aboard the NASA rovers *Spirit* and *Opportunity*.
- LEGO Town becomes LEGO World City.

2003

- The CLIKITS™ line of buildable jewelry is released.
- The BIONICLE film *Mask of Light* is released to DVD.
- LEGO Designer and LEGO Gravity Games lines are launched.
- A record-breaking 1.63 million people visit LEGOLAND Billund.

2003

- LEGO® Dora the Explorer™ sets are released under LEGO Explore.
- Little Robots™ toys are released in Europe based on the TV series.
- www.LEGO.com receives about 4 million visitors per month.

2004

- The second LEGO KNIGHTS' KINGDOM series features an original story, complete with story and activity books, online comics and a collectible card game.
- *BIONICLE 2: Legends of Metru Nui* is released on DVD.

2005

- LEGO *Star Wars*: Revenge of the Brick airs on television.
- LEGO Racers shrinks race cars down into pocket-sized Tiny Turbos.

2006

- The new LEGO® EXO-FORCE™ theme begins, inspired by Japanese giant-robot comics and animation.
- LEGO® MINDSTORMS® NXT is launched.
- LEGO® Batman™ leaps onto the scene.

2006

- LEGO sets based on the Nickelodeon cartoons *SpongeBob SquarePants*™ and *Avatar: The Last Airbender*™ are released.
- Remote-controlled LEGO Trains replace the classic electric system.

2006

- LEGO *Star Wars* II: The Original Trilogy video game is released.

And Beyond!

THE COMPANY CELEBRATED its 75th anniversary in 2007, and things only got bigger from there. LEGO® construction returned to outer space, and classic Castle, Pirates, and underwater themes made triumphant comebacks as well. Licensed lines were a huge success with blockbuster video games and sets based on some of the biggest properties around, from comic books to hobbits. These years also saw a boom for ninja, the debut and demise of LEGO Universe, and the 30th anniversary of the one and only LEGO minifigure ●

2007
- The LEGO Group celebrates its 75th anniversary.
- LEGO Mars Mission brings back LEGO Space sets for the first time since 2001's Life on Mars.
- More classic themes return in the form of new LEGO Castle and LEGO Aqua Raiders product lines.

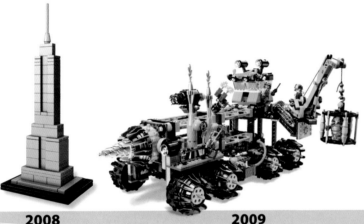

2008
- LEGOLAND Discovery Center Chicago opens in Schaumberg, IL.
- LEGO Stores begin offering a monthly mini-model build event.
- The LEGO Architecture theme introduces special-edition microscale models of famous buildings.

2009
- LEGO Power Miners is launched.
- LEGO Pirates and LEGO Space Police return with all-new sets.
- LEGO Games is launched.

2009
- The LEGO *Star Wars* theme celebrates its 10th anniversary with special packaging and minifigures.
- The LEGO Indiana Jones 2: The Adventure Continues video game adds new levels from the fourth movie and the original trilogy.
- LEGO Rock Band puts a minifigure spin on the Rock Band series of music video games.

2009
- The LEGO Agents upgrade to Agents 2.0.
- LEGO City branches out into the countryside with LEGO Farm sets.
- LEGO fans use the LEGO Design byME program to build virtual 3D models and then order them online with a custom box and building instructions.

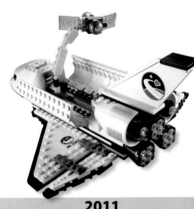

2011
- LEGO® *Pirates of the Caribbean*™ sets include ships, locations, and characters from the blockbuster movies.
- The LEGO Games sub-theme of Heroica introduces buildable games that can be combined into one giant adventure.

2011
- Hero Recon Team lets builders create their own Hero Factory characters online and order the parts through the mail.
- Hero Factory and Ninjago specials air on television.
- After a decade, LEGO® DUPLO® Winnie the Pooh™ sets return.

2011
- LEGOLAND® Florida becomes North America's second LEGOLAND theme park.
- A LEGOLAND Discovery Center opens in Texas.
- LEGOLAND California adds a new *Star Wars* section to its MINILAND display.
- LEGO *Star Wars* III: The Clone Wars introduces video game missions based on the computer-animated television series.

2011
- LEGO *Pirates of the Caribbean*: The Video Game includes gameplay from all four movies.
- LEGO City gains a new spaceport with sets developed in conjunction with NASA.
- LEGO sets are launched into space aboard the Space Shuttle *Endeavour*.
- The LEGO Master Builder Academy program teaches how to build like the LEGO professionals.

Indy's whip, hat, and bag were all-new pieces for 2008.

2007

- The LEGO® *Star Wars*™: The Complete Saga video game lets gamers play through a brick-ified version of all six films.
- The Modular Buildings series of models for advanced builders launches with the Café Corner set.
- *Mr. Magorium's Big Book*, a set containing nine different models, is released to coincide with the movie *Mr. Magorium's Wonder Emporium*.
- LEGO Creator sets introduce LEGO Power Functions, electronic modules that add motors, lights, and remote-controlled movement to models.

2008

- Kjeld Kirk Kristiansen is inducted into the Toy Industry Hall of Fame, USA.
- *LEGO Magazine* becomes *LEGO Club Magazine*.
- The first issue of *LEGO Club Jr.* magazine is sent to younger club members in the US.

2008

- The LEGO® Indiana Jones™, LEGO® Speed Racer™, and LEGO Agents themes are launched.
- LEGO Indiana Jones and LEGO Batman™ videogames are released.

2008

- The 50th anniversary of the patent of the stud-and-tube LEGO brick is celebrated with a worldwide building contest.
- The 30th birthday of the LEGO minifigure is commemorated with the "Go Miniman Go!" internet campaign and fan-video showcase.

2010

- The LEGO Group and Disney resume their partnership with the release of sets based on the *Toy Story* films, *Cars* (in LEGO® DUPLO® form) and *Prince of Persia*.
- Underwater action returns with LEGO Atlantis sets.
- The LEGO Castle theme continues with new LEGO Kingdoms sets.
- The LEGO Minifigures line launches with its first series of 16 characters.

2010

- LEGO World Racers takes builders on a frenetic, action-packed race through different environments.
- The long-running BIONICLE line comes to an end with the release of six BIONICLE Stars commemorative sets, each including a piece of extra golden armor to upgrade the Tahu figure.
- The Hero Factory theme continues the BIONICLE building style with an all-new universe and story.
- Harry Potter sets are produced for the first time since 2007.

2010

- LEGO® Ben 10™ buildable action figures are made in conjunction with Cartoon Network.
- Video game players magically build their way through the first four movies in LEGO® Harry Potter™: Years 1–4.
- The LEGO Universe massively multiplayer online game lets players create minifigure avatars and adventure together in a world of quests and construction.
- A direct-to-video movie, *The Adventures of Clutch Powers*, is the first full-length film to star minifigures.

2011

- Extraterrestrials invade Earth in the LEGO Alien Conquest theme.
- LEGO Ninjago puts a whole new spin on martial-arts action.
- The legacy of the LEGO Adventurers lives on with the heroes of the Pharaoh's Quest theme.

2011

- The LEGO CUUSOO partnership lets fans vote for models to be considered for release as LEGO sets.
- LEGO Harry Potter: Years 5–7 completes the video game retelling of the movie series.
- Life of George is released as an iPhone/iPod Touch application that interacts with a LEGO set.
- The year ends with the opening of LEGO ReBrick, a social media platform for LEGO fans aged 13 and over.

2012

- World-famous heroes and villains take the LEGO world by storm with the debut of the LEGO DC Universe Super Heroes and LEGO Marvel Universe Super Heroes themes.
- The new LEGO® *The Lord of the Rings*™ theme brings the epic movie world of Middle-earth to life with bricks, battling, and lots of short-legged minifigures.
- The LEGO Friends theme introduces a new line of building sets aimed at girls.

2012

- The LEGO City Police move out to the forest.
- Dinosaurs threaten the modern world once again with LEGO Dino.
- The LEGO Monster Fighters battle classic monster villains to prevent the sun from being forever extinguished.
- LEGO Ninjago gets an entire season of half-hour television episodes.

2012

- LEGO Universe, LEGO Design byME, and Hero Recon Team close down.
- LEGO CUUSOO voting leads to the production of a LEGO® Minecraft™ licensed model.
- LEGO DUPLO Disney Princess sets are released.
- New LEGOLAND Discovery Centers open in Kansas City and Atlanta.

The LEGO® Brick Patent

WHEN THE LEGO GROUP launched the LEGO® System of Play in 1955, it realized that the new LEGO brick had to be as perfect a building toy as possible. Bricks needed to lock together firmly to make stable models, but also come apart easily. CEO Godtfred Kirk Christiansen was determined to perfect the brick's quality and clutch power and fulfill the company's belief that it should be possible to build virtually *anything* with LEGO elements. At 1:58 pm on January 28, 1958, he finally submitted an application in Copenhagen, Denmark, for a patent for the improved LEGO brick and its building system ●

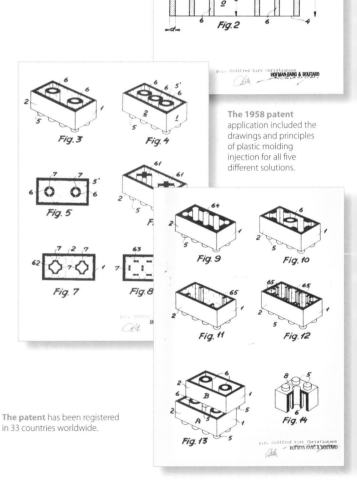

The **1958 patent** application included the drawings and principles of plastic molding injection for all five different solutions.

The **patent** has been registered in 33 countries worldwide.

THE STUD-AND-TUBE SOLUTION

The company developed several possible ways to improve the brick's clutch power. The first added three tubes to the underside of the current LEGO brick, creating a perfect three-point connection with the studs on top of the next brick below. Alternative solutions included bricks with two tubes or even crosses inside, with a total of five potential connection methods.

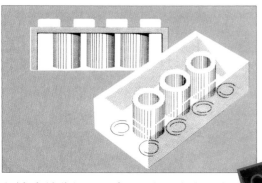

Godtfred Kirk Christiansen's favorite solution, the three-tube clutching system devised in 1957, became the final model for the new and improved LEGO brick.

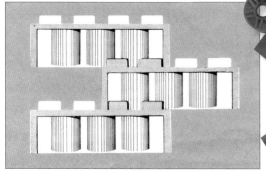

All 2 x 4 LEGO bricks manufactured since 1958 have been produced to the exact same measurements as the three-tube version described in the original patent.

BRICK VARIATIONS

Godtfred Kirk Christiansen's stud-and-tube solution continues to form the cornerstone of LEGO building. Today, LEGO elements are produced in thousands of different shapes, colors, and sizes, but each and every one of them is precisely designed to connect with the original brick, two studs wide and four studs long, that was patented on that famous day in 1958.

UNLIMITED POSSIBILITIES

The patented clutching ability of the LEGO brick gives builders of all ages an almost infinite variety of ways to express their imagination and creativity through construction. Each brick in the system can be connected to every other brick in multiple configurations, and as more bricks are added, the possibilities grow exponentially.

Two eight-stud LEGO bricks can be combined in 24 ways.

Three eight-stud LEGO bricks can be combined in 1,060 ways.

Six eight-stud LEGO bricks can be combined in 915,103,765 ways.

With eight bricks, the possibilities are virtually endless.

THE LEGO® BRICK

● LEGO® elements are part of a universal system and are all compatible with each other; bricks from 1958 fit bricks made 50 years later ● At 1:58 pm on January 28th, 1958, the company received a patent to manufacture LEGO bricks ● Since 1963, LEGO elements have been manufactured from ABS (acrylonitrile butadiene styrene), which is scratch and bite-resistant ● Bricks are made using small-capacity, precision-made molds ● Inspectors check the bricks for shape and color; only an average of 18 out of every million fails the test ● 36 billion LEGO bricks are produced each year. That's 68,000 every minute ● Six red eight-stud bricks can be combined in 915,103,765 different ways ● There are 4,200 different LEGO brick shapes ● The LEGO brick's 50th anniversary was celebrated in 2008 ● 40 billion LEGO bricks stacked together would reach the Moon ● There are 80 LEGO bricks for every person in the world

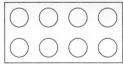

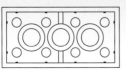

Top view showing studs.   **Bottom view** showing tubes.

LEGO® Elements to Remember...

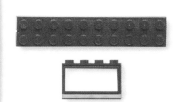

1949	**1953**	**1954**	**1955**
The first plastic bricks are launched. Forerunners of the true LEGO® brick, they are named Automatic Binding Bricks.	The first LEGO baseplate for building.	LEGO beams and windows.	Trees and small plastic vehicles for LEGO System of Play.

1968	**1969**	**1970**	**1974**	**1977**
Magnetic coupling brick.	LEGO® DUPLO® brick.	Cogwheel.	LEGO Family building figures.	LEGO DUPLO people.

1986	**1989**	**1990**	**1990**	**1990**	**1993**
LEGO Light & Sound elements.	LEGO Pirates parrot and monkey.	Coupling.	LEGO DUPLO zoo animals.	LEGO Technic motor.	LEGO Castle series dragon.

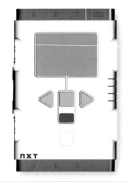

2003	**2003**	**2004**	**2005**	**2006**	**2006**
LEGO Technic motor.	CLIKITS™ elements.	LEGO QUATRO brick.	LEGO DUPLO figures become more realistic.	LEGO® EXO-FORCE™ elements.	LEGO® MINDSTORMS® NXT programmable brick.

1957

Flags and lights.

1958

The modern interlocking
brick is patented (January 28th).

1962

Wheel.

1963

One-third elements.

1966

4.5-volt train motor.

1977

LEGO Technic element.

1978

LEGO minifigures.

1980

LEGO Technic shock
absorber.

1981

Clockwork
engine.

1984

Knight's horse.

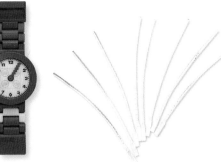

1994

LEGO® BELVILLE™
figures.

1996

Wristwatch
elements.

1997

Fiber-optic element.

1998

LEGO MINDSTORMS
programmable brick.

1999

LEGO® *Star Wars*™ elements.

2001

BIONICLE® elements.

2007

Power Functions
motor.

2008

LEGO DUPLO animals.

2009

LEGO Games.

2010

Rideable ostrich.

2011

Brain-sucking Alien
Clinger.

2012

LEGO Friends mini-dolls.

THE LEGO® MINIFIGURE

● The first LEGO® minifigures were made in 1978 for the new Town, Castle, and Space themes ● Minifigures are also known as "minifigs" ● Minifigure feet and legs have holes to let them connect to LEGO bricks when standing or sitting. Their heads have a stud on top to attach hair, hats, helmets, or other LEGO pieces ● Minifigures are made up of nine pieces, but are usually packaged in 3: head, body with arms, and legs ● Until 1989, all minifigures had the same smiling expression. That year, the new Pirates series added different faces as well as hook-hands and peg legs ● The first non-yellow standard minifigures were released in 2003 when the LEGO Group launched licensed characters from sports, television, and movies with more realistic skin tones ● Minifigures with two-sided faces that could change expression by turning their heads around were introduced with the LEGO® Harry Potter™ Professor Quirrell minifigure ● In 2005, electronics were added to minifigures, letting *Star Wars™* lightsabers and police flashlights light up when the figure's head was pressed down ● Some characters have their own unique bodies, such as the skeletons from LEGO Castle, droids from LEGO® *Star Wars™*, BIONICLE® heroes and villains, and aliens from Life on Mars and Mars Mission ● In 2008, the LEGO Group celebrated the 30th birthday of the minifigure with the worldwide "Go Miniman Go!" multimedia event. Fans joined in by uploading their own minifigure movies ● About 4 billion minifigures have been produced—more than 10 times the population of the USA!

An early ancestor of the LEGO minifigure, with a simple three-piece body, a faceless yellow head and no separate arms or legs, first appeared in sets in 1975.

Making LEGO® Bricks

THE LEGO® Kornmarken factory at the company headquarters in Billund, Denmark, opened on June 24th, 1987 after 18 months of construction. Today, the giant factory is constantly in motion, operating 24 hours a day and seven days a week. Its workers and state-of-the-art machinery produce about 2.4 million plastic bricks every hour. Approximately 16 billion LEGO elements were made there in the year 2007 alone ●

The Kornmarken factory building is big enough for a 20 km half-marathon race to be run inside it. It's so big inside that employees often use special scooters and other vehicles to get from place to place quickly.

1

2

3

4

BRICK BY BRICK BY BRICK...

1 A LEGO brick begins life as a pile of tiny plastic granules, each about the size of a grain of rice. The granules are shipped to Denmark from Italy, the Netherlands, and Germany. There are currently about 55 basic granule colors, which can be mixed to make additional colors.

2 The granules are sucked up from large plastic containers into one of the factory's 14 silos.

A silo can hold up to 33 tons (30 tonnes) of granules, but usually contains about 29 tons (26 tonnes). 50 tons (45 tonnes) of granules can be processed every 24 hours.

3 The granules travel along pipes to one of the 12 molding halls, which contain a total of 775 molding machines.

4 The granules are fed down pipes directly into the molding machines. A single person, backed

5

6

7

8

up by maintenance technicians, looks after 72 molding machines. The machines are computer-controlled and made in Germany and Austria. A warning light on top of the machine turns on to indicate any problems in the molding process.

5 Inside the molding machines, the granules are heated to a temperature of 455°F (235°C), which melts them together into a toothpaste-like mass of gooey plastic. The molds then apply 28 to 165 tons (25 to 150 tonnes) of pressure (depending on the element being produced) to shape each individual brick to an accuracy of 0.0002 in (0.005 mm), which is necessary to make sure that every LEGO brick fits together with the rest. In 10–15 seconds, the bricks harden and cool. Leftover plastic is recycled.

Bricks that chance to fall onto the factory floor are also recycled. The new bricks are automatically ejected from the molds.

6 The bricks travel along a short conveyor belt, dropping into boxes at the end.

7 When a box is full of newly made bricks, the molding machine transmits a signal to a nearby robot along wires embedded in the floor of the factory.

8 The robot travels to the machine, collects the box, puts a lid on it, stamps the box with the all-important barcode that enables this particular batch to be identified in future operations, and places it on a conveyor belt. This leads to the distribution warehouse.

9

9 The box travels along the conveyor belt to the distribution warehouse. The high-level warehouse has space for 424,000 boxes of LEGO® bricks. A logical motion machine, powered by compressed air, finds the boxes according to their barcodes and selects which ones are needed for an order. When certain boxes of bricks are needed to make up a LEGO set, the logical motion machine selects and grabs the correct ones.

10 The machine places the boxes on a conveyor belt that leads to a truck. The boxes are then driven to the packing, assembling, and decoration department.

11, 12 Assembly machines then attach arms and hands to minifigure bodies, tires to wheels, and so on.

13 Painting machines add faces to heads and complex patterns to decorated elements.

14 The finished LEGO pieces are then

13

From 1978 to 1989, all LEGO minifigures had the same expression: a smile and two dots for eyes. Today, there are so many different faces that the factory has to keep track of all the ones being made on a particular day!

Some heads even get an extra face painted on the back so you can turn it around and change our mood!

Printing inks used to make up colors for different features on bodies and faces.

14

15

16

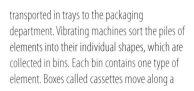

17

18

19

transported in trays to the packaging department. Vibrating machines sort the piles of elements into their individual shapes, which are collected in bins. Each bin contains one type of element. Boxes called cassettes move along a

conveyor belt beneath the bins. As each cassette arrives beneath a bin, the correct number and type of element drops into it.

15 The elements are then bagged or stored in clear plastic display trays. Each bag is weighed

twice to make sure that it contains the right number and type of elements.

16 Machines send the bags of elements, along with the set's instruction booklet, down chutes to fall into boxes on a packing line.

17 LEGO workers check that the bags of elements lie flat so that box lids close tightly.

18, 19 The boxed LEGO sets are picked up by robotic arms and packed into cardboard boxes for transportation to stores.

Designing a LEGO® Set

HOW DO THE LEGO® set designers come up with all of those wonderful models and minifigures? The first step is finding inspiration. The design team gathers material from many different sources—even from their own experiences. The LEGO City team worked at a fire station for a day to learn more about fire-fighting and fire trucks, and the LEGO Power Miners team took a trip to an underground mine ●

BRAINSTORMING

Once they have their inspiration, the LEGO design team members get together for a Design Boost session, where they come up with ideas for story, models, characters, and any new elements that might be needed. The Design Lead and Marketing Lead refine the models and agree on their price points, making sure that each model is unique, but works as part of the overall series.

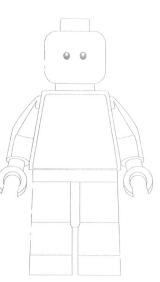

New LEGO characters start out as a blank minifigure template.

A graphic designer makes a quick sketch and adds color with markers or a computer.

Once the design is approved, the decoration is finalized on the computer so a test print can be made.

CREATING NEW ELEMENTS

If the set needs a new LEGO element, the model designer works with a part designer or engineer to produce it. Rounded pieces like animals and minifigure hair are hand-sculpted and scanned into a computer for the engineer to finalize, while simple shapes like bricks and wheels are built directly on the computer using 3D software.

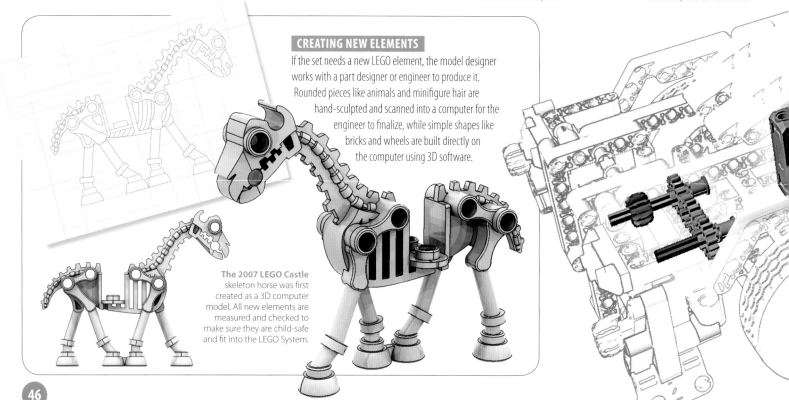

The 2007 LEGO Castle skeleton horse was first created as a 3D computer model. All new elements are measured and checked to make sure they are child-safe and fit into the LEGO System.

MODEL DEVELOPMENT

A team of four to eight Model Builder designers is assigned to start developing the final models. They make multiple versions of each one to test different functions and colors. All through the process, the models are tested with kids to find out what they like best or want to see added —it's their opinions that matter the most when designing a new LEGO set!

Realistic exhaust stack, light, and horn details

EARLY CONCEPTS

After the initial brainstorming, some ideas for new sets and minifigures are turned into hand-drawn illustrations or clay character models, while others are built out of LEGO bricks as conceptual "sketch models." If an element isn't available in the right color, the designers paint it themselves.

8258 Crane Truck (2009)

Gears and transmissions control crane functions

Creating a LEGO Technic model is one of the toughest challenges there is for a set designer. All of the parts have to line up with perfect precision to make the mechanical functions work properly when the model is put together.

V8 engine pistons move when vehicle rolls

Built-in safety clutch protects gears from damage

FINAL STEPS

The model is nearly done! Now it has to be approved by a Model Committee of expert builders, engineers, part designers, and building-instruction developers. If they find any problems, the designer has to start over again. Once approved, the model is taken apart piece by piece by the instructions team, who use a 3D computer program to create the building steps.

The LEGO® Logo

SINCE ITS CREATION in 1934, the LEGO® logo has undergone many changes. By 1953, what was affectionately nicknamed the "sausage logo"—rounded, black-outlined white letters, and a red background—already resembled today's distinctive brand. By the early 1970s, the logo looked almost as it does today; a slight modification in 1998 brought it up to date ●

1934

1946

1950

1953

1955

1955

1958

1958

1936

1946

1953

1953

1956

1958

1958

1964

1972

1998

Inspirational building leaflet included in LEGO model boxes between 1963 and 1964.

LEGO® Play Themes

EVEN THOUGH all of the sets in the LEGO® System of Play were designed to be compatible within one big creative LEGO universe, there were some types of models that kids wanted more and more of. More trains! More castles! More cities! More spaceships! Answering the call in 1978 were the first three LEGO Play Themes, each full of sets based on a popular subject and populated by the brand-new, fully-posable LEGO minifigures. LEGO Castle had medieval knights, kings, and fortresses. LEGO Town had buildings, roads, cars, and trucks. LEGO Space had rockets, rovers, and lunar bases. No matter what your favorite theme was, now you could collect and construct it to build your own LEGO world ●

LEGO® City

IT TAKES A TOWN to make a city. A LEGO® Town, that is! In contrast to fantastical themes like LEGO Castle and LEGO Space, LEGO Town has offered a familiar slice of real life ever since it first came on the scene in 1978. Spinning out of sets like 1972's Police Heliport and the original 1955 Town Plan, the Town theme let builders create their own modern cities full of airports, police stations, construction sites, shops, restaurants, and more. Known today as LEGO City, this once-little town is bigger and busier than ever before ●

LEGO® Town & City

With a moving piston and bucket, the Fire Station truck's folding, telescoping ladder worked just like the real thing.

Fire truck from 7945 Fire Station (2007)

SOME THINGS never go out of style in the big city. While LEGO® Town and LEGO City sub-themes may have come and gone over the years, no brick-built metropolis is complete without these classic civic fixtures: a police department, a fire station, an airport, a hospital, and a busy construction crew to ensure the city keeps on growing ●

FIRE

For more than 50 years, the fearless firefighters of LEGO City have been extinguishing blazes and saving LEGO cats from LEGO trees with the help of extending ladders, wind-up hoses, and an ever-growing assortment of fire trucks, fire stations, and rescue gear!

Not everyone rides in the truck. When there's an emergency in LEGO City, the Fire Chief speeds to the scene in his personal car.

POLICE

When danger calls, the LEGO City Police are always on the scene. These dedicated officers never stop patrolling the streets of LEGO City, protecting its citizens night and day. From their modern police station, they can monitor radio bands, dispatch vehicles to emergencies, scan the crime computer, and keep watch on the prison in case of break-outs.

7744 Police Headquarters (2008)

Radio mast

7892 LEGO City Hospital (2006)

The most common procedure at this hospital? Emergency minifigure reassembly!

The operating room had everything a LEGO doctor could need. Just don't ask about the chainsaw in the corner.

HOSPITAL

Though it's had fewer releases than the other major sub-themes, the LEGO City Hospital is a vital part of city life. Complete with all the latest innovations in minifigure medical care, it even had a helicopter pad and off-road vehicle for the biggest emergencies in and out of town.

7893 Passenger Plane (2006)

Angled wing tips

Tool kit

Did you know that the airport has its own fire department? 7891 Airport Firetruck (2006) and others are always on hand in case of emergencies.

AIRPORT

Whether you're taking a vacation or just arriving in town for the first time, the LEGO City Airport is the place to go when you need to fly. With dozens of different helicopters, passenger planes, and jumbo jets to choose from, not to mention baggage carts, runway strips, air traffic control towers, and a friendly crew of pilots, mechanics, and flight attendants, you'll never have a delayed departure!

In 2008, the police department finally got something it had needed for a long time: the first-ever LEGO City handcuffs.

Searchlight

The 2008 Police Headquarters featured 953 elements, including five police officers, one crook, and a police dog.

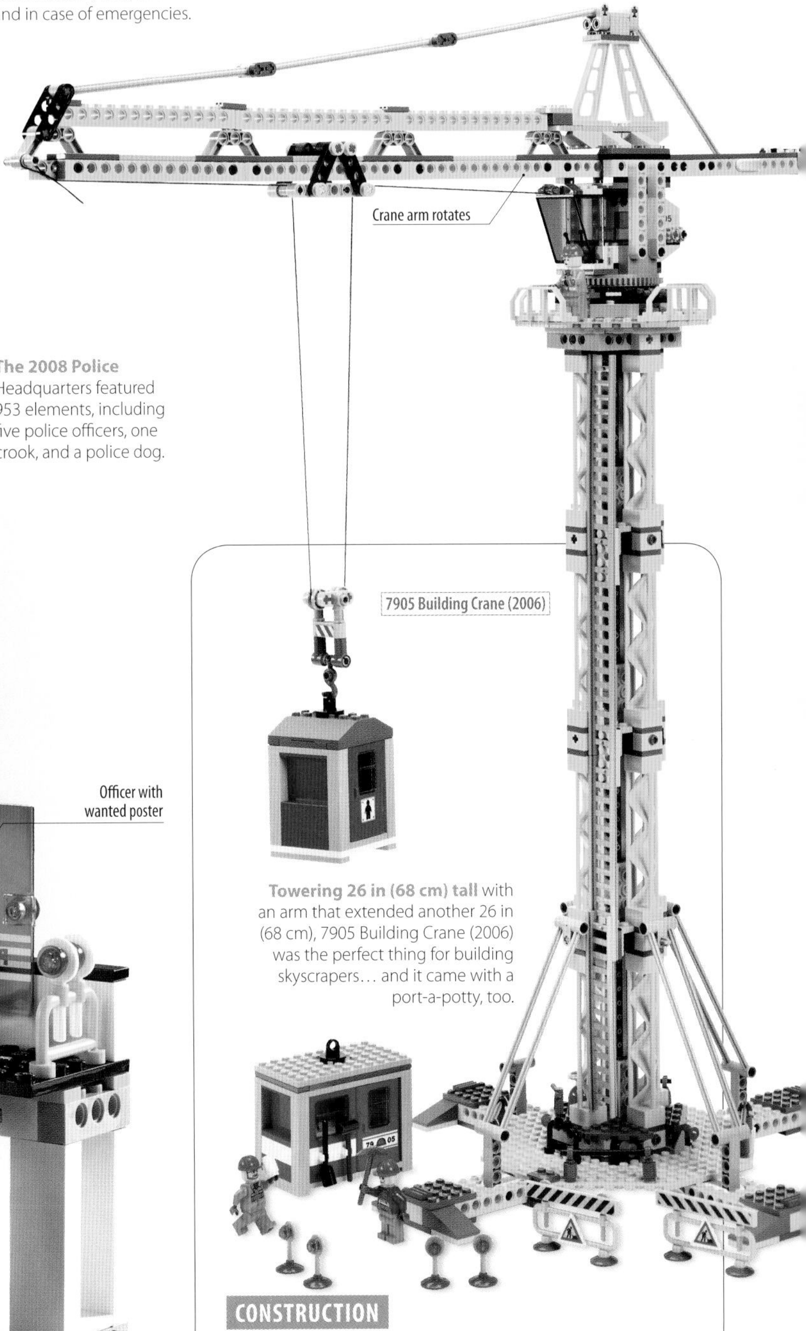

POLICE

Crane arm rotates

7905 Building Crane (2006)

Towering 26 in (68 cm) tall with an arm that extended another 26 in (68 cm), 7905 Building Crane (2006) was the perfect thing for building skyscrapers… and it came with a port-a-potty, too.

Officer with wanted poster

WANTED

POLICE

CONSTRUCTION

They may not have a station of their own, but these hard-working, hard-hatted city heroes make up for it by building all the rest. With cranes, bulldozers, cement mixers, dump trucks, haulers, loaders, and more to use in their projects, it's a wonder the LEGO City Construction crew ever gets any sleep at all!

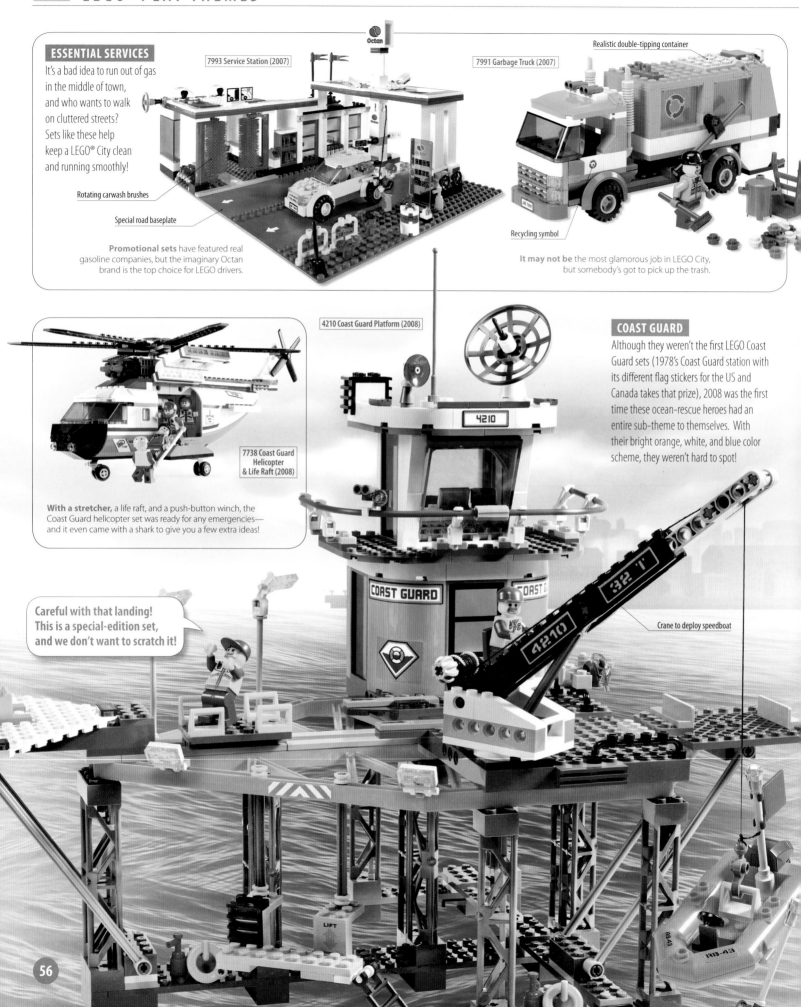

ESSENTIAL SERVICES

It's a bad idea to run out of gas in the middle of town, and who wants to walk on cluttered streets? Sets like these help keep a LEGO® City clean and running smoothly!

7993 Service Station (2007)

Rotating carwash brushes

Special road baseplate

Promotional sets have featured real gasoline companies, but the imaginary Octan brand is the top choice for LEGO drivers.

7991 Garbage Truck (2007)

Realistic double-tipping container

Recycling symbol

It may not be the most glamorous job in LEGO City, but somebody's got to pick up the trash.

7738 Coast Guard Helicopter & Life Raft (2008)

With a stretcher, a life raft, and a push-button winch, the Coast Guard helicopter set was ready for any emergencies— and it even came with a shark to give you a few extra ideas!

4210 Coast Guard Platform (2008)

COAST GUARD

Although they weren't the first LEGO Coast Guard sets (1978's Coast Guard station with its different flag stickers for the US and Canada takes that prize), 2008 was the first time these ocean-rescue heroes had an entire sub-theme to themselves. With their bright orange, white, and blue color scheme, they weren't hard to spot!

Crane to deploy speedboat

Careful with that landing! This is a special-edition set, and we don't want to scratch it!

COAST GUARD

4210

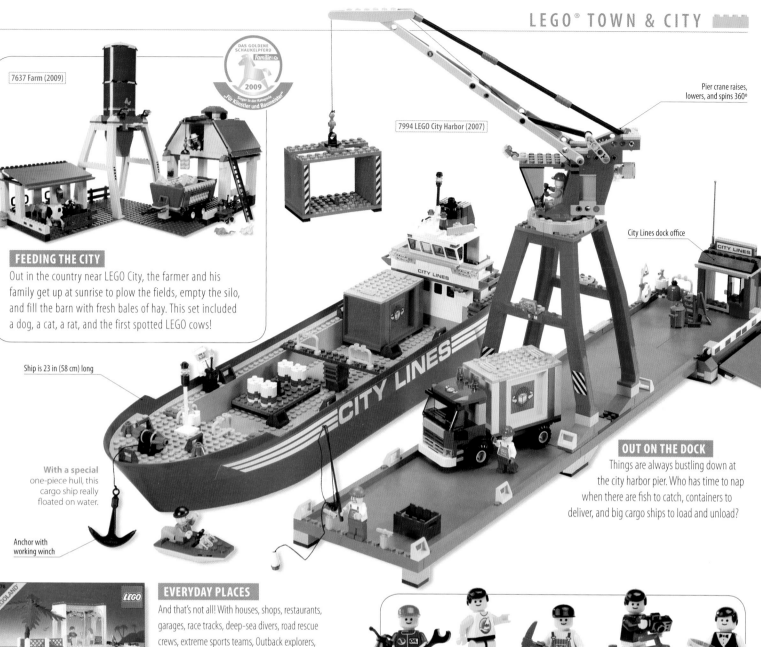

7637 Farm (2009)

7994 LEGO City Harbor (2007)

Pier crane raises, lowers, and spins 360º

City Lines dock office

CITY LINES

FEEDING THE CITY
Out in the country near LEGO City, the farmer and his family get up at sunrise to plow the fields, empty the silo, and fill the barn with fresh bales of hay. This set included a dog, a cat, a rat, and the first spotted LEGO cows!

Ship is 23 in (58 cm) long

With a special one-piece hull, this cargo ship really floated on water.

Anchor with working winch

OUT ON THE DOCK
Things are always bustling down at the city harbor pier. Who has time to nap when there are fish to catch, containers to deliver, and big cargo ships to load and unload?

6376 Breezeway Cafe (1990)

EVERYDAY PLACES
And that's not all! With houses, shops, restaurants, garages, race tracks, deep-sea divers, road rescue crews, extreme sports teams, Outback explorers, and even a space port or two, there have probably been enough LEGO Town and LEGO City sets released since 1978 to fill a real city!

The busy City Corner set included a skater and bike shop, a 2-story pizzeria, and a businessman to chase after the bus when he was running late for work.

7641 City Corner (2009)

6372 Town House (1982)

| Auto mechanic | Skateboarder | Builder | Photographer | Waiter |

| Swimmer | Security guard | Firefighter | Robber | Pedestrian | Doctor |

CITIZENS OF THE CITY
Meet the inhabitants of LEGO Town and LEGO City! They include cooks, crooks, divers, drivers, mailmen, mechanics, news reporters, office workers, delivery boys, and lots of other familiar city faces. And they always do their jobs with a smile!

7731 Mail Van (2008)

City Outskirts

THERE'S MORE TO LEGO® City than just what's in the city. From a bustling modern space center where rockets and space shuttles blast into orbit, to a forest full of cops, robbers, and the occasional hungry bear, these sets are just a small sampling of the activity and fun that you can discover outside the city limits •

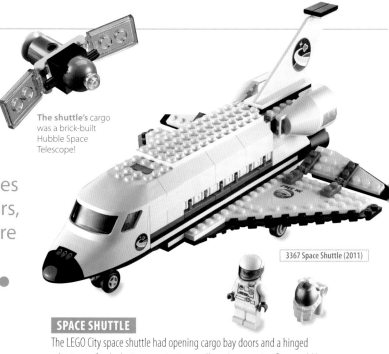

The shuttle's cargo was a brick-built Hubble Space Telescope!

3367 Space Shuttle (2011)

CITY IN SPACE

Built on a LEGO road baseplate, the biggest set in 2011's LEGO City space sub-theme starred a 14 in (35 cm) tall rocket. Builders could fuel it up, use tools to make last minute changes, roll it into position at the launch platform, load a pilot or cargo on board, count down, and then blast off for adventure.

SPACE SHUTTLE

The LEGO City space shuttle had opening cargo bay doors and a hinged robotic arm for deploying or retrieving satellites. Its rear wing flaps could be angled for landing maneuvers when it returned to Earth. The included space-suited astronaut had alternate helmets for piloting the shuttle or taking part in missions outside.

J - L336 - 8

Accessed by a launch platform elevator, the cockpit had interchangeable parts to hold an astronaut or a folded-up satellite.

Rocket ready for launch

3368 Space Center (2011)

Control center

Launch tower

Satellite

Back-up crew

Astronaut with helmet

COUNTRY TRIP

Released as a special-edition set in the City Farm line, this four-wheel drive auto pulled a trailer with a LEGO horse inside. The horse's rider wore a smart riding jacket and helmet, while the 4WD driver was more relaxed in plaid. The model also included a fence for jumping.

Horse could wear a saddle

7635 4WD with Horse Trailer (2009)

WIND POWER

LEGO City went green with this model, which let you drive the disassembled wind turbine to its destination on the extending transport truck with escort traffic car, then connect the blades, motor, and tower together to start generating clean wind power for the city.

7747 Wind Turbine Transport (2009)

FLYING IN STYLE

Whether driving or flying, this is the way to travel! Another special-edition model in the US, this set featured a private helicopter and a stretch limousine to carry its V.I.P.s (very important passengers). To get them there, they had both a chopper pilot and their very own chauffeur.

3222 Helicopter and Limousine (2010)

LEGO building got a little recursive with this 2010 model of a LEGO delivery truck. Its trailer was full of tiny LEGO City boxes… including one for the truck itself!

INTO THE WOODS

The LEGO City theme took a detour off the beaten path in 2012, which saw a change of scene from the city streets to the trees of the nearby LEGO City Forest. Builders were introduced to a brave team of forest police, who used their off-road vehicles and knowledge of nature to track down fugitive crooks.

The woodsy-looking forest police station had a tall communications tower for keeping in touch with civilization.

Secret mailbox escape hatch

3221 LEGO® Truck (2010)

LEGO set boxes made from bricks with stickers

Hollow rock for hiding stolen loot

The forest police sets introduced a brand-new LEGO bear. Its hind legs and neck were jointed to let it walk on four or two legs—much to the dismay of these crooks.

Police helicopter

Police truck

4440 Forest Police Station (2012)

4438 Robbers' Hideout (2012)

Working crane

MINE, ALL MINE

LEGO City struck gold with its 2012 mining sets. At the big mine, you could use the drilling machine to break up rocks, drive them out to the crane, load them onto the conveyor belt, and haul them away.

4204 The Mine (2012)

Drilling machine

What do you get when you build flame elements onto trees? A forest fire! Fortunately, the Fire Plane could dump a tank-full of clear blue "water" bricks to put out the blaze.

4209 Fire Plane (2012)

Sets to Remember

374 Fire Station (1978)

6335 Indy Transport (1996)

6414 Dolphin Point (1995)

600 Police Car (1978)

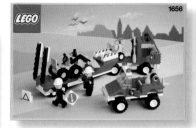

1656 Evacuation Team (1991)

376 Town House With Garden (1978)

1572 Super Tow Truck (1986)

6356 Med-Star Rescue Plane (1988)

6365 Summer Cottage (1981)

6380 Emergency Treatment Center (1987)

6336 Launch Response Unit (1995)

6441 Deep Reef Refuge (1997)

10159 City Airport (2004)

6473 RES-Q Cruiser (1998)

7239 Fire Truck (2004)

6435 Coast Guard HQ (1999)

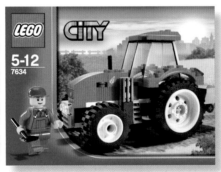

7634 Tractor (2009)

7734 Cargo Plane (2008)

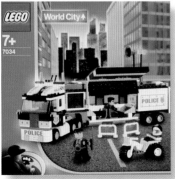

7034 Surveillance Truck (2003)

7631 Dump Truck (2009)

7279 Police Minifigure Collection (2011)

61

LEGO® Train

ALL ABOARD!

Train conductor (2003)

This conductor's jacket bears the LEGO Train logo.

IT'S BEEN SPEEDING down the tracks since 1966. It's driven on blue rails, gray rails, metal rails, and plastic rails. It's been powered by hand, clockwork, batteries, electricity, and remote control. From old-time steam locomotives to modern bullet trains, here comes that classic among classics: the famous LEGO® Train ●

7740

INTER-CITY EXPRESS

This German inter-city engine with an electric 12-volt motor and two passenger cars was introduced in 1980, the year when the LEGO Train theme was redesigned with gray tracks and a more realistic model style.

7740 12V Passenger Train (1980)

Most LEGO train cars were connected to the engine and each other by articulated magnetic couplers; the earliest trains used a hook-and-eye system.

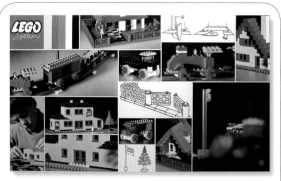

080 Basic Building Set with Train (1967)

RIGHT ON TRACK

This 700-piece Universal Building Set model included one of the first LEGO trains. It had to be pushed along by hand, but could be motorized with a 4.5-volt battery box borrowed from another train set.

RUNNING ON BLUE RAILS

Between 1966 and 1979, LEGO train sets ran on blue rails. The first models were basic push-along trains, but 4.5-volt battery motors quickly followed, and in 1969, the latest LEGO trains were powered by 12-volt electrified tracks. Trains of this period were small and low on detail.

182 4.5v Train Set with Signal (1975)

116 Starter Train Set with Motor (1967)

Thanks to the LEGO System of Play, boats, aircraft, buildings, and trains from different years combine together.

Blue LEGO train tracks were simple rails with white cross-tie bricks to hold them off the ground.

113 Motorized Train Set (1966)

SANTA FE SUPER CHIEF

Originally sold as a numbered limited edition of 10,000, this locomotive was based on the real *Super Chief* luxury passenger train. It could be upgraded with additional cars or a motor.

LEGO Train logo

4513 Grand Central Station (2003)

Track-side pizzeria

10020 Santa Fe Super Chief (2002)

RAIL NETWORK

Along with train engines and cars of all shapes and sizes, LEGO Train sets have included a number of stations, level crossings, cargo cranes, a train wash, and an engine shed.

6399 Airport Shuttle (1990)

9-VOLT MONORAIL

This LEGO Town monorail was powered by the 9-volt electric current that would become a new standard for LEGO Train rails starting in 1991.

NIGHT TRAIN

Inspired by classic steam engines, the Emerald Night was a LEGO Train fan's dream come true. It measured 27 in (68 cm) long, featured piston-action wheels and an opening coal tender and dining car, and could be motorized by adding Power Functions parts.

The Emerald Night took a year and a half to develop with input from top train fans. It included two new sizes of big train wheels and elements in new and rare colors.

10194 Emerald Night (2009)

This motorized train would start and stop automatically when you blew the whistle (lying on rear car).

118 Electronic Train (Forward-Stop) (1968)

REMOTE CONTROL

In 2006, LEGO Trains returned to plastic rails and battery-powered motors, but now they had infrared remote controls that could turn on an engine's lights, change its speed, and even toot its horn. 2009 saw the further introduction of Power Functions technology, rechargeable motor batteries, and new flexible tracks.

My Own Train was hosted by Engineer Max and Conductor Charlie, who also came with the 10133 BNSF GP-38 Locomotive set in 2005.

7897 Passenger Train (2006)

MY OWN TRAIN

From 2001 to 2003, the LEGO My Own Train website let builders create and order their own custom trains from two sizes and five colors of classic steam locomotives, as well as several types of rolling stock cars.

10205 My Own Train (2002)

Conductor Charlie

Engineer Max

LEGO® Castle

1978 WAS A HISTORIC YEAR
for the LEGO Group—it embarked on
a fantasy-filled journey back to the days
of kings, queens, knights, and legends.
Starting with a simple yellow fortress,
the world of LEGO® Castle soon grew
to include entire kingdoms, as well as
armies of sword-wielding warriors that
were at times chivalrous, villainous,
swashbuckling, or downright spooky.
Prepare for a blast from the past with
these sets straight from the days of
knightly yore ●

For King
and Castle!

For a big shiny trophy!

Classic Castles

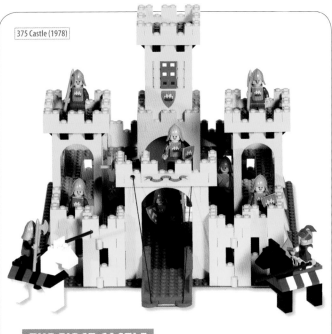

375 Castle (1978)

THE FIRST CASTLE

Here's where it all began! The famous "Yellow Castle" was the very first castle made for the LEGO System of Play. With its tall towers, crank-raised drawbridge and four factions of knights to attack or defend it, it already had many of the classic features of later LEGO castles.

FROM THE ORIGINAL yellow castle with its brick-built horses to today's catapult-covered fantasy fortresses, the LEGO® Castle theme has been letting builders create their own medieval kingdoms for more than 30 years. Take an historical tour of some of the most famous castles of the past and present, and then turn the page to discover even more of the world of LEGO Castle ●

You might think that this piece only works as a dragon's wing, but see p. 190 and you might just spot it somewhere else!

6086
Black
Knight's
Castle
(1992)

One of the most realistic LEGO castles, the home of the Black Knights included rare yellow Tudor-patterned wall pieces and four knights with lances and flags, mounted on horses and ready to joust.

7094 King's Castle Siege (2007)

KING'S CASTLE SIEGE

Besieged by an evil wizard's skeleton warriors and a fire-breathing dragon, the King of the Western Kingdom fought back with knights, catapults, and a golden sword. The 2007–2009 LEGO Castle series was praised by fans for its return to classic building styles and castle design, including a working drawbridge and portcullis.

The 2007 Skeleton Warriors were redesigned from the original loose-limbed LEGO Castle skeletons to have scarier skulls and more posable limbs.

66

Bad guys need homes, too. When the evil Vladek conquered the kingdom of Ankoria, he built his own fortress, complete with launching fireballs and an enchanted mask for the heroes to knock off its central tower.

Watch out if you walk from the treasure room to the prison tower. This bridge is booby-trapped to flip upside-down and send attackers flying!

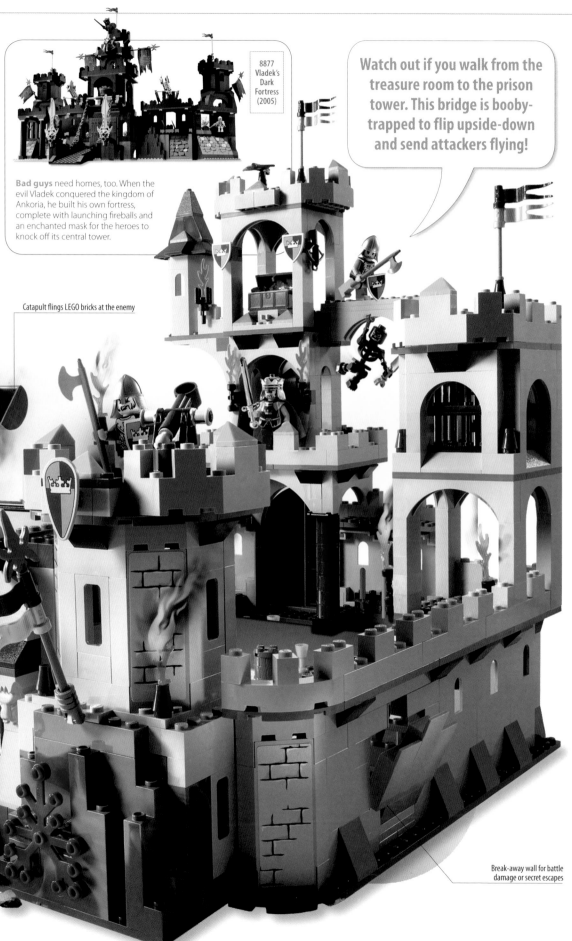

Catapult flings LEGO bricks at the enemy

Break-away wall for battle damage or secret escapes

6097
Night Lord's
Castle
(1997)

The lair of the dreaded Fright Knights and their leader, Basil the Bat Lord, was also home to Willa the Witch and a black dragon. Spooky surprises included a secret rotating wall, a locking dungeon door, and a skull that appeared inside a crystal ball.

8781 Castle of
Morcia (2004)

From the second LEGO® KNIGHTS' KINGDOM™ series, King Mathias's magical castle had reversible details to let you transform it from good and blue to evil and red when the villainous Vladek took control.

6082 Fire Breathing Fortress (1993)

Starring Majisto the wizard and his glow-in-the-dark wand, the Dragon Masters series jumped into the world of fantasy and magic. This set featured a rock-dropping dragon head, a cage for captured dragons, and a sneaky spy from the Wolfpack Renegades.

6098
King Leo's Castle
(2000)

From the first LEGO KNIGHTS' KINGDOM series, this fairy tale-style castle had modular towers on a raised baseplate. It belonged to the Lion Knights, who defended it with the sword-swinging Princess Storm against Cedric the Bull's warriors.

Knights & Legends

THERE'S MUCH MORE to LEGO® Castle than just castles! The theme has included hundreds of buildings, vehicles, and scenes, as well as more than a dozen groups of minifigure characters, from the chivalrous Royal Knights and the swashbuckling Forestmen to the savage Wolfpack Renegades and the creepy Fright Knights ●

7093 Skeleton Tower (2007)

WILY WIZARDRY

The first LEGO Castle theme to be titled "LEGO Castle" on the packaging launched in 2007. It featured a kingdom under attack by The Evil Wizard, who was served by a horde of skeleton warriors and dragons.

6067 Guarded Inn (1986)

A CASTLE CLASSIC

Hailed by many fans as the best LEGO Castle set of all time, 1986's Guarded Inn is a rare civilian setting with a cozy tavern and section of wall that can be connected to other castle models. It includes a knight on horse, two guards, and a maiden to tend the inn and pour refreshments. It proved so popular that it was re-released in 2001 as the first in a series of LEGO Legends.

| LEGOLAND Castle (1978–1983) | Black Falcons (1984–1992) | Crusaders (1984–1992) | Forestmen (1987–1990) | Black Knights (1988–1994) | Wolfpack Renegades (1992–1993) | Basil the Bat Lord Fright Knights (1997–1998) | Cedric the Bull KNIGHTS' KINGDOM I (2000) | Jayko KNIGHTS' KINGDOM II (2004–2006) |

A-VIKING WE SHALL GO

The LEGO Vikings set sail in 2005 with a collection of sets full of bold, bearded warriors, vehicles built for battle, and a mighty walled fortress. With their horned helmets, fireball launchers, and monsters from the mists of Norse mythology like the Fenris Wolf and Nidhogg dragon, these Vikings may not have been quite historically accurate, but they did have some of the longest LEGO set names of all time!

7018 Viking Ship Challenges the Midgard Serpent (2005)

Flexible sea serpent

Longboat measures 19 in (48 cm) long with a 12-in (30-cm) sail

3053 Emperor's Stronghold (1999)

NINJA KNIGHTS

Despite their unusual non-European setting, the Ninja sets were an official part of the LEGO Castle theme. With their ornate temples, sword-wielding samurai, and bands of stealthy (and occasionally flying) ninja mercenaries, they added a distinctly Eastern flair and plenty of brand-new pieces to the Castle collection.

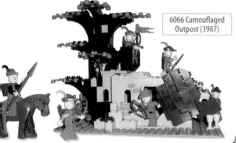

6066 Camouflaged
Outpost (1987)

8701 King Jayko (2006)

Once a reckless young knight, Jayko the Swift became King of Morcia.

LEGO® KNIGHTS' KINGDOM™

The second of two LEGO Castle themes named KNIGHTS' KINGDOM, the 2004–2006 series revolved around the magical kingdom of Morcia. The tale was told through storybooks and online comics, and the sets included both minifigure-scale models, and larger action figures with thumb-driven battle moves.

8702 Lord Vladek (2006)

The scorpion-themed Vladek had mystical powers and a legion of Shadow Knights at his command.

MERRY MEN

With their feathered caps, green clothes, bows and arrows, and treetop hideouts, the Forestmen bore quite a resemblance to a famous merry band of outlaws from English folklore!

8780 Citadel of Orlan (2004)

Each knight had his own animal icon, armor color, and special skill.

PERILOUS PITFALLS

When the dark knight Vladek took over the kingdom and kidnapped the king, Jayko the Swift, Santis the Strong, Danju the Wise, and Rascus the Joker had to brave the traps of this ancient ruin—including whirling axes, swinging vines, a collapsed bridge, and a giant serpent—to find the one magical artifact that could defeat their foe.

7009 The Final Joust (2007)

The king's finest knight and the wizard's black skeleton rider battled for the fate of the kingdom in this set that included a new skeleton horse element.

NEW FRIENDS AND FOES

Originally made up entirely of humans and the occasional dragon, the population of LEGO Castle swelled with the introduction of the evil Skeleton Warriors, the stout and stalwart Dwarves, the greedy Trolls, and the huge but dim-witted Giant Trolls.

7036 Dwarves' Mine (2007)

LEGO® Kingdoms

WHEN THE THEME CALLED LEGO® Castle ended, the question on every castle-builder's mind was: what next? The answer arrived in 2010 with LEGO Kingdoms. Gone were the trolls and dwarves of the fantasy era. In their place came a tale of two rival medieval kingdoms, the good Lion Knights and the wicked Dragon Knights—not to mention the villagers stuck in the middle ●

7947 Prison Tower Rescue (2010)

PRINCESS IN PERIL

Smart and brave but a bit clumsy, the Princess of the Lion Kingdom had a habit of getting captured by the Dragon Knights and locked up in their prison tower. Fortunately, there were always loyal Lion Knights ready to ride to the rescue. LEGO Kingdoms introduced new armor that transformed knightly horses into horned battle-steeds.

The princess also had a habit of escaping on her own if the knights didn't arrive fast enough.

KING'S CASTLE

The castle of the Lion Knights had a modular design that let builders arrange its walls and towers in different configurations. Its drawbridge could be raised and lowered, and a turning crank controlled the gatehouse's portcullis to keep enemies outside—such as the three Dragon Knights who came in the set.

King's royal tower

Drawbridge mechanism

Lion Knight with crossbow

What would a modern LEGO Castle be without catapults? The King's Castle was defended by three of them.

Blazing torch

Dragon Knight

Lion Knight with glaive

7946 King's Castle (2010)

Rotating windmill blades

Spinning the rooster weathervane raised or lowered the barn's basket, and the crank-powered windmill had moving gears and a tipper box inside.

Farmer

Milkmaid

Dragon Knight raiders

Goats

Chickens

Pig

Horse-drawn cart

7189 Mill Village Raid (2011)

VILLAGERS

The Dragon Knights didn't limit their plundering to castles. They also raided this village mill and farm in search of hidden treasure. The brave farmers fought back with pitchforks, apples, booby traps, and a barnyard full of animal friends, including brand-new LEGO goats and chickens. The barn could open up on a secret flowerbox hinge.

THE BIG EVENT

With 1,575 pieces, this was the largest model to date in the LEGO Kingdoms theme. The Kingdoms Joust set included a six-roomed castle, nine minifigures, two weapon tents, a royal viewing box, a jousting fence, and two horses. Even better, you could combine two sets to make an even bigger scene!

Among the contents: a nobleman, a princess, a squire, a frog, and a knight who resembled the classic Black Falcons.

Spectator box

Two combined 10223 Kingdoms Joust (2012) sets

Wall extension hut

Jousting fence

YE OLDE SMITHY

Those Dragon Knights just didn't give up! This set depicted a Dragon Kingdom knight's attack on a blacksmith's shop. Spinning the water-wheel made the hammer pound on the anvil to forge new weapons.

6918 Blacksmith Attack (2011)

Given all of the fighting gear in the shop, the evil knight might have made an error in judgment.

A KINGLY CARRIAGE

The King's Carriage Ambush set introduced new torso and leg decoration for the wise and noble Lion King. He'd need his chromed sword when a pair of Dragon Knights launched a forest sneak attack with their lever-activated hammer in an attempt to capture a king's ransom in treasure.

The royal treasure chest was filled with gold, jewels, and precious trinkets.

7188 King's Carriage Ambush (2011)

A Medieval Village

PRODUCED IN 2008 as a special-edition exclusive for the online LEGO® Shop and LEGO Brand Stores, the Medieval Market Village was the biggest town-themed LEGO Castle set ever made. The designers consulted with Castle fans and filled the model with colorful characters, brand-new animals, and rare and classic elements •

Cock-a-doodle doo! We're the first buildable LEGO chickens!

10193 Medieval Market Village (2008)

Both buildings open up to show the furnished rooms inside!

Mm-mm. I'm glad they rediscovered this classic LEGO turkey piece!

Male and female villagers

Peasant boy

Medieval peasant

King's soldier

Tavern maid

Village blacksmith

VILLAGE PEOPLE
The 1,601-piece set featured a tavern, a blacksmith's shop, a feast of plastic food, the return of the original LEGO Castle hood element, and eight minifigures including a pair of soldiers to guard the king's treasure... or fill themselves up with turkey!

We've also got the first LEGO cow, a brick-built tree, stables, tables, a duck, and more!

Spinning the water-wheel makes my hammer strike the anvil!

Sets to Remember

375 Castle (1978)

383 Knight's Tournament (1979)

6074 Black Falcon's Fortress (1986)

6077 Forestmen's River Fortress (1989)

6034 Black Monarch's Ghost (1990)

6030 Catapult (1984)

6059 Knight's Stronghold (1990)

6049 Viking Voyager (1987)

1584 Knight's Challenge (1988)

6062 Battering Ram (1987)

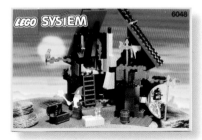
6048 Majisto's Magical Workshop (1993)

6090 Royal Knight's Castle (1995)

6037 Witch's Windship (1997)

LEGO Blacksmith Shop
Schmiedewerkstatt

3739

AGES/EDADES
10+

Building Toy
Jouet de Construction
Juguete para Construir

Cont. **622** pcs/pzs

Original design by Daniel Siskind

3739 Blacksmith Shop (2002)

8702 Lord Vladek (2006)

8823 Mistlands Tower (2006)

6093 Flying Ninja Fortress (1998)

8780 Citadel of Orlan (2004)

7041 Troll Battle Wheel (2008)

8876 Scorpion Prison Cave (2005)

6096 Bull's Attack (2000)

7187 Escape from the Dragon's Prison (2011)

7094 King's Castle Siege (2007)

7949 Prison Carriage Rescue (2010)

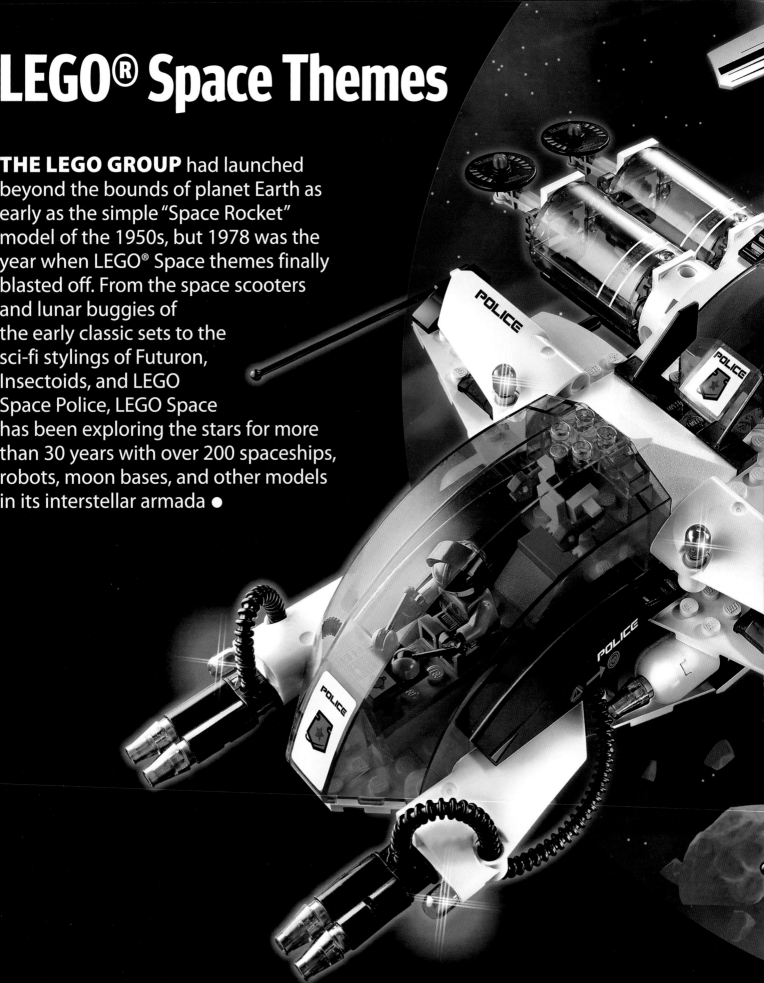

LEGO® Space Themes

THE LEGO GROUP had launched beyond the bounds of planet Earth as early as the simple "Space Rocket" model of the 1950s, but 1978 was the year when LEGO® Space themes finally blasted off. From the space scooters and lunar buggies of the early classic sets to the sci-fi stylings of Futuron, Insectoids, and LEGO Space Police, LEGO Space has been exploring the stars for more than 30 years with over 200 spaceships, robots, moon bases, and other models in its interstellar armada ●

Classic LEGO® Space Sets

THE EARLIEST LEGO® Space sets in 1978 let kids build a future that seemed just around the corner. The theme became more sci-fi in 1984 with Blacktron and Futuron, the first of many Space sub-series with their own unique vehicle designs, colors, astronauts, and model functions. With new series released almost every year through 2001, these sets are the classic era of LEGO Space and beyond ●

6954 · BLACKTRON

Ages 8-12

302 interlocking pieces

The sleek black spaceships of Blacktron made it one of the most popular LEGO Space sub-themes. It later provided bad guys for the 1989 Space Police, and was revisited with a second series in 1991.

6954 Renegade (1987)

6990 Monorail Transport System (1987)

6990 · LEGOLAND · LEGO

FAST FORWARD
Futuron carried on in the spirit and color scheme of the original Space sets. Its battery-powered, 9-volt monorail transported blue and yellow astronauts around their home base on a distant moon or planet.

1789 Star Hawk II (1995)

TO THE STARS
The Unitron theme saw only four sets released in 1994 and 1995, but even this short-lived series had a distinct style. With their translucent blue windows and yellow-green weapons, the high-tech Star Hawk II spaceship, crater cruiser, monorail transport base and Zenon space station were unified by cockpit pods that could be detached and exchanged between vehicles.

Communications dish

Rear laboratory section

OUT OF THIS WORLD
The earliest LEGO Space sets were a mix of simple science-fiction spaceships, lunar bases, rockets and rovers that weren't too far removed from the real space technology of the 1970s and 1980s, like the Uranium Search Vehicle with its 16 wheels.

6928 Uranium Search Vehicle (1984)

All-terrain wheels

HEY, MISTER SPACEMAN!
With space suits, helmets, and air tanks in white, red, yellow, blue, and black, the colorful astronauts of the original LEGO Space series explored the universe in peace and harmony, with no names or stories beyond what builders imagined themselves.

MINIFIGURE ASTRONAUTS

From M:Tron to Exploriens, U.F.O., and RoboForce, each LEGO Space series had its own astronauts. One rare pair was Biff Starling and Sandy Moondust, "astrobots" produced as a tie-in with NASA's 2003 Mars Exploration Rover mission.

Space Police II (1992)

Insectoids (1998)

Biff Starling (2002)

6986 Mission Commander (1989)

SPACE POLICE

Piloting blue and black vehicles with clear red windows and interchangeable prison cells, the Space Police arrived in 1989 to battle the villains of Blacktron. They returned with a second series in 1992, and again in 2009 after LEGO Space was relaunched.

Rocket booster

Classic Space logo

497 Galaxy Explorer (1979)

LL 928

EXPLORING A GALAXY

The classic of classic LEGO spaceships and a favorite for Space fans, the Galaxy Explorer was built in the traditional blue and grey color scheme with yellow windows and details. It included a decorated base plate with a communications tower and launch pad.

7314 Recon-Mech RP (2001)

RED PLANET ADVENTURE

Life on Mars brought things closer to home with the story of a crashed shuttle team and a planet of mech-driving Martians for them to battle or befriend. Apart from a licensed Discovery Channel theme in 2003, it was the last LEGO Space series for six years.

Double cockpit

Extending grabber arm

6939 Saucer Centurion (1994)

DEEP FREEZE

In 1993, LEGO builders went on an interstellar journey to the distant future of 2002. Ice Planet 2002 took place on the frozen world of Krysto, where clear neon orange parts reigned supreme, jetpacks gave way to skis, and lasers were replaced by ice-cutting chainsaws.

Magnetic rocket crane

6898 Ice-Sat V (1993)

SPY GUYS

In 1994, Spyrius joined the bad guys of Blacktron as the latest villains to menace the LEGO Space universe. Until 1996, these data-stealing agents used giant and minifigure-sized robots to do their dirty work all over the galaxy. The Saucer Centurion, the Spyrius flagship, could split down the middle to deploy an android-driven space buggy.

LEGO® Mars Mission

THE LAST TIME LEGO® space explorers traveled to Mars in 2001's LEGO Life on Mars theme, they encountered a friendly Martian civilization. In 2007, they returned to a Red Planet filled with precious energy crystals and menaced by a mysterious alien armada. The result was the first new LEGO Space theme in six years: Mars Mission ●

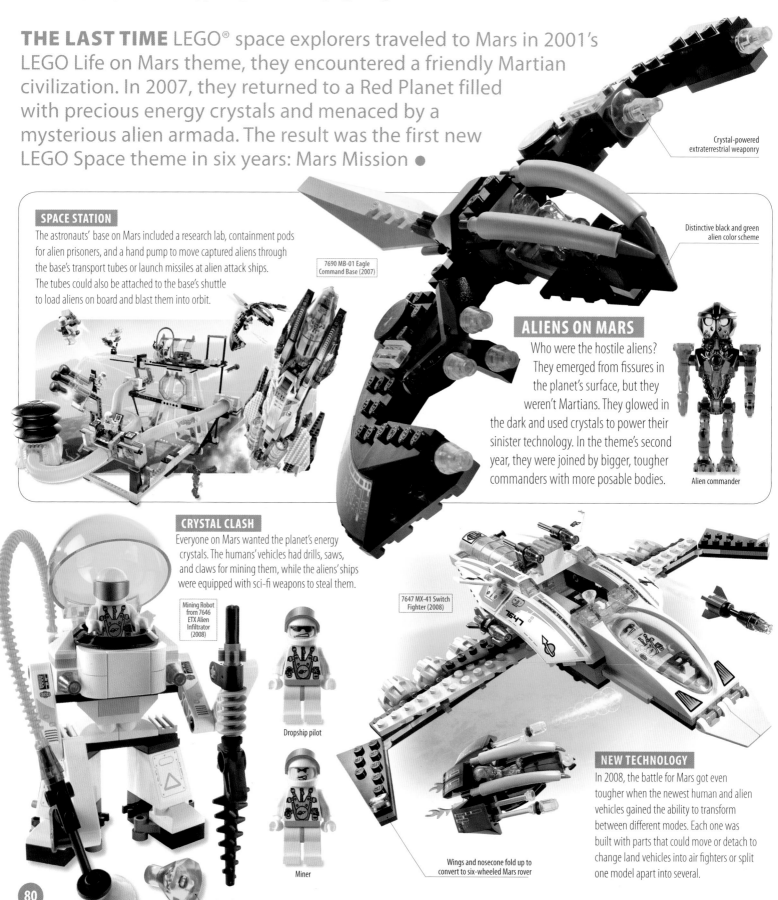

Crystal-powered extraterrestrial weaponry

Distinctive black and green alien color scheme

SPACE STATION

The astronauts' base on Mars included a research lab, containment pods for alien prisoners, and a hand pump to move captured aliens through the base's transport tubes or launch missiles at alien attack ships. The tubes could also be attached to the base's shuttle to load aliens on board and blast them into orbit.

7690 MB-01 Eagle Command Base (2007)

ALIENS ON MARS

Who were the hostile aliens? They emerged from fissures in the planet's surface, but they weren't Martians. They glowed in the dark and used crystals to power their sinister technology. In the theme's second year, they were joined by bigger, tougher commanders with more posable bodies.

Alien commander

CRYSTAL CLASH

Everyone on Mars wanted the planet's energy crystals. The humans' vehicles had drills, saws, and claws for mining them, while the aliens' ships were equipped with sci-fi weapons to steal them.

Mining Robot from 7646 ETX Alien Infiltrator (2008)

7647 MX-41 Switch Fighter (2008)

Dropship pilot

Miner

Crystal

Wings and nosecone fold up to convert to six-wheeled Mars rover

NEW TECHNOLOGY

In 2008, the battle for Mars got even tougher when the newest human and alien vehicles gained the ability to transform between different modes. Each one was built with parts that could move or detach to change land vehicles into air fighters or split one model apart into several.

ALIEN TECH

The aliens' ultimate attack vehicle included five glowing alien warriors and could split apart into a command saucer, two scout ships, and a strike fighter. To combat it, the set came with a defense station with two astronauts and pump-blasted foam missiles.

7691 ETX Alien Mothership Assault (2007)

Shuttle attaches as cockpit and drill becomes top-mounted cannon

7649 MT-201 Ultra-Drill Walker (2008)

MULTI-PURPOSE WALKER

Another special-edition set, the MT-201 could be converted from a mining base with a powerful spinning drill into a 4-legged mech walker with a detachable observation shuttle and a launching missile. It also came with a small enemy vehicle to fight.

Gear-driven rotating drill

THREE VEHICLES IN ONE

With independent suspension for its six wheels, a giant drill for mining crystals, a firing launcher and the ability to separate into three vehicles to fight an alien attack ship, the special-edition MT-101 was one of the most popular Mars Mission sets.

7699 MT-101 Armored Drilling Unit (2007)

Instructions included for motorizing with LEGO Power Functions parts

Cockpit becomes armed flying vehicle

7645 MT-61 Crystal Reaper (2008)

CRYSTAL REAPER

The MT-61 was designed to collect crystals from Martian rocks, but with its giant spinning saw blades, blasters, and gripping hands, it was no slouch in the alien-fighting department. It included three astronauts, two aliens, an alien commander, an alien strike-ship, and a deploying rover.

MT 61-REAPER

Treads rotate and saw-blades and crystal scoops spin when model rolls

LEGO® Space Police

IN 2009, the Space Police made their long-awaited return. Piloting sleek black-and-white patrol spaceships and packing an arsenal of freeze-ray blasters and prison pods, these brave defenders of the interplanetary peace had the tough job of chasing down an assortment of crooks from all sectors of the galaxy and bringing them to justice ●

Space Biker Gang markings

LIGHT-SPEED HEIST

Toting a safe full of stolen gold bars, the Skull Twins thought they could make a quick getaway aboard their Skull Interceptor. But even though the alien brothers broke every speed limit in the universe, they couldn't evade the long arm of the intergalactic law.

SPACE CHASE

The nano-second the First Galactic Bank's alarm sounded, the Space Police were on the move in the VX-Falcon Pursuit Cruiser. Siren blazing and lights flashing, the pilot hit his turbo-rockets and blasted off at near-lightspeed after the fleeing space criminals. All it took was a few well-placed freeze-rays and both the pilfered gold and the Skull Twins were safely back in Space Police custody.

5973 Hyperspeed Pursuit (2009)

Modular prison pod

Freeze-ray blasters

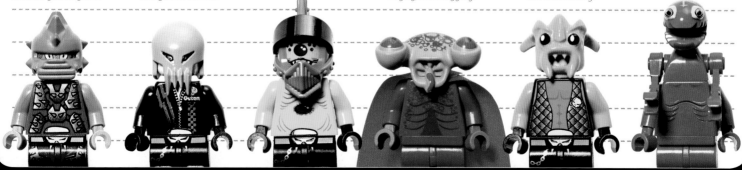

COSMIC CROOKS

Slizer, heavy-metal hyper-crook with a penchant for satellite theft and galactic graffiti.

The Skull Twins, identical clone brothers with a double dose of disregard for the law.

Snake, arachnoid astro-punk who once stole a prototype Space Police laser.

Squidman, gold-crazed mollusk menace wanted for gold robbery, forging, and smuggling.

Kranxx, Space Biker leader wanted galaxy-wide for grand theft spacecraft and robot rustling.

Frenzy, four-armed space lizard known for illegally impersonating a Venusian.

Detachable escape craft

LEGO® Alien Conquest

THE HISTORY of LEGO® Space is full of astronauts blasting off from Earth to explore the outer reaches of the galaxy and encountering all kinds of alien life forms along the way. But in 2011, for the first time ever, they came to visit us—and they weren't friendly. As saucers and tripods swept across the world, only the A.D.U. stood between our planet… and alien conquest ●

7051 Tripod Invader (2011)

Clinger and Alien Trooper

Panicked human citizen

Alien Pilots have hyper-tuned reflexes

Transparent neon-green elements

WALK AND RULE

The three-legged Tripod Invader had posable legs, a swiveling disintegrator cannon, a prison pod for captured humans, and a bumper sticker reading, "WE'VE BEEN TO EARTH." Removing the civilian's hair and attaching an Alien Clinger (a.k.a. Pluuvian Brain-Beast) over his head would drain his brainpower and control him.

Brainpower-fueled technology

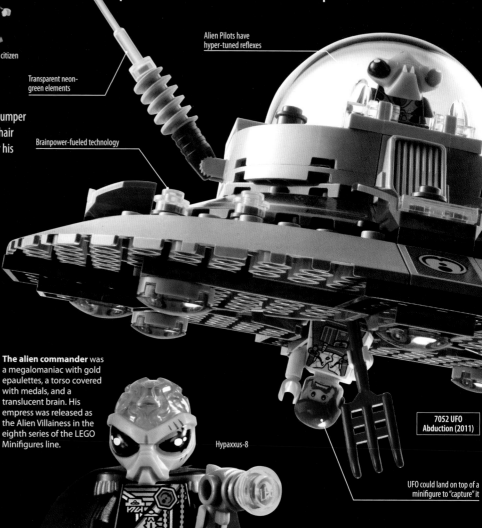

7065 Alien Mothership (2011)

The alien commander was a megalomaniac with gold epaulettes, a torso covered with medals, and a translucent brain. His empress was released as the Alien Villainess in the eighth series of the LEGO Minifigures line.

Hypaxxus-8

7052 UFO Abduction (2011)

UFO could land on top of a minifigure to "capture" it

MOTHERSHIP

Hypaxxus-8 oversaw the invasion from his giant saucer along with his pet Clinger, Captain Ploovie. Spinning the mothership's outer ring (built from curved track elements) produced an eerie electronic sound. It also had a jointed capture claw to grab a reporter for an exclusive interview.

The News Reporter may have gotten a little too close to her story this time.

THE INVADERS

Under the leadership of the tentacled Commander Hypaxxus-8, the invasion fleet included dim-witted Alien Troopers, hyperactive Alien Pilots, and the cybernetic Alien Android. They came to kidnap humans and steal our brainpower to use as spaceship fuel.

THE A.D.U.

Earth's protectors were the Alien Defense Unit (A.D.U.), an elite fighting force that used the latest tech to strike back against the invaders. Their base was the Earth Defense HQ, a massive armored truck with firing rockets in front and a mobile laboratory in back. The articulated sections could snap together for a compact transport mode.

The shuttle's decals included an homage to a late fan builder who went by the nickname "nnenn".

Interceptor Shuttle on launch rack

The HQ's lab trailer was loaded with equipment and scanners for studying captured aliens and freeing Clinger victims. Panels on its sides could be folded out to reveal flip-up satellite dishes for detecting alien attacks.

Rescue vehicle with stretcher

Mini UFO

7066 Earth Defense HQ (2011)

Alien containment pod

OUR HEROES

The A.D.U. forces included the grizzled Sergeant, the cocky Pilot, the loyal Soldier, the brainy Computer Specialist, the eccentric Scientist (in white), and the enthusiastic but hapless Rookie. Most wore uniforms in a brand-new shade of blue and carried a double-barreled blaster.

Alien Troopers had big mouths and tiny brains

7049 Alien Striker (2011)

CONQUEST'S END

The Alien Conquest story reached its climax in the November 2011 issue of *LEGO Club Magazine*, which resulted in the extraterrestrial invaders' (seemingly temporary) defeat… and tied it together with the Atlantis, Pharaoh's Quest, and LEGO Dino themes!

The Computer Specialist's small scout car battled an even smaller alien mini hover-bike.

Alien prisoners could be stowed in the Jet-Copter's detachable pod.

SKY PROTECTOR

The Jet-Copter was the only vehicle fast enough to catch flying saucers, though it might have met its match in a UFO that could split into a pair of flyers. Although the website listed this as the A.D.U. Pilot's favorite vehicle, it actually came with the Rookie.

7067 Jet-Copter Encounter (2011)

Wingtip cannons

LEGO ALIEN CONQUEST 7-14 7050

7050 Alien Defender (2011)

85

Sets to Remember

493 Space Command Center (1978)

305 2 Crater Plates (1979)

6954 Renegade (1987)

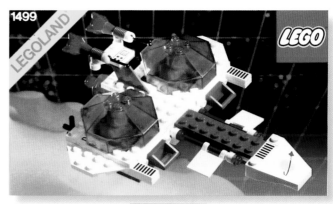

1499 Twin Starfire (1987)

454 Landing Plates (1979)

LIGHT SYSTEM

Licht System
Mit elektrischen Leucht- und Blinkelementen, die auch in andere LEGOLAND® Modelle eingebaut werden können.

Système Lumineux
Ce modèle LEGOLAND® est muni de flashes lumineux. Les éléments lumineux peuvent être incorporés dans d'autres modèles LEGOLAND.

Sistema luce
Questo modello LEGOLAND ha luci intermittenti. Gli elementi luce possono essere inseriti anche in altri modelli LEGOLAND.

6781 SP-Striker (1989)

483 Alpha-1 Rocket Base (1979)

6930 Space Supply Station (1983)

6989 Mega Core Magnetizer (1990)

6877 Vector Detector (1990)

6887 Allied Avenger (1991)

6991 Monorail Transport Base (1994)

7315 Solar Explorer (2001)

7699 MT-101 Armored Drilling Unit (2007)

6939 Sonar Security (1993)

6982 Explorien Starship (1996)

1793 Space Station Zenon (1995)

7697 MT-51 Claw-Tank Ambush (2007)

7647 MX-41 Switch Fighter (2008)

5972 Space Truck Getaway (2009)

6975 Alien Avenger (1997)

6907 Sonic Stinger (1998)

8399 K-9 Bot (2009)

7052 UFO Abduction (2011)

LEGO® Pirates

YO HO HO! The first eleven
LEGO® Pirates sets set sail
in 1989, and they quickly
became the most popular
LEGO theme of the time.
Filled with daring
buccaneers with hook-
hands and peg-legs,
square-sailed sailing
ships, tropical islands
full of hidden treasure,
and imperial soldiers in
hot high-seas pursuit,
LEGO Pirates is still an
enduring favorite for
kids and grown-up fans
alike. Best of all, it was
up to you to decide
which of the scurvy
swashbucklers were the
good guys and which
were the bad guys ●

On The High Seas

SHIPS AHOY! A pirate captain has to have a ship, and the LEGO® Pirates theme was filled from the start with gallant galleons, cutlass-laden clippers, and ramshackle rafts. Through more than 20 years of ocean-going excitement and fun, these stalwart sea vessels have helped their crews do what they do best: loot, fight, and have a swashbucklingly good time on the high seas.

A PIRATE'S PRIZE

The fan-favorite Black Seas Barracuda is considered by many to be the best classic LEGO pirate ship. With Captain Redbeard at the helm, it sailed the Seven Seas with four cannons, five secret compartments, and seven piratical crew members, plus a parrot and monkey.

6286 Skull's Eye Schooner (1993)

A SKULL'S EYE BROADSIDE

Even bigger than the Black Seas Barracuda, this three-masted pirate ship boasted a quartet of deck cannons that could rotate from one side to the other, making it a dangerous foe to sail alongside.

Fabric sails

7070 Catapult Raft (2004)

Eight years after the last LEGO Pirates set, the 2004 LEGO 4+ Pirates series reintroduced the theme for younger deckhands with bigger figures and models for quicker, easier construction.

6285 Black Seas Barracuda (1989)

IMPERIAL SOLDIERS

When the LEGO Pirates first set sail in 1989, they were opposed by the blue-uniformed Imperial Soldiers. The soldiers were led by Governor Broadside, whose Caribbean Clipper was named the Sea Hawk in its UK release.

6274 Caribbean Clipper (1989)

After an absence of 12 long years (apart from three 2001 re-releases), minifigure-scale LEGO Pirates sets finally returned in 2009 with an all-new series of models and a new pirate captain.

6240 Kraken Attackin (2009)

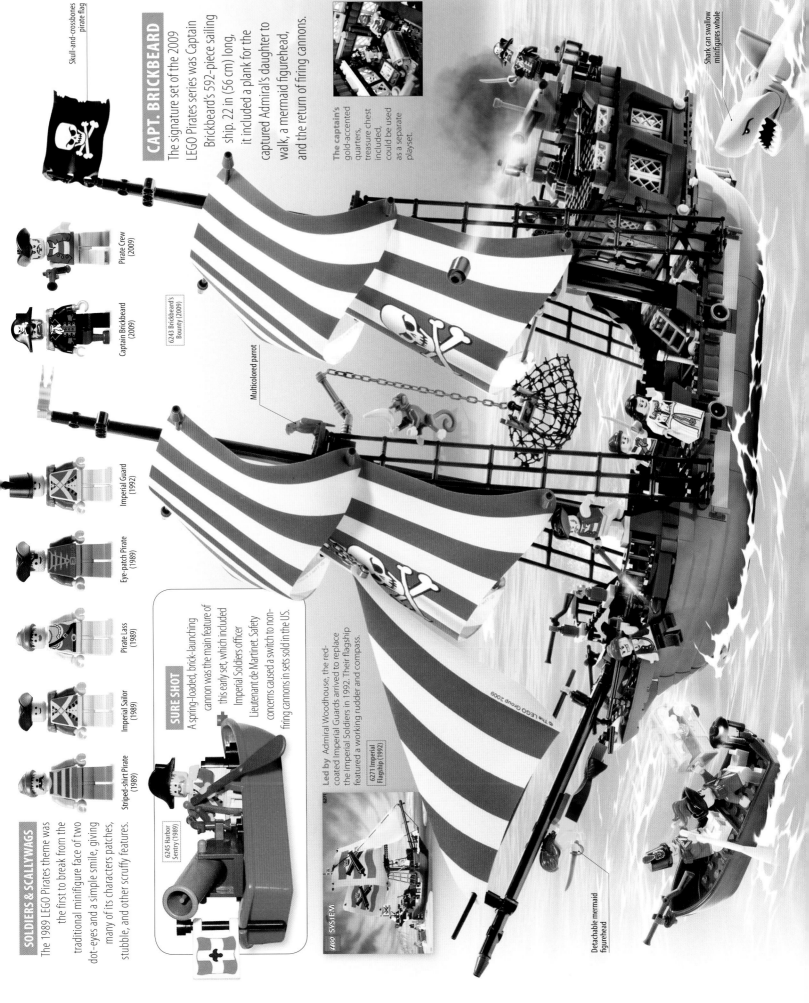

CAPT. BRICKBEARD

The signature set of the 2009 LEGO Pirates series was Captain Brickbeard's 592-piece sailing ship. 22 in (56 cm) long, it included a plank for the captured Admiral's daughter to walk, a mermaid figurehead, and the return of firing cannons.

The captain's gold-accented quarters, treasure chest included, could be used as a separate playset.

Shark can swallow minifigures whole

Pirate Crew (2009)

Captain Brickbeard (2009)

6243 Brickbeard's Bounty (2009)

Multicolored parrot

SOLDIERS & SCALLYWAGS

The 1989 LEGO Pirates theme was the first to break from the traditional minifigure face of two dot-eyes and a simple smile, giving many of its characters patches, stubble, and other scruffy features.

Imperial Guard (1992)

Eye-patch Pirate (1989)

Pirate Lass (1989)

Imperial Sailor (1989)

Striped-shirt Pirate (1989)

SURE SHOT

A spring-loaded, brick-launching cannon was the main feature of this early set, which included Imperial Soldiers officer Lieutenant de Martinet. Safety concerns caused a switch to non-firing cannons in sets sold in the US.

6245 Harbor Sentry (1989)

Led by Admiral Woodhouse, the red-coated Imperial Guards arrived to replace the Imperial Soldiers in 1992. Their flagship featured a working rudder and compass.

6271 Imperial Flagship (1992)

LEGO SYSTEM

© The LEGO Group 2009

Detachable mermaid figurehead

Treasure Islands

What good is plundered pirate treasure without somewhere to bury it? The world of the LEGO® Pirates is full of exotic desert islands, pirate hideouts, and soldier outposts, forts, and prisons. The theme has even had a band of tropical islanders, who weren't too thrilled about their new piratical neighbors digging up their beautiful beaches ●

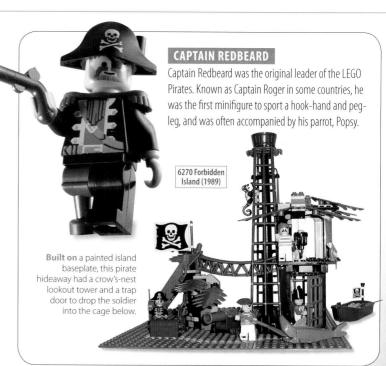

CAPTAIN REDBEARD

Captain Redbeard was the original leader of the LEGO Pirates. Known as Captain Roger in some countries, he was the first minifigure to sport a hook-hand and peg-leg, and was often accompanied by his parrot, Popsy.

6270 Forbidden Island (1989)

Built on a painted island baseplate, this pirate hideaway had a crow's-nest lookout tower and a trap door to drop the soldier into the cage below.

Governor Broadside

6276 Eldorado Fortress (1989)

MEET THE GOVERNOR

One of only two sets to include the rare Governor Broadside figure, this sturdy portside fortress swarmed with loyal Imperial Soldiers, each of them ready to arrest and imprison any pirates daring or foolish enough to try to steal the Governor's treasure.

"Cannonball" launched by pulling and releasing a spring-loaded knob on the cannon

SHIPWRECKED

Long ago, the pirate king's ship ran aground on an uncharted island, and Captain Brickbeard built his hideout inside the wreck. Invading soldiers had to get past a collapsing bridge, a slashing sword trap, and a skull launcher.

6253 Shipwreck Hideout (2009)

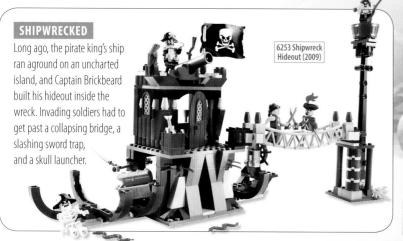

NEW ENEMIES

Although they wore red coats like the 1992 Imperial Guards, the 2009 theme's soldiers were not given a formal name. They did, however, get their own base: a fortress prison built above the sea, complete with a new Admiral figure to lead the troops, a Captain Brickbeard wanted poster, and a jail cell with a monkey guard that the pirate prisoner could bribe with a banana.

Crane with working winch to load and unload treasure

6242 Soldiers' Fort (2009)

Following the Imperial Soldiers and Imperial Guards came the Imperial Armada, a new faction of soldiers inspired by Spanish conquistadors.

6244 Armada Sentry (1996)

6278 Enchanted Island (1994)

In 1994, the pirates met the Islanders. Led by King Kahuka, the Pacific Islands-inspired tribe didn't take kindly to trespassing buccaneers.

CAPTAIN IRONHOOK

The second LEGO Pirates captain was Captain Ironhook, introduced in 1992 and shown in command of the 6268 Renegade Runner in 1993. Not as stylishly dressed as Captains Redbeard or Brickbeard, the tattered Ironhook battled the Royal Guards and Islanders, and occasionally gained or lost a peg-leg. He was last seen aboard 1996's 6289 Red Beard Runner.

This set included a new island baseplate, a fish roasting over a fire, a catapult, and a treasure map.

6241 Loot Island (2009)

TREASURE HUNTERS

A skull marked the spot on this almost-deserted island where a castaway guarded a hidden treasure. When both a pirate and soldier arrived, it was a three-way race to find the golden chest.

Dark green crocodile with moving jaw and tail

Imperial Flagship

AFTER YEARS of the LEGO® Pirates ruling the seas, the Imperial navy finally struck back in 2010 with the biggest LEGO sailing ship of them all. Stretching 30 in (75 cm) from bowsprit to stern and standing 24 in (60 cm) tall at the top of its main-mast, the enormous Imperial Flagship was built from 1,664 LEGO pieces ●

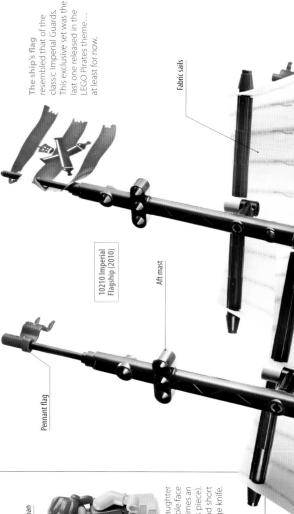

The ship's flag resembled that of the classic Imperial Guards. This exclusive set was the last one released in the LEGO Pirates theme... at least for now.

Fabric sails

10210 Imperial Flagship (2010)

Aft mast

Pennant flag

PIRATE PURSUIT

Watch out, Captain Brickbeard! The flagship was crewed by its captain, four soldiers, a lieutenant, the ship's cook, and the captain's daughter. No wonder the famous pirate ended up shackled in the brig—but could he get loose, steal the captain's gold, and make his escape?

Frying pan

The captain's daughter had a reversible face (and sometimes an alternate dress piece). The cook had short legs and a large knife.

Rifle

Peg leg

The ship included four firing, wheeled cannons, eight cannon hatches (four on each side), and plenty of ammunition.

DECK TOUR

Realistic and detailed in its design, the Imperial Flagship was covered with doors and hatches, railings, and intricately assembled decorations. It had a working anchor winch, a captain's quarters, a galley, and a brig (with a resident rat to keep the pirate prisoners company).

Clips on the base of the ship's wheel held a golden telescope and a sextant for plotting a safe course across the waves.

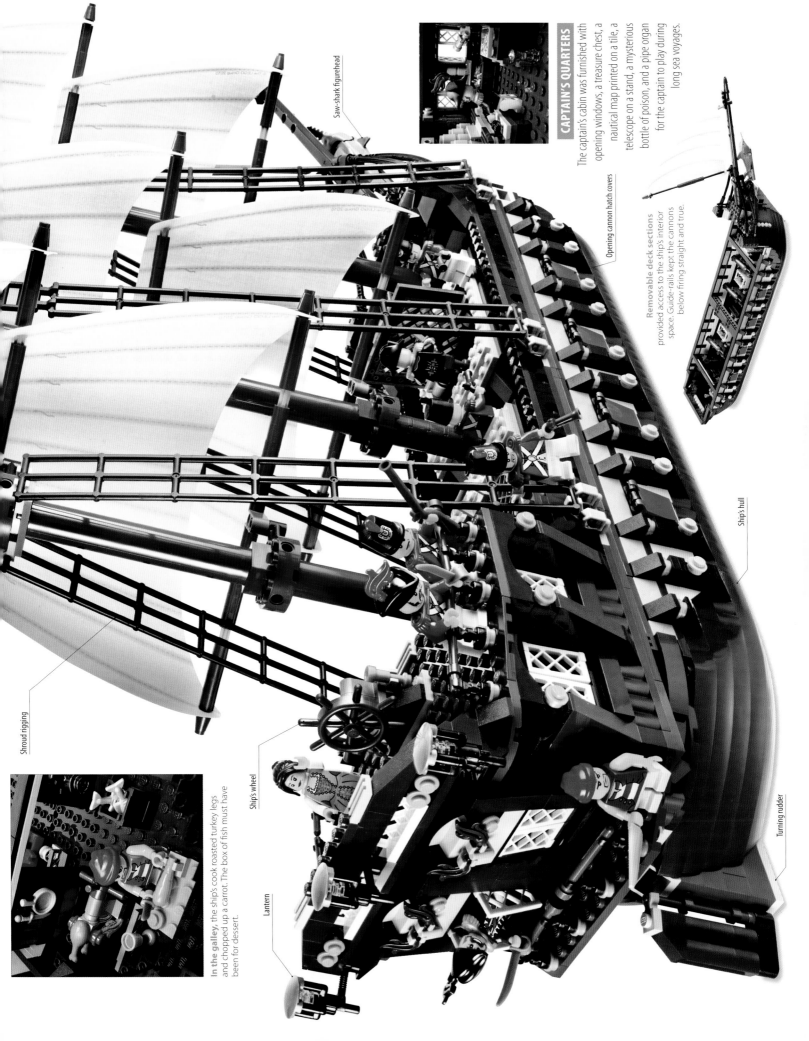

Shroud rigging

Ship's wheel

Lantern

In the galley, the ship's cook roasted turkey legs and chopped up a carrot. The box of fish must have been for dessert.

Saw-shark figurehead

Opening cannon hatch covers

CAPTAIN'S QUARTERS

The captain's cabin was furnished with opening windows, a treasure chest, a nautical map printed on a tile, a telescope on a stand, a mysterious bottle of poison, and a pipe organ for the captain to play during long sea voyages.

Removable deck sections provided access to the ship's interior space. Guide-rails kept the cannons below firing straight and true.

Ship's hull

Turning rudder

Sets to Remember

6235 Buried Treasure (1989)

1696 Pirate Lookout (1992)

6268 Renegade Runner (1993)

6285 Black Seas Barracuda (1989)

6256 Islander Catamaran (1994)

6262 King Kahuka's Throne (1994)

6236 King Kahuka (1994)

6273 Rock Island Refuge (1991)

6237 Pirates' Plunder (1993)

6267 Lagoon Lock-up (1991)

6252 Sea Mates (1993)

6279 Skull Island (1995)

6280

8-12

6290

5-12
8397

6280 Armada Flagship (1996)

6290 Pirate Battle Ship / Red Beard Runner (2001)

8397 Pirate Survival (2009)

INCLUDES 6 MINIFIGURES
INCLUT 6 FIGURINES

Ages/edades
6-12
6253
Shipwreck Hideout
Cont. 310 pcs/pzs

LIMITED EDITION

1747

6296

1747 Pirates Treasure Suprise (1996)

6296 Shipwreck Island (1996)

6253 Shipwreck Hideout (2009)

6248

6232

5-12
8396

6248 Volcano Island (1996)

6204 Buccaneers (1997)

6232 Skeleton Crew (1996)

8396 Soldier's Arsenal (2009)

Cont. 155 pcs/pzs

4+
7072

4+
7071

7071 Treasure Island (2004)

4+
7074

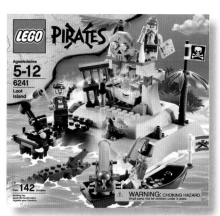

Ages/edades
5-12
6241
Loot Island

Cont. 142 pcs/pzs

6249 Pirates Ambush (1997)

7072 Captain Kragg's Pirate Boat (2004)

7074 Skull Island (2004)

6241 Loot Island (2009)

LEGO® Adventures

JOURNEY TO A WORLD of buildable adventures, where the good guys are good, the bad guys are bad, and there's always another battle for the fate of the city, the ocean, or the planet waiting just around the corner. These classic and modern LEGO® themes have taken kids of all ages from the Earth's inner core to a near future filled with rampaging dinosaurs, and even on a wild trip through time itself. Fasten your supercar seat belt and power up your giant robot, because the LEGO adventures are just getting started ●

Another adventurer?

Around the Globe

YOU CAN'T HAVE ADVENTURE without adventurers! From 1998 until 2003, the LEGO® Adventurers traveled the globe in search of discoveries and danger—and they found plenty of both. Though the names of his friends and enemies often changed, you always knew that wherever Johnny Thunder and company went, exciting adventure was sure to follow ●

This hot-air balloon carried the Adventurers over the Himalayas in the 2003 LEGO Orient Expedition series.

Crate of adventure tools

7415 Aero Nomad (2003)

LEGO ADVENTURERS

In 1998, a new hero arrived in the LEGO universe. Johnny Thunder, dashing explorer from Australia, was joined by the wise Dr. Kilroy and intrepid reporter Miss Pippin Reed. Together, they were the LEGO Adventurers, and for five years and four series of LEGO sets, their travels took them on exciting 1920s-era adventures all over the world.

LEGO ORIENT EXPEDITION

The final LEGO Adventurers theme saw Johnny and his friends journey across India, China, and Tibet as they faced a tyrannical Maharaja, a ruthless emperor, a wild Yeti, and their old enemy Lord Sam Sinister in search of explorer Marco Polo's long-lost treasure.

ADVENTURES IN EGYPT

The first series to feature the Adventurers took place in Egypt during the golden age of archaeology. Joined by their pilot friend Harry Cane, Johnny and his friends explored tombs, temples, and pyramids, encountering mummies, skeletons, scorpions, and nefarious criminals along the way.

5988 Pharaoh's Forbidden Ruins (1998)

AMAZON

In 1999, the Adventurers returned for a journey deep into the Amazon jungle. There, they braved colorful tribal warriors and perilous pitfalls while racing to find treasures before the villainous Señor Palomar and Rudo Villano could get their hands on them. At least Pippin had a good story to take back to World Magazine!

1271 Jungle Surprise (1999)

5934 Track Master/Dino Explorer (2000)

DINO ISLAND

2000 saw Johnny and his friends visit a lost island inhabited by dinosaurs, where they built a research compound and kept Lord Sinister and his allies from stealing the creatures.

7414 Elephant Caravan (2003)

To find the Golden Dragon statue, the Adventurers had to make it past the traps and guards in Emperor Chang Wu's Dragon Fortress.

The Adventurers' new friend Babloo and his elephant Giri.

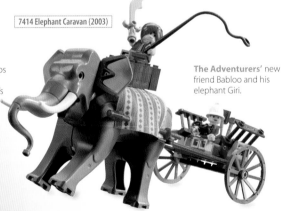

Fireworks

Lord Sinister

Printed 3-D baseplate

7419 Dragon Fortress (2003)

ALSO KNOWN AS...

The Adventurers often had different names in different countries. Johnny Thunder was also known as Sam Grant and Joe Freemann, Dr. Kilroy as Dr. Charles Lightning and Professor Articus, and Pippin Reed as Pippin Read, Gail Storm, and Linda Lovely. Even in the same country, things could change: the original Sam Sinister later became Slyboots, while the second Lord Sinister also went by Baron von Barron, Sam Sanister, Evil Eye, and Mr. Hates!

One place you don't expect to find evil mummies is up in the sky—but that's exactly where Jake Raines ran across them in his search for the Soul Diamond.

7307 Flying Mummy Attack (2011)

ANCIENT TREASURES

Each of the treasures gave Amset-Ra a different power, like the Golden Staff that increased the might of his mummy servants. If he could gather all six, the pharaoh would become unstoppable. That's why it was up to the luckless Mac to get it first!

7306 Golden Staff Guardians (2011)

PHARAOH'S QUEST

The Adventurers' spirit lived on in the 2011 theme Pharaoh's Quest, which pitted a new team of period adventure heroes against a resurrected Egyptian king with an army of mummy warriors and living stone monsters. The heroes' task was to find six ancient treasures and prevent Pharaoh Amset-Ra from conquering the world.

Like Johnny Thunder, Gail Storm and Professor Lightning before them, Jake Raines, Mac McCloud, Professor Hale and Helena Skvalling all had weather-related names.

7327 Scorpion Pyramid (2011)

MUMMIES

Amset-Ra's legions included Mummy Warriors, winged and falcon-helmeted Flying Mummies, a Mummy Snake Charmer, and the elite, jackal-headed Anubis Guards who protected his pyramid. Each type was stronger than the last.

Scarab shield

Mummy Warrior from 7306 Golden Staff Guardians (2011)

CREATURES OF STONE

7326 Rise of the Sphinx (2011)

Even more dangerous than the pharaoh's warriors were the ancient guardians that protected his treasures: giant beasts that looked like stone statues until they sprang to life to attack the enemies of Amset-Ra. They included a mighty sphinx that crouched above the Temple of Anubis, hiding place of the Golden Sword.

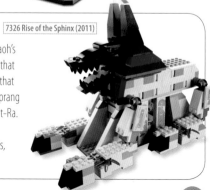

Worlds of Adventure

FROM THE ROOTIN', tootin' cowboys of the Wild West to the dangerous world of 2010, from the time-cruising travels of the eccentric Dr. Cyber to battles with dinosaurs in the modern-day jungle… when you're building a LEGO® adventure, your imagination can take you anywhere you want to go, or even anywhen—past, present, or future ●

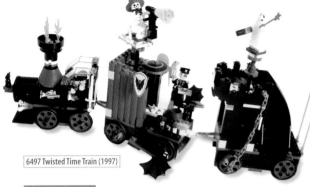

6497 Twisted Time Train (1997)

TIME TRAVEL

In 1996, Dr. Cyber, his sidekick Tim, and their monkey friend were the LEGO Time Cruisers, bold adventurers who traveled across the centuries in wacky hat-powered contraptions with parts that moved and spun when their wheels turned. 1997 introduced their rivals, Tony Twister and Professor Millennium, also known as the artifact-stealing Time Twisters.

WILD WESTERN

From 1996 to 1997, the LEGO Western theme took builders back to the American frontier of the 1800s and the age of round-ups, showdowns, and cattle rustling. With models full of cowboy minifigures, locations, and accessories but no official story to set the scene, kids were free to make up their own tall tales and adventures set in the exciting days of the Wild West.

6755 Sheriff's Lock-Up (1996)

The infamous outlaw Flatfoot Thompson

The brave sheriff and his faithful steed

Card shark Dewey Cheatum

Z-1 Kinetic Launcher

7476 Iron Predator vs. T-Rex (2005)

LEGO DINO ATTACK

In the near future, mutated monsters from the prehistoric past suddenly appeared and started laying waste to cities all across the globe. Enter the LEGO Dino Attack team: a rag-tag band of scientists, adventurers, and soldiers whose mission was to fight back against the rogue reptiles and end their threat once and for all.

LEGO DINO 2010

In the year 2010, science finally brought extinct dinosaurs back to life. When they broke loose and escaped into the jungle, it was up to a team of fearless dino hunters to track down and recapture the gigantic creatures before they could cause any harm to the outside world.

Light-up eyes and mouth

7297 Dino Track Transport (2005)

In an unusual split launch, these 2005 themes offered two different spins on the same basic models. Some countries received the conflict-heavy Dino Attack, with vehicles covered in sci-fi weaponry and firing projectiles, while others had the more peaceful Dino 2010 with its nets, cages, and capture gear.

Rotating treads

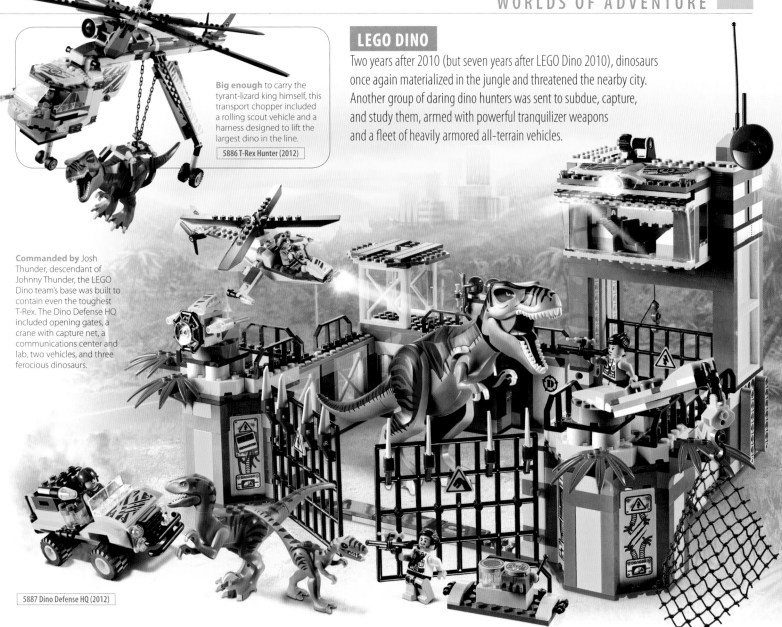

Big enough to carry the tyrant-lizard king himself, this transport chopper included a rolling scout vehicle and a harness designed to lift the largest dino in the line.

5886 T-Rex Hunter (2012)

LEGO DINO

Two years after 2010 (but seven years after LEGO Dino 2010), dinosaurs once again materialized in the jungle and threatened the nearby city. Another group of daring dino hunters was sent to subdue, capture, and study them, armed with powerful tranquilizer weapons and a fleet of heavily armored all-terrain vehicles.

Commanded by Josh Thunder, descendant of Johnny Thunder, the LEGO Dino team's base was built to contain even the toughest T-Rex. The Dino Defense HQ included opening gates, a crane with capture net, a communications center and lab, two vehicles, and three ferocious dinosaurs.

5887 Dino Defense HQ (2012)

JUNGLE CHASE

Sometimes it takes more than tranq rifles to catch a dinosaur. This off-roader's crew had to lure a ravenous Raptor in close with the most low-tech trap of all: a roasted turkey leg. Then they just needed to snare it with the lasso and somehow get it back to base.

5884 Raptor Chase (2012)

Flick-fire missiles

Lasso snare

Rotating boom

5885 Triceratops Trapper (2012)

THREE-HORNED TROUBLE

The spikes on the bumper of this heavy-duty truck were no match for the horns of an angry Triceratops. That's why it carried a set of flick-fire tranquilizer missiles in front and a reinforced cage in back. Dino team member "Tracer" Tops was just the minifigure for the job.

Where did the dinosaurs come from, and why were they here? The answer was revealed in the pages of *LEGO® Club Magazine*: it was all part of a plot by Commander Hypaxxus-8 of the Alien Conquest theme!

5883 Tower Takedown (2012)

Pteranodon bait stick

Tranq refilling station

Jet boat

Under the Sea

THE VAST OCEANS of the LEGO® world are filled with mysteries to explore, unknown dangers to face, and amazing new discoveries to make. Forget about outer space—for these brave divers, the deep blue sea is the real final frontier ●

LEGO SYSTEM   6160

7-12

6160 Sea Scorpion (1998)

LEGO AQUAZONE

Running from 1995 to 1998, LEGO Aquazone was the overall name for several underwater sci-fi themes, including the crystal-hunting Aquanauts, their enemies the Aquasharks, the Aquaraiders, the Hydronauts, and the fearsome fish-like Stingrays.

LEGO SYSTEM   6180

8-12

6180 Hydro Search Sub (1998)

LEGO AQUA RAIDERS

In 2007, the popular LEGO underwater theme returned when the Aqua Raiders dove into danger deep within the mysterious Bermuda Triangle. Piloting hi-tech submarines and other undersea vehicles, this team of valiant explorers searched every cave and fissure on the ocean floor in their quest for long-lost sunken treasure.

With snapping claws, spiny legs, and an armored shell, this giant lobster was one tough crustacean…

… but the Aqua Raiders underwater exploration rover took it on with the help of working treads, a robot arm, and a saw-blade drill.

7772 Lobster Strike (2007)

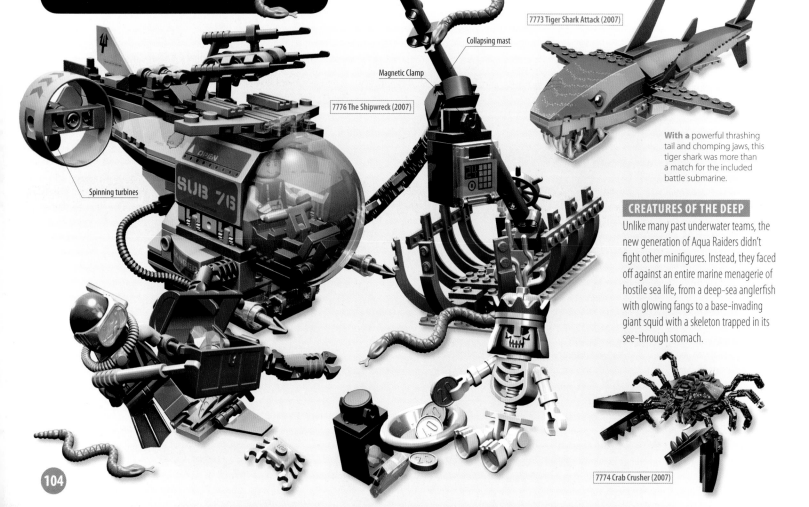

7773 Tiger Shark Attack (2007)

With a powerful thrashing tail and chomping jaws, this tiger shark was more than a match for the included battle submarine.

Collapsing mast

Magnetic Clamp

7776 The Shipwreck (2007)

Spinning turbines

SUB 76

CREATURES OF THE DEEP

Unlike many past underwater teams, the new generation of Aqua Raiders didn't fight other minifigures. Instead, they faced off against an entire marine menagerie of hostile sea life, from a deep-sea anglerfish with glowing fangs to a base-invading giant squid with a skeleton trapped in its see-through stomach.

7774 Crab Crusher (2007)

8077 Atlantis Exploration HQ (2010)

Sea-scooter docking platform

Spinnning drill

Primary viewing dome

In the second year of the Atlantis theme, the crew were joined by excavation specialist Dr. Brains from the LEGO Power Miners. Yellow parts replaced neon green on the team's new vehicles.

7984 Deep Sea Raider (2011)

THE CREW

The Atlantis crew were mission commander Captain Ace Speedman, first mate Lance Spears, tech pro Axel Storm, apprentice Bobby Buoy, marine biologist Dr. Jeff "Fish" Fisher, and Atlantis expert Professor Samantha (Sam) Rhodes.

Treasure keys could be used to activate special functions in Atlantis models. This one revealed the legendary Golden King, ruler of the lost city.

7985 City of Atlantis (2011)

8061 Gateway of the Squid (2010)

LEGO ATLANTIS

In 2010, the LEGO Atlantis theme sent a team of bold salvage divers on a mission to locate the famous sunken city of Atlantis. In futuristic undersea vehicles, they combed the ocean for long-lost treasure keys, battling fish-men and monstrous sea beasts that were determined to keep them from finding their goal.

8079 Shadow Snapper (2010)

The Shadow Snapper was an oversized turtle with a spiked shell and massive claws. It was available in a limited-edition set along with a small combat sub, diver, and treasure key.

RUINS OF ATLANTIS

The Gateway of the Squid was the team's first major archaeological find. A treasure key unlocked its gates, though you'd think they could just swim over them. Either way, they'd have to escape the giant squid's rotating jaws and the Squid Warrior's octopus prison cage.

8060 Typhoon Turbo Sub (2010)

The spectacular Portal of Atlantis featured an opening shark-jaw entrance, detachable shark statue guardians, a Portal Emperor minifigure, and a gateway that opened with five treasure keys.

8078 Portal of Atlantis (2010)

WARRIORS AND GUARDIANS

The crew faced fierce underwater humanoids such as the Manta Warrior, Shark Warrior, and Squid Warrior; 2011's evil Dark Guardians; and giant sea creatures covered with glowing Atlantean runes, including a huge black shark known as the Guardian of the Deep. The beginning of the LEGO Atlantis story was told in a half-hour television special, and other parts in magazine comics and online games.

A slider flipped the Typhoon Turbo Sub's propellers around to reveal a grabber claw and a firing torpedo. It would need them to defeat the Shark Warrior that guarded the yellow Atlantis treasure key!

Rough and Tough

WHETHER THEY'RE MINING for energy crystals in deep space, battling monsters at the Earth's core, or racing across the planet's most hostile terrain, these hard-working heroes laugh at danger and don't mind getting down and dirty. It's all part of a day's work when you're on one of the roughest, toughest teams of LEGO® minifigures around ●

THE CRYSTALS

Underwater, underground, or in outer space, LEGO explorers always seem to run into energy crystals. These ones packed some serious power —if a rock monster ate one, it would vibrate so much it created earth-shaking rumblings!

LEGO POWER MINERS

In 2009, mysterious rumblings from deep beneath the ground threatened to shake apart the surface world. To fix the problem, a courageous team of miners tunneled down to a subterranean kingdom full of glowing crystals and mischievous rock monsters. It was up to the Power Miners to dig up the crystals, stop the monsters, and save the planet!

8-12

4970

LEGO ROCK RAIDERS

A decade before the Power Miners took on their mission, the space-traveling LEGO Rock Raiders were flung across the galaxy to a distant planet, where they dug for energy crystals and battled alien rock creatures. Their adventures were chronicled in books and video games.

4970 Chrome Crusher (1999)

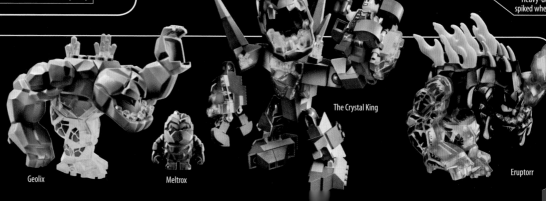

Double-geared rotating planetary drill

Adjustable drilling platform

Team leader Doc

Heavy-duty spiked wheels

THE MONSTERS

The underground world of the Power Miners was filled with monsters of all sizes, shapes, and colors. Each had its own troublemaking personality, from the pint-sized rock monsters and their hot-headed lava cousins, to the boulder-tossing bullies Geolix and Tremorox, all the way up to the titanic Crystal King and Eruptorr, ruler of the molten core.

Geolix

Meltrox

The Crystal King

Eruptorr

Cavern-illuminating floodlights

TITANIUM COMMAND RIG

The LEGO Power Miners' mobile base was this gigantic digging machine. Its forward-mounted drill had sections that rotated in different directions as the massive vehicle rolled forward. A few quick turns and snaps converted it into a vertical drilling platform built to bore into the cave floor below in search of crystals.

Veteran miner Duke

World-famous scientist Brains

Rock monster containment cage

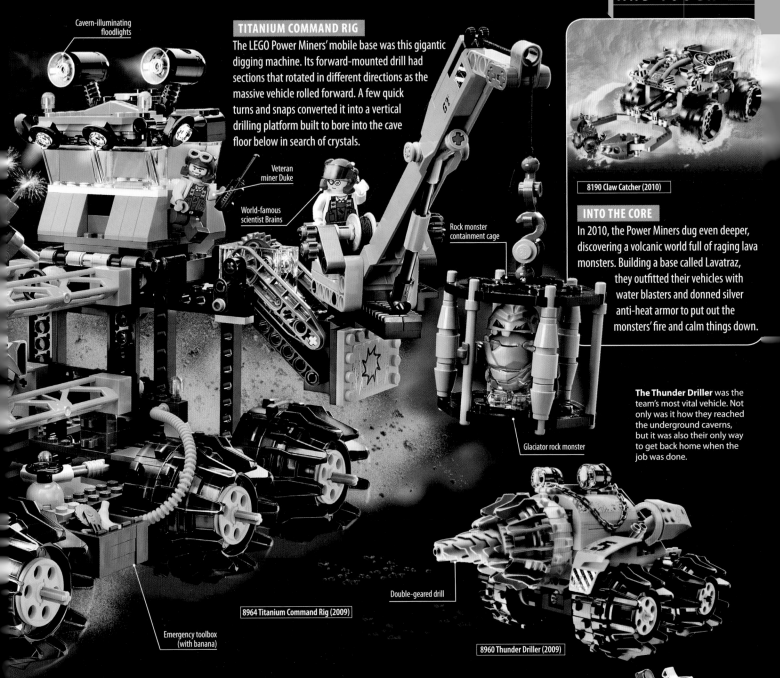

8190 Claw Catcher (2010)

INTO THE CORE

In 2010, the Power Miners dug even deeper, discovering a volcanic world full of raging lava monsters. Building a base called Lavatraz, they outfitted their vehicles with water blasters and donned silver anti-heat armor to put out the monsters' fire and calm things down.

The Thunder Driller was the team's most vital vehicle. Not only was it how they reached the underground caverns, but it was also their only way to get back home when the job was done.

Glaciator rock monster

Double-geared drill

8964 Titanium Command Rig (2009)

Emergency toolbox (with banana)

8960 Thunder Driller (2009)

LEGO WORLD RACERS

The World Racers theme of 2010 pitted the fearless X-treme Daredevils team against the lowdown, cheating Backyard Blasters in high-speed racing competitions in different vehicles and environments all over the globe. With set names like Snake Canyon, Wreckage Road, and Jagged Jaws Reef, you knew

Missiles, harpoons, chainsaws, mines, dynamite, fish-launchers, and ball-blasting cannons were all within the rules for the World Racers' armed and armored rides.

REX-Treme, DEX-Treme, and MAX-Treme faced off against Bart, Billy Bob, and Bubba Blaster.

Extreme Action

WHEN EVIL MASTERMINDS hatched sinister schemes… when giant robots rampaged through the streets… when mad scientists threatened to take over the world… these LEGO® themes were there! Filled with battle-function models and larger-than-life heroes, they took adventure to a new level of excitement ●

4791 Alpha Team Sub-Surface Scooter (2002)

4791

MISSION DEEP SEA

In 2002, LEGO Alpha Team: Mission Deep Sea brought our heroes beneath the waves, where the newly hook-handed Ogel was creating an army of mutated sea life to do his bidding.

In 2004, the LEGO Alpha Team took a trip south to icy Antarctica, where Ogel was plotting to freeze time itself. A secret Alpha Mode let the team's latest vehicles reveal new forms and hidden weapons.

Orb-collecting crane

Evil skeleton drone

4746 Mobile Command Center (2004)

Dash Justice, the heroic leader of LEGO Alpha Team.

LEGO ALPHA TEAM

On the land, in the air, even at the bottom of the sea, Dash Justice and the agents of LEGO Alpha Team were always ready to foil the planet-conquering schemes of the evil Ogel (say it backwards!) and his mind-control orbs.

4742 Chill Speeder (2004)

ALPHA MODE

With Agent Flex at the controls, the speedy Chill Speeder could convert from a snowmobile into an all-terrain walker to help the team search for Ogel's ice orbs.

8634 Mission 5: Turbocar Chase (2008)

TURBO POWER

Move over, bad guys—Agent Chase was at the wheel of his turbocar with a stolen laptop full of Dr. Inferno's latest evil plans! The spider-legged Spy Clops was only one of the villains Chase and his fellow agents fought. They also crossed paths with the likes of Break Jaw, Gold Tooth, and Slime Face.

Rare silver-coated elements

Pop-up laser blasters

TGD-2000

HOT SPOT

In true evil-genius fashion, Dr. Inferno made his super villain base inside an active volcano. The set included Agents Chase, Trace, and Fuse, as well as the spiky-haired doctor and hench-persons Fire Arm and Claw-Dette. Lots of translucent orange elements simulated blazing-hot lava.

8637 Mission 8: Volcano Base (2008)

Giant laser cannon

Satellite dish

Remote-controlled arm

The other Agents had to rescue the captured Fuse before Claw-Dette dropped him into the lava pit.

Articulated robo-limbs

8635 Mission 6: Mobile Command Center (2008)

Stealth plane

The Agents' headquarters was packed with spy gear, a light-up mission projector, and a prison for Dr. Inferno.

Armor plating

Spy car 1

Spy car 2

Jet-boat stores under trailer

8970 Robo Attack (2009)

In the theme's second year, its name changed to Agents 2.0 and the action moved to the city. The Agents got new body armor… and Dr. Inferno got a giant robot to crush his enemies.

LEGO AGENTS

Wherever the maniacal Dr. Inferno struck, the LEGO Agents were on the case. The specially trained super-spies battled the bad doctor and his cybernetic henchmen with an arsenal of cutting-edge vehicles and gadgets. Their missions took them all over the world, from jetpack battles on snowy mountaintops to high-speed escapes from secret lairs.

8971 Aerial Defense Unit (2009)

The Agents 2.0 got a big new toy, too: a helicopter with a geared dual rotor and a mission to destroy Magma Commander's satellite broadcaster and magma-drones.

LEGO® Monster Fighters

9461 The Swamp Creature (2012)

Spear

Green LEGO frog

SPOOKY CREATURES have been a part of the LEGO® universe since the first ghost minifigure appeared in 1990, but this is definitely their biggest starring role. Monsters of all kinds abound in 2012's LEGO Monster Fighters theme, including vampires, swamp creatures, mummies, werewolves, and zombies. Standing against them was a band of heroes who battled to save the world from eternal night ●

VAMPYRE'S CASTLE

When Lord Vampyre collected the six moonstones and placed them in his castle's tower window, he would gain the power to eclipse the sun forever. It was up to Dr. Rodney Rathbone, Major Quinton Steele, Jack McHammer, Ann Lee, and Frank Rock to shine some light on his dark designs.

FISHY FIEND

LEGO Monster Fighters sets included decorated, transparent moonstones for the heroes to try to capture. The amphibious Swamp Creature guarded its stone from biker Frank Rock and his swamp boat. Its mask could be removed to reveal a fully painted face underneath, and its small section of underwater terrain included a clipped-on fish for a forever-midnight snack.

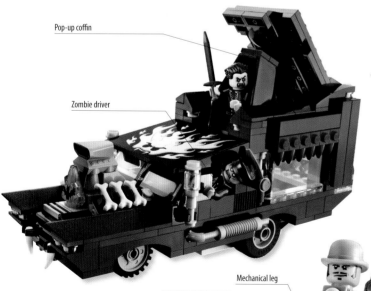

Pop-up coffin

Zombie driver

Man-bat henchman

9468 Vampyre Castle (2012)

An unfortunate guest

Mechanical leg

9464 The Vampyre Hearse (2012)

Red moonstone

Single driving glove

Dueling rapier

REVVED-UP RIDE

Lord Vampyre's personal hot-rod hearse had a pair of fangs in front and a six-bone-cylinder engine on its hood that was powered by the red moonstone. Turning a lever made the main villain pop up through the top of the car in his coffin to launch a surprise attack on his foes.

Dr. Rodney Rathbone, the bowler-hatted British leader of the heroes, had a mechanical right leg to replace the one lost in a past monster battle.

The Zombie Driver, Lord Vampyre's most loyal and obedient servant, was rotten to the core… literally.

Spire bat

A special mechanism built into the castle tower made the moonstones swing open simultaneously to activate their evil power when the moon-dish in the middle was pushed forward.

Vampyre's Bride

Dr. Rodney Rathbone

Moonstone eclipse device

Lord Vampyre

Jack McHammer

Lord Vampyre's coffin

The heroes customized their vehicles with special gear to help them battle the monsters and counter their fearsome supernatural powers. Mixing vintage and hi-tech elements gave the models a steampunk flair.

Double-barreled bumper blasters

This auto's back-mounted cannon could aim and fire a net to snare Lord Vampyre's winged minions.

GHOST BUSTERS

Pulling three cars full of glow-in-the-dark ghosts, the ghoulish Ghost Train locomotive could only be stopped by the heroes' flick-missile-firing airplane. The barrel on the plane's back was designed for containing captured ghosts. The Monster Fighters also faced a werewolf, a crazy scientist and his monster, a chariot-driving mummy, and a graveyard full of zombies.

Ghost-sucking vacuum

Frank Rock

Ann Lee carried a spare crossbow bolt in her hair in case of emergencies.

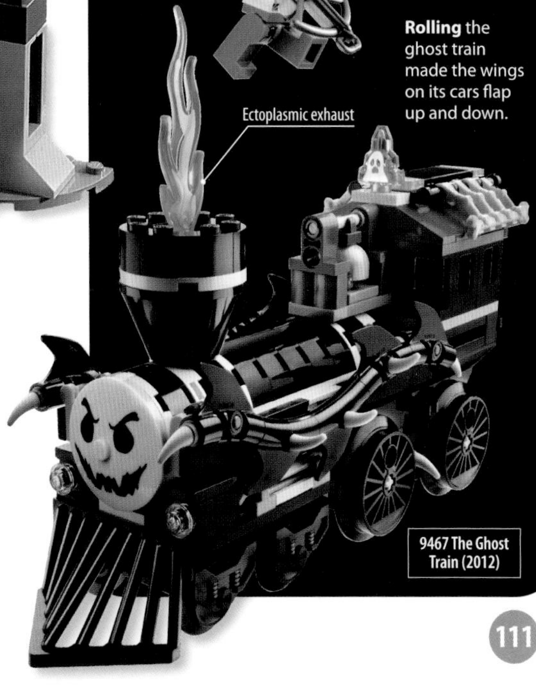

Rolling the ghost train made the wings on its cars flap up and down.

Ectoplasmic exhaust

9467 The Ghost Train (2012)

LEGO® EXO-FORCE™ Universe

INSPIRED BY Japanese manga and animation, the LEGO® EXO-FORCE™ theme introduced a new world of giant robot action in 2006. With courage, skill, and pointy hair, the human pilots used battle machines to fight an evil robot army for control of their mountain home ●

THE EXO-FORCE comics were illustrated in the popular style of Japanese manga. Pictured here are Takeshi (left) and Hikaru (right).

Something's wrong. We need to get back to the Golden City!

POWERING UP
The LEGO EXO-FORCE story was told through books, TV mini-episodes, and a series of comics on the LEGO.com website. The 40 comic chapters formed a three-year saga that brought the battle for Sentai Mountain to life for readers all over the world.

Many EXO-FORCE sets featured instructions for alternate and combination models. The giant Mountain Warrior was assembled out of the pieces of the Stealth Hunter and Grand Titan battle machines.

Double-strength armor plating

Battlefield repair tool

Two light-up bricks for twice the firepower

Pilot Takeshi

Most of the 2006 EXO-FORCE sets had a built-in light-up brick. Pulling a lever on the battle machine pressed the button on the brick, sending light through a flexible clear tube to make weapons glow red.

Mountain Warrior

MOUNTAIN OF MYSTERY
The LEGO EXO-FORCE story took place on Sentai Mountain, a towering peak split in two by unknown forces during the first robot rebellion. With humans trapped on one side and robots on the other, their battle machines clashed on the narrow bridges that spanned the divide. What lay at the base of the mountain was unrevealed.

7701 Grand Titan (2006)

7700 Stealth Hunter (2006)

Although the theme's models also included vehicles and buildings, most sets were battle machines, piloted robotic combat armor that could walk, run, fight hand-to-hand, and sometimes fly. Both sides in the conflict tried to create stronger battle machines to win the war between the humans and the robots.

THE GOOD GUYS
Presenting the heroes of the LEGO EXO-FORCE team: cool-headed marksman Hikaru, reckless warrior Takeshi, eccentric inventor Ryo, and fun-loving flyer Ha-Ya-To. They were joined by Hitomi, the proud, sword-wielding granddaughter of Sensei Keiken, the team's wise commander and mentor.

Hitomi

Sensei Keiken

Ha-Ya-To

Hikaru

Ryo

Takeshi

EXO-FORCE pilot

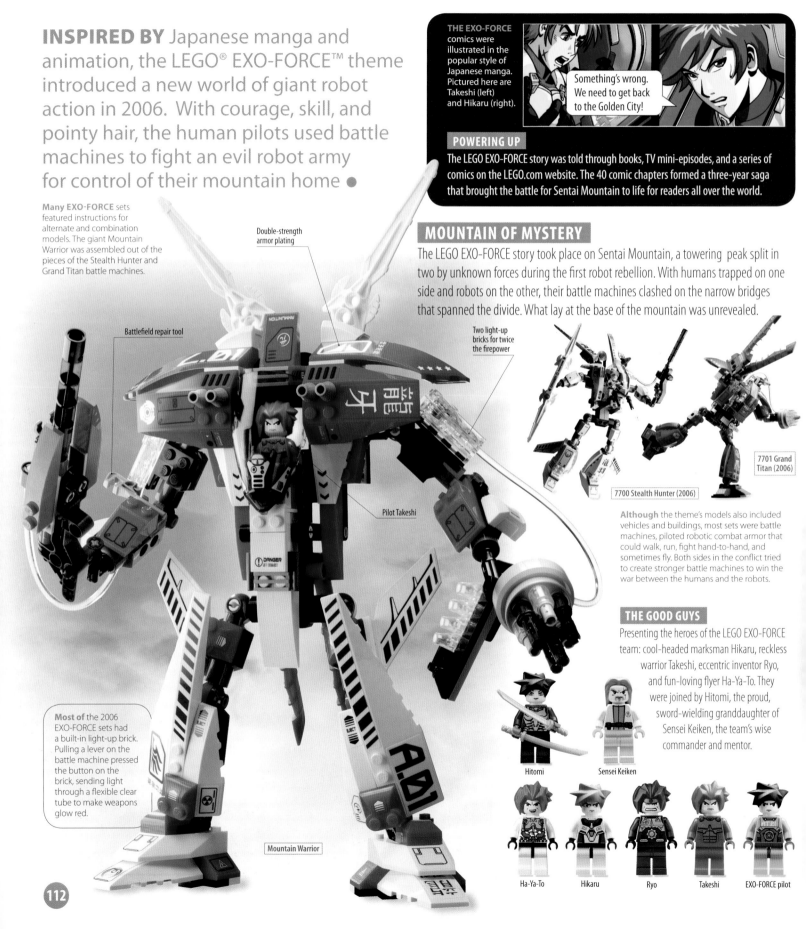

8113 Assault
Tiger (2008)

2008 battle machine sets included weapons that could transform into mini-robots to help the pilots.

INTO THE JUNGLE

The 2008 LEGO EXO-FORCE story ended on a cliffhanger: with Sensei Keiken captured by the robots and taken deep into the mountain's jungle, could the heroes and their newest battle machines rescue their leader in time?

With just a quick turn of the head, my expression changes from calm to battle-rage!

THE GOLDEN CITY

In 2007, with their Sentai Fortress HQ in ruins, the EXO-FORCE team retreated to the legendary Golden City, home of an ancient civilization. There they discovered more powerful battle machines to fight the robots, and codes to unlock the city's secrets.

Triple turbojet engines

Heavy laser cannon

Ha-Ya-To upgraded his ride in a major way with the Aero Booster, a battle machine with a huge detachable rocket pack.

Firing missile launcher

8106 Aero
Booster (2007)

The first year's story ended with a climactic battle as Meca One unleashed his ultimate weapon, the Striking Venom battle tank. Only the courage of the entire EXO-FORCE team—and a lucky shot from Takeshi's Grand Titan—saved the day.

Rotating laser machine cannons

Rapid-fire energy disc launcher

Light-up brick

11 in (28 cm) tall

18 in (46 cm) wide

Piledriver legs

Iron Drone defender

Meca One pilot

Shovel claw

7707 Striking Venom (2006)

THE BAD GUYS

There were three main types of robots: mass-produced, copper-colored Iron Drones, smarter silver Devastator commanders (available with several different secondary colors), and Meca One, the golden leader of the robot forces.

Meca One

Devastator

Iron Drone

GOLDEN IDOL

Built as a simple mining machine, Meca One gained awareness and reprogrammed his fellow robots to revolt. Not content with driving humanity off his half of the mountain, the mechanical tyrant sent wave after wave of battle machines across the bridges to destroy LEGO EXO-FORCE once and for all.

LEGO® Ninjago

LONG AGO, the mystical world of Ninjago was created by the first Spinjitzu master using four golden weapons: the Scythe of Quakes, the Nunchucks of Lightning, the Shurikens of Ice, and the Sword of Fire. Launched in 2011, the LEGO® Ninjago: Masters of Spinjitzu theme took classic LEGO ninja figures and gave them a whole new spin ●

Removable ninja mask

Golden katana

2111 Kai (2011)

Spinjitzu spinner

SPINNERS

Kai and his fellow ninja warriors could be found in standard LEGO construction sets, but they were also sold individually with top-like spinners. The rules: two players spin their minifigures toward each other while shouting "Ninja GO!" The ninja that stayed on its spinner was the winner of the showdown.

Individualized skull features

Separate body armor

2174 Kruncha (2011)

2173 Nuckal (2011)

Double chain whip

2175 Wyplash (2011)

GENERALS

The ninja team's skeleton enemies were available with spinners as well, including the bigger and tougher generals who served their arch-enemy, Lord Garmadon. Spinner sets included a variety of weapons, cards, and bricks that could be used to modify play for more challenging duels.

Bone hand with jointed fingers

Driver's seat

2506 Skull Truck (2011)

SKELETON VEHICLES

Although the world of Ninjago was based on a fantasy version of feudal Japan, the Skulkin villains emerged from the underworld with their own fleet of skeleton-themed vehicles. The massive Skull Truck featured chomping jaws, a bone hand that could be launched to capture ninja, two rib-cages, and a working suspension system.

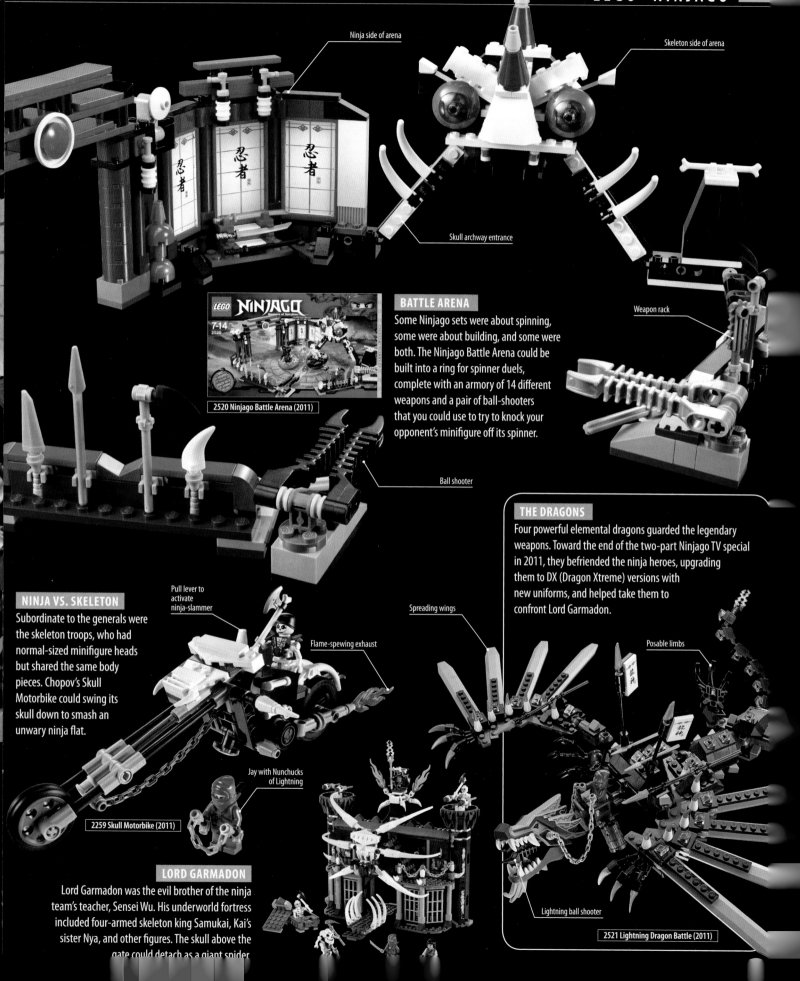

Ninja side of arena

Skeleton side of arena

Skull archway entrance

Weapon rack

BATTLE ARENA

Some Ninjago sets were about spinning, some were about building, and some were both. The Ninjago Battle Arena could be built into a ring for spinner duels, complete with an armory of 14 different weapons and a pair of ball-shooters that you could use to try to knock your opponent's minifigure off its spinner.

2520 Ninjago Battle Arena (2011)

Ball shooter

THE DRAGONS

Four powerful elemental dragons guarded the legendary weapons. Toward the end of the two-part Ninjago TV special in 2011, they befriended the ninja heroes, upgrading them to DX (Dragon Xtreme) versions with new uniforms, and helped take them to confront Lord Garmadon.

Spreading wings

Posable limbs

NINJA VS. SKELETON

Subordinate to the generals were the skeleton troops, who had normal-sized minifigure heads but shared the same body pieces. Chopov's Skull Motorbike could swing its skull down to smash an unwary ninja flat.

Pull lever to activate ninja-slammer

Flame-spewing exhaust

2259 Skull Motorbike (2011)

Jay with Nunchucks of Lightning

LORD GARMADON

Lord Garmadon was the evil brother of the ninja team's teacher, Sensei Wu. His underworld fortress included four-armed skeleton king Samukai, Kai's sister Nya, and other figures. The skull above the gate could detach as a giant spider.

Lightning ball shooter

2521 Lightning Dragon Battle (2011)

Sets to Remember

6195 Neptune Discovery Lab (1995)

6190 Shark's Crystal Cave (1996)

6769 Fort Legoredo (1996)

6494 Magic Mountain Time Lab (1996)

5978 The Sphinx Secret Surprise (1998)

5956 Expedition Balloon (1999)

4980 Tunnel Transport (1999)

6776 Ogel Control Center (2001)

4797 Ogel Mutant Killer Whale (2002)

7419 Dragon Fortress (2003)

7475 Fire Hammer vs. Mutant Lizards (2005)

7298 Dino Air Tracker (2005)

7713 Bridge Walker and White Lightning (2006)

8107 Fight for the Golden Tower (2007)

8118 Hybrid Rescue Tank (2008)

8634 Mission 5: Turbocar Chase (2008)

7775 Aquabase Invasion (2007)

8961 Crystal Sweeper (2009)

8898 Wreckage Road (2010)

7985 City of Atlantis (2011)

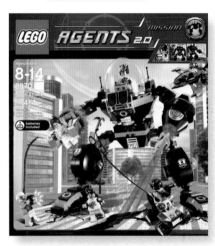

8970 Robo Attack (2009)

8191 Lavatraz (2010)

7327 Scorpion Pyramid (2011)

9464 The Vampyre Hearse (2012)

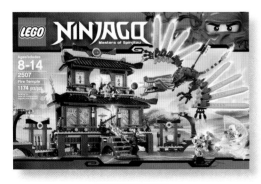

2507 Fire Temple (2011)

9450 Epic Dragon Battle (2012)

5887 Dino Defense HQ (2012)

LEGO® Racers

LEGO® RACING started with a Formula 1 car model in 1975 and a racetrack-themed Town series in the 1980s, but it wasn't until LEGO Racers revved up in 2001 that brick-built cars and trucks were designed with real speed and competition in mind. With vehicles that have ranged from pint-sized Tiny Turbos to stunt-driving Power Racers, LEGO Racers just keeps on going ●

Built to burn rubber!

4584 Hot Scorcher (2002)

DROME RACERS

In 2002, everything had a story—even LEGO Racers! Set in the year 2015, its racecar-driver heroes and villains vied for fame and fortune in the dangerous Drome, run by the mysterious Dromulus and his pet robot monkey Monkulus. A video game and comics told the tale of these multi-scaled race cars with pull-back motors.

R/C RACING

With an infrared remote control, this 133-piece RC racer set included instructions for building it as a 4x4 off-road vehicle, a dune buggy for pit racing, or a fast track car. It could swap wheels with other LEGO Racers sets for different surfaces and speeds.

4589 RC-Nitro Flash (2002)

Three infrared channels let up to three people race their cars at the same time without interference.

RADICAL RACERS

The first LEGO Racers sets were very different from the rest. Shredd, Surfer, Spiky, Duster, and their rivals were toothy monsters whose simple, eight-piece cars were built to send their drivers flying on impact.

Each set came with a storage container that doubled as a high-speed slammer launcher.

4570 Shredd (2001)

6111 Street Chase (2006)

TINY TURBOS

The Tiny Turbos sub-theme of LEGO Racers launched in 2005. Similar in scale to other small race car toys, these pocket-sized cars and trucks came in tire-shaped transport cases and had smooth, free-spinning tires for maximum speed when pushed or rolled down a ramp. Releases have included classic muscle cars, police cruisers, and city street racers with glow-in-the-dark elements.

The different fold-out tracks could be combined and rebuilt into even bigger and better raceways!

BUILDABLE RACETRACKS

The 2009 Tiny Turbos series included vehicle two-packs with storage containers that unfolded to make T-shaped stretches of racetrack. LEGO pieces and racing signs were included to build environment-themed tracks, including an ice rally, a bumpy desert road, and a stock car raceway.

EXTREME ICE RALLY

STAGE 5

8124 Ice Rally (2009)

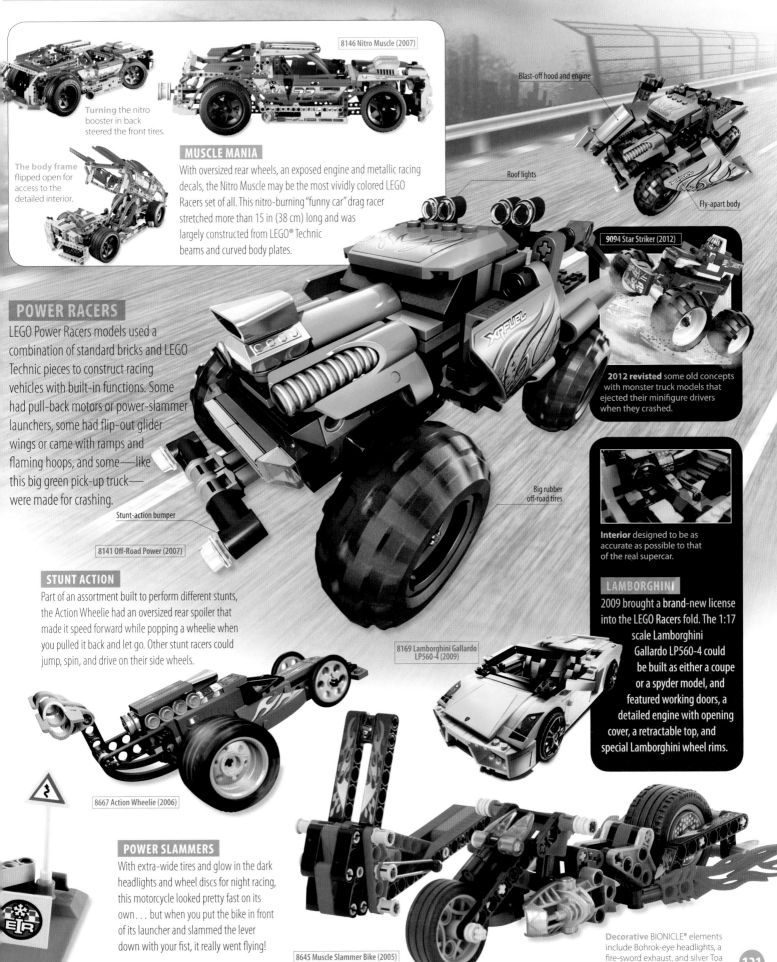

8146 Nitro Muscle (2007)

Turning the nitro booster in back steered the front tires.

The body frame flipped open for access to the detailed interior.

MUSCLE MANIA

With oversized rear wheels, an exposed engine and metallic racing decals, the Nitro Muscle may be the most vividly colored LEGO Racers set of all. This nitro-burning "funny car" drag racer stretched more than 15 in (38 cm) long and was largely constructed from LEGO® Technic beams and curved body plates.

Blast-off hood and engine

Roof lights

Fly-apart body

9094 Star Striker (2012)

2012 revisted some old concepts with monster truck models that ejected their minifigure drivers when they crashed.

POWER RACERS

LEGO Power Racers models used a combination of standard bricks and LEGO Technic pieces to construct racing vehicles with built-in functions. Some had pull-back motors or power-slammer launchers, some had flip-out glider wings or came with ramps and flaming hoops, and some—like this big green pick-up truck— were made for crashing.

Big rubber off-road tires

Interior designed to be as accurate as possible to that of the real supercar.

LAMBORGHINI

2009 brought a **brand-new license** into the LEGO Racers fold. The 1:17 scale Lamborghini Gallardo LP560-4 could be built as either a coupe or a spyder model, and featured working doors, a detailed engine with opening cover, a retractable top, and special Lamborghini wheel rims.

Stunt-action bumper

8141 Off-Road Power (2007)

STUNT ACTION

Part of an assortment built to perform different stunts, the Action Wheelie had an oversized rear spoiler that made it speed forward while popping a wheelie when you pulled it back and let go. Other stunt racers could jump, spin, and drive on their side wheels.

8667 Action Wheelie (2006)

8169 Lamborghini Gallardo LP560-4 (2009)

POWER SLAMMERS

With extra-wide tires and glow in the dark headlights and wheel discs for night racing, this motorcycle looked pretty fast on its own . . . but when you put the bike in front of its launcher and slammed the lever down with your fist, it really went flying!

8645 Muscle Slammer Bike (2005)

Decorative BIONICLE® elements include Bohrok-eye headlights, a fire-sword exhaust, and silver Toa feet on the sides.

LEGO® Ferrari

IN 2004, Italian sports car manufacturer Ferrari S.p.A. joined the LEGO® Racers team, and brought Ferrari's famous Formula One race cars, premium sports cars, and an international reputation for speed and quality. The bright red Ferrari sets quickly became a popular LEGO license for both young auto fans and grown-up enthusiasts, with a growing collection of racing toys and detailed replicas in multiple scales, and even a pair of LEGO® DUPLO® sets for the youngest builders ●

8375 Ferrari F1 Pit Set (2004)

The classic yellow minifigure face means that this Scuderia Ferrari racing team member isn't based on a real person.

8142 Ferrari 248 1:24 (2007)

Details and functions included working jacks and a mid-mounted engine with support frame.

Special racing tires

8143 Ferrari 1:17 F430 Challenge (2007)

COLORS OF VICTORY

The LEGO model of the aerodynamic Ferrari F430 included optional parts to make either the standard sports car version in yellow or the lighter, faster racing-edition F430 Challenge with a red body, sponsor logos, and different rims on the wheels.

FERRARI FORMULA ONE

In 2004 and 2007, the series included 1:24 scale versions of Ferrari's famous Formula One race cars with pull-back motors. The 2007 version had an updated construction and sponsorship decals to match the latest real vehicle. Despite appearances, there are no minifigures included with the set, as it's too large to be in-scale; instead, the driver's head and helmet are directly attached to the cockpit.

RACING CREW

Everybody may know the drivers, but the hard-working Scuderia Ferrari pit crew received their due at last in several garage and pit sets that included them and all their tools and equipment. After all, somebody has to keep those race cars tuned-up and ready to break records!

This set also came with two Ferrari F1 racers and a full garage with fuel pit, driver stations, and a service bike.

8144 Ferrari 248 F1 Team (2007)

8155 Ferrari F1 Pit 1:55 (2008)

SMALLER SPEEDSTERS

In 2008, Ferrari sets went pocket-sized with a garage, fuel pit, trucks, and F1 racers in the same small scale as the LEGO Racers Tiny Turbos.

4693 Ferrari F1 Race car (2004)

PIT STOP

This set from the first year of LEGO Ferrari featured a racing pit with a custom road plate, six helmeted mechanics, spare tires for quick mid-race replacements, tools for on-the-go repairs, and instructions for rebuilding it into a Ferrari F1 starting grid.

8375 Ferrari F1 Pit Set (2004)

LEGO DUPLO FERRARI

Little kids like to race, too! This officially licensed Ferarri car for ages 3-6 came pre-assembled as a single piece, but young builders could build on top of the rear spoiler or put together the winner's stand and stack the shining trophy on top when they won the preschool championship. 4694 Ferrari F1 Racing Team, released the same year, included a car, truck, mechanic, and race pit.

Driver and passenger seats

Technic body frame

2556 Ferrari Formula 1 Racing Car (1997)

FIRST OFF THE GRID

Meet the very first LEGO Ferrari set! This Model Team racer (above) for experienced builders was only available at Shell gas stations as a special promotional purchase.

GRAND TOURER

This model of Ferrari's 2-seat Gran Turismo flagship coupe used flexible LEGO Technic rod elements to replicate the real auto's curves. Built from 1,340 pieces, it was 18 in (46 cm) long and had a working front-wheel steering system and a V12 engine with moving pistons.

8156 Ferrari FXX 1:17 (2008)

8145 Ferrari 599 GTB Fiorano 1:10 (2007)

Doors, hood, and trunk all opened for access to interior details.

RARE RACER

Only 30 of the real Ferrari FXX racing cars were ever produced. Fortunately, it was a lot easier to get hold of the LEGO version, which had an opening rear engine cover and front trunk, and doors that swung up just like the ones on the real thing.

Some builders bought this set just to get the rare chrome-coated winner's trophy!

8389 M. Schumacher & R. Barrichello (2004)

A DARING DUO

The 2009 LEGO Ferrari series starred the newest drivers on the Scuderia Ferrari racing team. Finnish driver Kimi Räikkönen won first place in the 2007 Drivers' World Championship, and Brazilian-born Felipe Massa took second place in 2008, making them the latest tough team to beat.

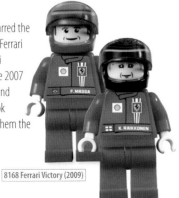

8168 Ferrari Victory (2009)

DESIGNATED DRIVERS

The 2004 Scuderia Ferrari racing team became LEGO minifigures in this all-star winner's podium set. It featured multiple-record-smashing driver Michael Schumacher and 2000 German Grand Prix winner Rubens Barrichello, both with flesh-toned faces, authentically decorated helmets and jackets, and approved real-world likenesses.

LEGO® Sports

LEGO Basketball minifigures had springs built into their legs and specially designed arms to let them hold, throw, and dunk balls.

Let's see your Castle figures do THIS!

3427 NBA Slam Dunk (2003)

ATHLETIC COMPETITION and brick construction go together better than you'd think. Between 2000 and 2006, the LEGO® Group produced several model series based on real sports. These licensed themes were filled with unique minifigures and action features to let builders show off their skills ●

LEGO SOCCER

Released as LEGO Soccer in some countries and LEGO Football in others, this was the first, largest, and longest-lived of the LEGO Sports themes. With over 25 sets made between 2000 and 2006, its models included international team buses, training stations, and fields with minifigure bases that could be rotated to aim and tapped with a finger to "kick" a ball.

3569 Grand Soccer Stadium (2006)

LEGO BASKETBALL

Launched in 2003, the NBA-licensed LEGO Basketball theme's models enabled builders to reproduce their favorite flashy basketball moves. Sets included street hoops with lever-activated slam-dunking features and courts with full teams.

3432 NBA Challenge (2003)

Stadium measures 22 in (55 cm) long and 14 in (35 cm) wide

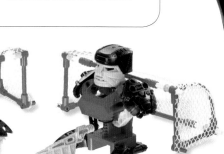

3544 Game Set (2003)

LEGO HOCKEY

Licensed by the NHL and NHLPA, the first LEGO Hockey sets in 2003 used chunky BIONICLE® style elements to build tough robotic players that swung their sticks when you slammed down on their heads. Different sets could execute slap shots, flip shots, passes, and other hockey moves.

The Basketball theme featured the first minifigures based on real personalities.

FAMOUS FIGURES

Although the generic team members in LEGO Basketball sets kept their familiar yellow faces, the company tried something new for minifigures based on real NBA players: realistic skin tones. This soon became standard for licensed figures across all LEGO themes.

Shaquille O'Neal (2003)   Paul Pierce (2003)

LEGO hockey puck

SECOND PERIOD

In its second year, LEGO Hockey shifted to a smaller scale. Similar to other LEGO Sports themes, the 2004 hockey sets let builders play against their friends by controlling rival minifigure players on a stadium-like base. No actual teams or players were licensed, and ice hockey figures wore only the NHL logo on their padded jerseys.

3578 NHL Championship Challenge (2004)

Long rods moved the hockey figures' bases and activated flippers to pass or shoot the puck.

Sliding base with flipper

URBAN SHOWDOWN

Only two LEGO Hockey sets were made in the new style: 3578 NHL Championship Challenge, with an ice rink and two four-figure teams, and 3579 NHL Street Hockey for those who favored a one-on-one face-off on the mean city streets.

3579 NHL Street Hockey (2004)

The street hockey set was also licensed from the NHL.

GRAVITY GAMES

In a tie-in with the summer edition of the extreme-sports Gravity Games, LEGO Sports released this skateboarding park with customizable vertical ramps and railings. The set included a special "stunt stick" that could be attached to a minifigure skater to create mid-air tricks and stunts.

Curved ramp pieces

3537 Skateboard Vert Park (2003)

Sets could be combined to make bigger parks.

Modular design

Snowboard launcher

3538 Snowboard Boarder Cross Race (2003)

Airborne snowboarder

COLD COMPETITION

Made for the winter Gravity Games, this competitive snowboarding set featured a snowy mountain slope with launchers at the top for two minifigures on boards. Set them loose and they slid down the hill toward the finish line at the bottom, flying and bouncing into the air thanks to the course's built-in obstacles and stunt ramps.

The snowboards were weighted to keep the minifigures upright and moving down the slope.

Each minifigure comes randomly packed inside a sealed bag (a different color for each series), so you never know which one you'll get!

Collectible Minifigures

FOR MORE THAN 30 YEARS, LEGO® themes have been filled with colorful minifigures. Kids and grown-up fans both love them—so why not give them even more to love? Starting in 2010, the LEGO Minifigures collection has swelled the population of the brick-built world, 16 collectible characters at a time ●

Cowboy

Twin six-irons

Nurse

Zombie

Deep Sea Diver

Flippers for swimming

Skater

Rolling skateboard

Super Wrestler

Forestman

Robot

Magician

Ninja

Demolition Dummy

PA7 70

Tribal Hunter

Caveman

Circus Clown

New pompom elements

Cheerleader

8683 LEGO Minifigures Series 1 (2010)

SERIES 1

Released in May 2010, the first series of LEGO Minifigures provided new citizens for classic themes such as City, Castle, Space, and Western, along with totally original creations like the Super Wrestler, Circus Clown, and Zombie. Common categories across multiple series include sports, monsters, sci-fi, and historical warriors.

Each minifigure includes a base and signature accessories. Some are classic LEGO elements, while others are totally new and exclusive.

126

Series 2 featured the sombrero-wearing Maraca Man, a Mime with two extra heads for added expressions, a Spartan Warrior, a Pop Star, and the totally retro Disco Dude.

8684 LEGO Minifigures Series 2

Breakout stars of Series 3 included the Hula Dancer, an Elf warrior, a cybernetic Space Villain with a Blacktron II logo, a Baseball Player, and the Gorilla Suit Guy.

8803 LEGO Minifigures Series 3

SERIES 4

To give some extra character to the characters, the collectible minifigures have their own individual bios on the LEGO website. Series 4's update revealed the Hazmat Guy's job concerns, the Artist's compulsion to paint (and paint on) everything he sees, the Kimono Girl's love of haiku verse, and the Monster's desire to help people build.

Lawn Gnome's fishing pole

Gold Viking horns

Silver Soccer Player trophy

8804 LEGO Minifigures Series 4

Street Skater board with new printing

Punk Rocker's new electric guitar

Spaceman

Electro-Zapp blast

8805 LEGO Minifigures Series 5

SERIES 5

Series 5 added lots of brand-new LEGO pieces, including the Small Clown's cream pie and bowler hat, the Lizard Man's removable mask and tail, the Gladiator's helmet and sword, the Detective's deerstalker cap, the Gangster's opening violin case, and the Zookeeper's chimpanzee.

SERIES 6

Things got even more wild in Series 6, which introduced a Leprechaun with a pot o' gold, a Clockwork Robot with a wind-up key, the universe-saving Intergalactic Girl, the pajama-clad Sleepyhead, a smoke-tailed Genie, and the torch-bearing Lady Liberty.

8827 LEGO Minifigures Series 6

Genie can hold or attach to his magic lamp

Removable tiara holds veil in place

SERIES 7

Still going strong as of 2012, Series 7's lineup featured (among others) a brave Aztec Warrior, a kilted Bagpiper, a Computer Programmer with a laptop, a Bride with a bouquet and veil, an armored member of the Galaxy Patrol, and the enigmatic Bunny Suit Guy.

8831 LEGO Minifigures Series 7

127

BIONICLE®

IT WAS A TRICKY PUZZLE: How could the LEGO Group break into the world of action figures without losing what made its products so distinctly LEGO® sets? The company tested the water with the Technic-themed, robotic Slizers (a.k.a. ThrowBots) in 1999, and the rolling RoboRiders the following year. The success of these "constraction" sets led to the development of an all-new, entirely original LEGO theme called BIONICLE®. Launched in 2001 to great acclaim, the "Biological Chronicle" blended technology with mythology to create a universe filled with buildable heroes, creatures, and villains, with a story that was told through comic books, novels, movies, and online games and animations. It quickly became one of the most unique and popular LEGO themes of all time ●

The Legend Begins

MONTHS BEFORE the first toys were released in 2001, the BIONICLE® story emerged through an intriguing series of teaser ads and a popular online adventure game. The setting was a mysterious tropical island called Mata Nui, where bio-mechanical villagers were under attack from fierce creatures controlled by an evil being called the Makuta. When all seemed lost, six heroes arrived who were prophesied to save the universe from darkness. The BIONICLE legend had begun ●

Each Toa Nuva's tools had a double function. The magma swords of Tahu Nuva, Toa of Fire, could also attach to his feet to make a lava surfboard.

THE ISLAND OF MATA NUI

Named after the islanders' sleeping Great Spirit, the island (pictured right) had ice fields, rocky deserts, underground catacombs, dense jungle, a great lake, and a volcano. The isle was home to living mechanical beings, who wore masks called Kanohi.

8544 Nuju (2001)

8540 Vakama (2001)

8543 Nokama (2001)

8542 Onewa (2001)

The wise Turaga were the elders of the island's villages and the keepers of its many secrets. Their toys raised their staffs at the push of a lever, and their Noble Kanohi masks gave them powers such as invisibility, mind control and telekinesis.

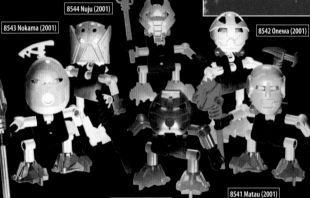

8545 Whenua (2001)

8541 Matau (2001)

THE TOA

The six Toa came to the island in canisters—matching their toys' packaging—that washed up on shore from the endless sea. Imbued with elemental powers and wearing Great Kanohi masks, they were figures of legend to the islanders, who believed that the heroes were destined to awaken the Great Spirit Mata Nui and save the universe from Makuta's evil.

8568 Pohatu Nuva (2002)

8567 Lewa Nuva (2002)

8566 Onua Nuva (2002)

THE VILLAGERS

The villagers of Mata Nui lived in six villages, one for each of the island's elemental themes. Originally known as Tohunga, they were renamed the Matoran in honor of Mata Nui following the defeat of the invading Bohrok.

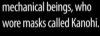

8595 Takua and Pewku (2003)

Once called the Chronicler, Takua would later be transformed by the Mask of Light into the Seventh Toa, Takanuva.

The Toa battled Makuta, the Rahi, and other threats to the island. In the theme's second year, they became the Toa Nuva (pictured below) and gained new armor, tools, and enhanced mask powers.

Collectible Kanohi came with sets and in assorted mask packs

THE RAHI

8538 Muaka & Kane-Ra (2001)

From the mosquito-like Nui Rama to the mighty Kane-Ra bull, the beasts of the BIONICLE universe were collectively called Rahi. In the theme's first year, five sets of Rahi were sold in two-packs, each with instructions for combining the pieces into a new, larger creature. The models were designed with Technic action features that let them battle Toa and each other by knocking off their opponents' masks.

Ice blades convert to skis

8571 Kopaka Nuva (2002)

8570 Gali Nuva (2002)

MAKUTA

The dark being known as the Makuta had been trying to dominate the inhabitants of Mata Nui for centuries before the arrival of the Toa. He used infected masks to control wild Rahi, set the Bohrok swarm loose on the island, and unleashed the reptilian Rahkshi to prevent the discovery of the Toa of Light.

8593 Makuta (2003)

THE SWARM

The six breeds of insect-like Bohrok were the first Toa-sized BIONICLE villain sets. They could curl up and hibernate inside their plastic containers, or attack with lunging heads and rubbery parasite "brains" called krana. These controlled heroes by taking the place of their masks.

8562 Gahlok (2002)

Aqua axes become swimming fins

131

New Islands, New Adventures

AT THE CONCLUSION of 2003's *BIONICLE®: Mask of Light* movie, the heroes of Mata Nui discovered a second island deep beneath their own. For the first time, the BIONICLE story departed from its original home, first in an ancient tale from the high-tech city of Metru Nui , and then with an epic quest that led from the imperiled island of Voya Nui to sunken Mahri Nui, and finally to Karda Nui at the heart of the BIONICLE world ●

8605 Toa Matau (2004)

TOA METRU

The rediscovery of Metru Nui led the Turaga to tell a tale from 1,000 years before, when they were the Toa Metru, guardians of the ancient island city. Like the Toa Nuva, their sets' tools could be reconfigured into travel forms, and their action figures were the first BIONICLE heroes to feature articulated elbows, knees, and heads.

THE VISORAK INVASION

The flashback continued as the Toa Metru were transformed into savage, mutated Toa Hordika and battled the spider-like Visorak. The Metru Nui chronicles were animated in the movies *BIONICLE® 2: Legends of Metru Nui* (2004) and *BIONICLE® 3: Web of Shadows* (2005).

The six Rahaga (2005), companions to the Toa Hordika

Lifeblade measures 5 in (13 cm) long

Axonn's axe could cut through stone, fire energy blasts, and return to his hand when thrown

8733 Axonn (2006)

The robotic guard Maxilos was secretly the evil Makuta in disguise

8924 Maxilos and Spinax (2007)

INTO THE DEEPS

In 2007, the Toa Inika followed the Mask of Life into the sea, transforming into the aquatic Toa Mahri and defending a lost underwater city from squid-launching Barraki warlords. Their sets featured air hoses, diving masks, and rapid-fire Cordak blasters. At the end of the year, Toa Matoro sacrificed himself to save Mata Nui, but the story wasn't over yet...

IGNITION

In 2006, the BIONICLE story returned to its present when six Matoran villagers traveled to Voya Nui and became the Toa Inika. They fought the mercenary Piraka for the Mask of Life that could save the Great Spirit Mata Nui. These BIONICLE figures lacked Technic-style gear mechanisms, focusing instead on new parts and posability.

A friend to the Toa Inika, Axonn even had articulated fingers.

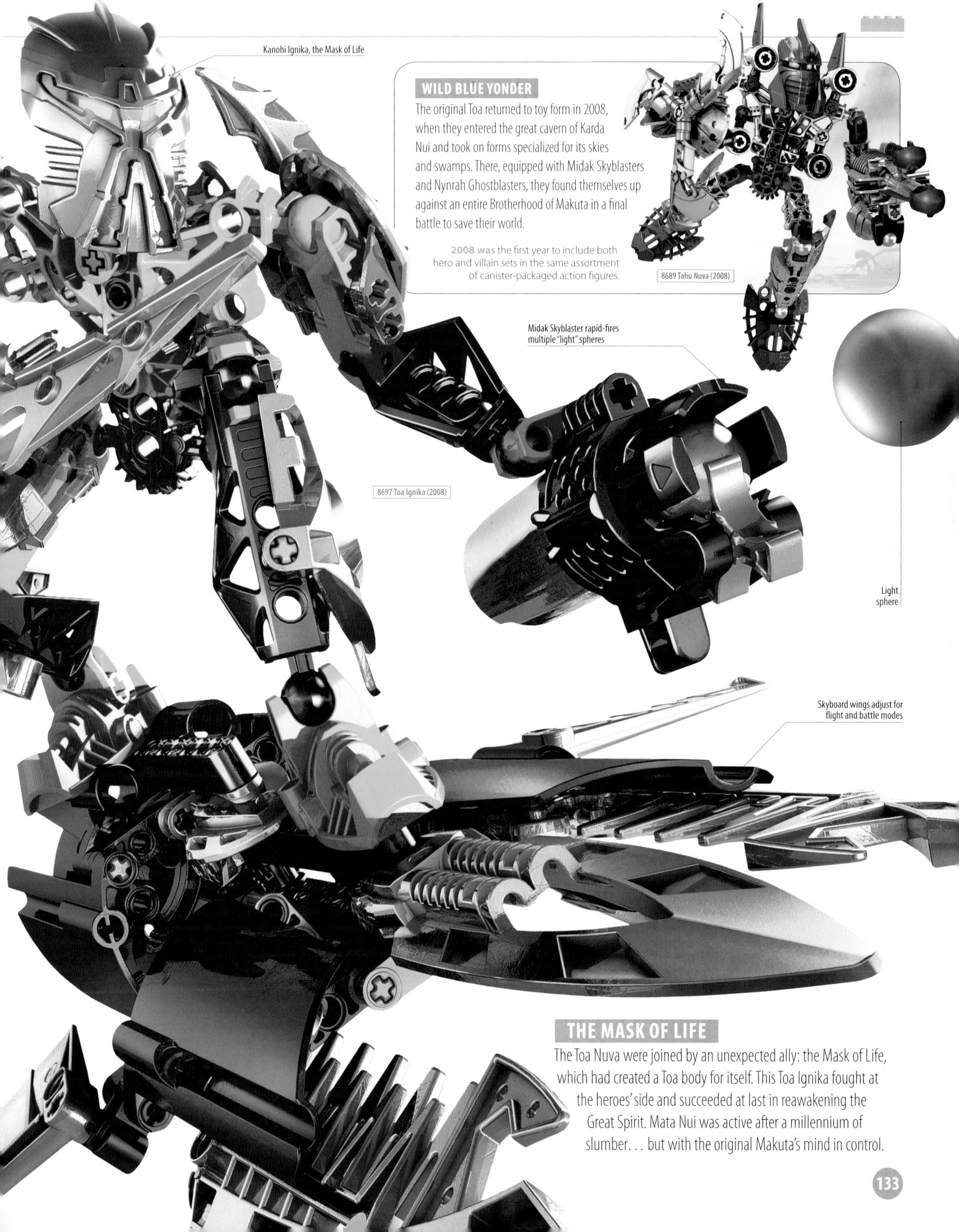

Kanohi Ignika, the Mask of Life

WILD BLUE YONDER

The original Toa returned to toy form in 2008, when they entered the great cavern of Karda Nui and took on forms specialized for its skies and swamps. There, equipped with Midak Skyblasters and Nynrah Ghostblasters, they found themselves up against an entire Brotherhood of Makuta in a final battle to save their world.

2008 was the first year to include both hero and villain sets in the same assortment of canister-packaged action figures.

8689 Tahu Nuva (2008)

Midak Skyblaster rapid-fires multiple "light" spheres

8697 Toa Ignika (2008)

Light sphere

Skyboard wings adjust for flight and battle modes

THE MASK OF LIFE

The Toa Nuva were joined by an unexpected ally: the Mask of Life, which had created a Toa body for itself. This Toa Ignika fought at the heroes' side and succeeded at last in reawakening the Great Spirit. Mata Nui was active after a millennium of slumber. . . but with the original Makuta's mind in control.

133

Endings and Beginnings

AFTER EIGHT YEARS of mystery, the biggest secret of the BIONICLE® universe was at last revealed: the Great Spirit Mata Nui was a space-faring robot 40 million feet (12,200 km) tall, and the story's islands and cities were all parts of his colossal body. Now, in 2009, Mata Nui would have an adventure of his own ●

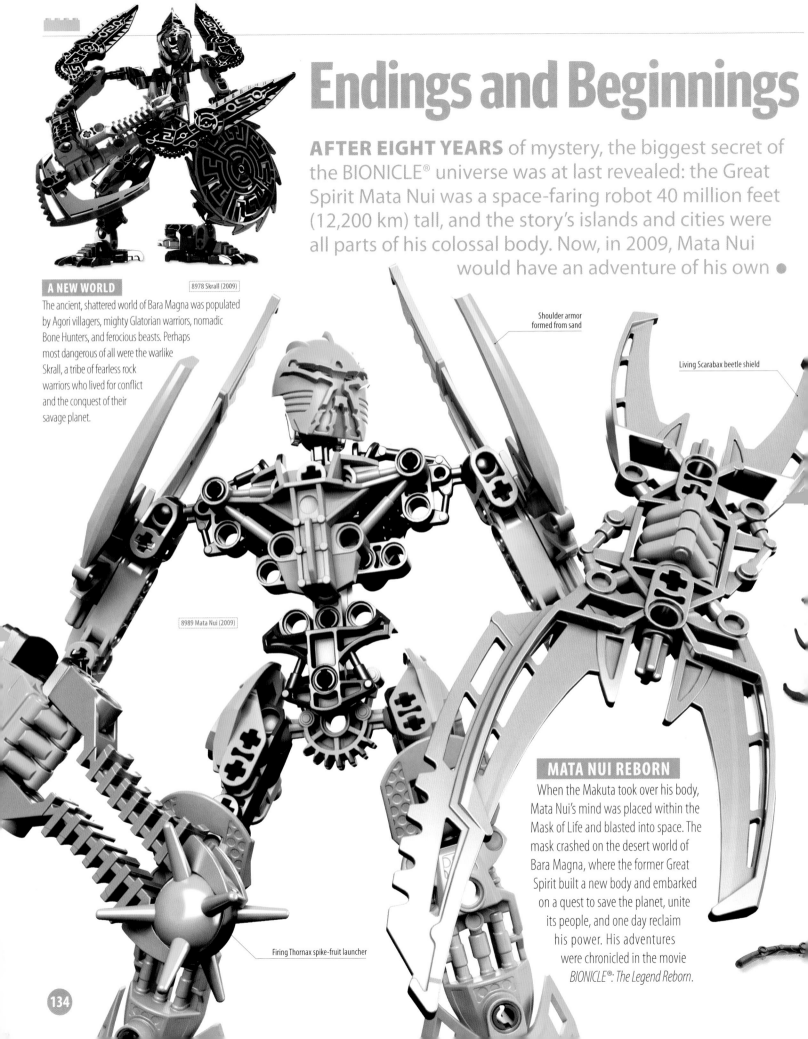

8978 Skrall (2009)

A NEW WORLD

The ancient, shattered world of Bara Magna was populated by Agori villagers, mighty Glatorian warriors, nomadic Bone Hunters, and ferocious beasts. Perhaps most dangerous of all were the warlike Skrall, a tribe of fearless rock warriors who lived for conflict and the conquest of their savage planet.

Shoulder armor formed from sand

Living Scarabax beetle shield

8989 Mata Nui (2009)

Firing Thornax spike-fruit launcher

MATA NUI REBORN

When the Makuta took over his body, Mata Nui's mind was placed within the Mask of Life and blasted into space. The mask crashed on the desert world of Bara Magna, where the former Great Spirit built a new body and embarked on a quest to save the planet, unite its people, and one day reclaim his power. His adventures were chronicled in the movie *BIONICLE®: The Legend Reborn.*

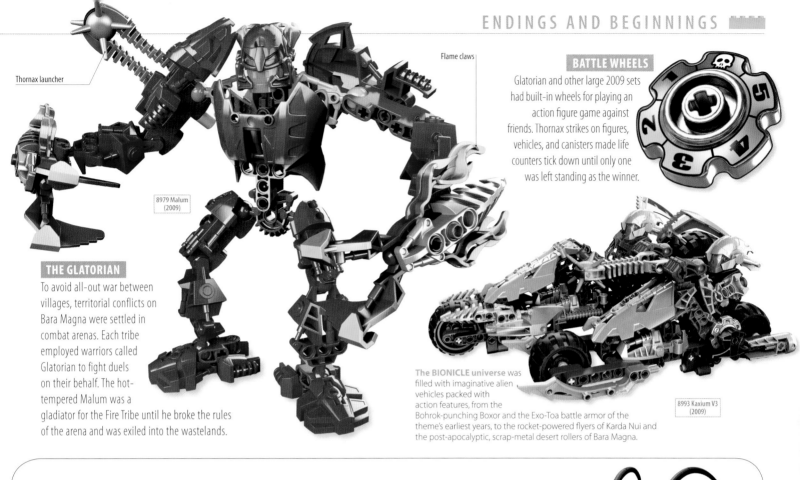

Thornax launcher

Flame claws

8979 Malum
(2009)

BATTLE WHEELS

Glatorian and other large 2009 sets had built-in wheels for playing an action figure game against friends. Thornax strikes on figures, vehicles, and canisters made life counters tick down until only one was left standing as the winner.

THE GLATORIAN

To avoid all-out war between villages, territorial conflicts on Bara Magna were settled in combat arenas. Each tribe employed warriors called Glatorian to fight duels on their behalf. The hot-tempered Malum was a gladiator for the Fire Tribe until he broke the rules of the arena and was exiled into the wastelands.

The BIONICLE universe was filled with imaginative alien vehicles packed with action features, from the Bohrok-punching Boxor and the Exo-Toa battle armor of the theme's earliest years, to the rocket-powered flyers of Karda Nui and the post-apocalyptic, scrap-metal desert rollers of Bara Magna.

8993 Kaxium V3
(2009)

SMALL HEROES, BIG BATTLES

It was difficult to create full-sized scenes featuring the large action figures, but minifigure-scaled BIONICLE sets enabled builders to create giant vehicles, huge monsters, fortresses, and battle scenes from the sagas of Metru Nui, Voya Nui, and Mahri Nui.

8927 Toa Terrain Crawler (2007)

Mutant sea squid

Rapid-fire Cordak blaster

Mini Toa Mahri with posable arms, waist, and head

LEGO® Hero Factory

IN EARLY 2010, the BIONICLE® universe came to an end with the release of the BIONICLE Stars, new versions of six characters from the nine-year history of the theme. In its place rose LEGO® Hero Factory, a new story about an immense factory in futuristic Makuhero City, where robot heroes were manufactured to protect the galaxy ●

7164 Preston Stormer (2010)

Preston Stormer, a.k.a. "The Pro," was a seasoned veteran and the leader of the Alpha 1 Team. The six main 2010 heroes had real first names and carried large weapons on their hands and arms.

FIRST GENERATION
The first Hero Factory heroes were smaller than traditional BIONICLE Toa and made use of the same construction style as the BIONICLE Stars, with snap-on armor and jointed heads, shoulders, wrists, hips, and ankles. In the center of the chest was the Hero Core that provided each robot's personality and power source.

FALLEN HERO
Von Nebula was once the hero Von Ness until his cowardice made him desert during a vital mission. Gaining a hatred for Hero Factory, he recruited a team of interplanetary villains and set in motion a grand scheme for revenge.

7145 Von Nebula (2010)

At 156 pieces, Von Nebula was the largest individual character released in the theme's first year. His Black Hole Orb Staff had spinning blades and in the story could generate black holes.

NEED A LIFT?
The Drop Ship was a light-speed transport vehicle that the factory used to carry heroes to their assigned missions on remote planets. It had trigger-activated wings and could pick up or drop the "Hero Pod" canisters that the heroes came inside. It included a pilot figure.

LEGO Technic structure

7160 Drop Ship (2010)

The Drop Ship was much bigger in the four-part *Hero Factory: Rise of the Rookies* animated miniseries, with a cockpit that had room for four.

H4 Force Ball shooter

NEW KID ON THE BRICK
A newly built, latest-model hero with a supercharged Hero Core, William Furno was placed in charge of a group of rookies under the training of the Alpha 1 Team. Competitive and impulsive, he was eager to prove himself to Stormer and the other veterans.

Furno was released twice in 2010: as a standard canister figure and with a different body design in the Furno Bike set, where he rode a fiery, ball-shooting motorcycle.

7158 Furno Bike (2010)

THE UPGRADE

In 2011, the heroes underwent an upgrade, gaining enhanced armor and abilities. Furno's fellow rookies Surge and Breez were joined by two new team members: tech-head Nex and weapons specialist Evo. The reinforcements really came in handy against renegade mining bots under the command of the powerful Fire Lord.

The characters' 2.0 upgrade was reflected in the hero figures' new, larger designs. These added elbow and knee articulation and armor that snapped onto ball joints instead of LEGO® Technic connections.

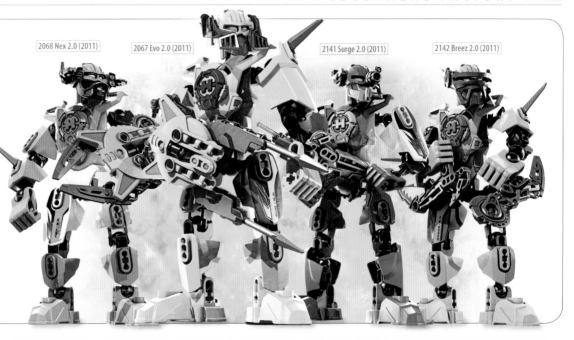

2068 Nex 2.0 (2011)

2067 Evo 2.0 (2011)

2141 Surge 2.0 (2011)

2142 Breez 2.0 (2011)

ORDEAL OF FIRE

The 2011 Hero Factory story kicked off with a mission to Tanker Station 22, which was under siege by a group of energy-siphoning fuel thieves. The mission was communicated in multiple ways: through a television episode, a comic book adapted by BIONICLE writer Greg Farshtey, and an online game on the Hero Factory website.

Drilldozer was one of the Fire Lord's three hench-bots. He carried a large turbine drill and a firing Lava Sphere shooter. His body was protected by molten spikes.

Nitroblast was the smartest of the three hench-bots and utterly loyal to the Fire Lord. His blowtorch was powered by the plasma container on his shoulder.

The insectile Jetbug had bladed mandibles and rocket-powered wings on his back. Like the others, he was a mid-sized model in between the smaller heroes and the giant Fire Lord.

2192 Drilldozer (2011)

2194 Nitroblast (2011)

2193 Jetbug (2011)

SAVAGE PLANET

In the second half of 2011, the heroes' new mission took them to the jungle world of Quatros, where the evil Witch Doctor was using Quaza spikes to control the local robotic wildlife.

The Witch Doctor had been Dr. Aldous Witch, a Hero Factory instructor who became obsessed with the Quaza Stone used to make Hero Cores.

2283 Witch Doctor (2011)

BEASTLY BOTS

Several of the heroes (including first-year veterans Stormer, Stringer, and Bulk) were upgraded again for their jungle assignment, gaining animal features and a new 3.0 designation. They also gained a new member: the lion-armored Rocka.

Starting in 2011, the Hero Factory sets included armor pieces with printed decoration specific to each character.

2143 Rocka 3.0 (2011)

KING-SIZED HERO

To deal with the titanic Witch Doctor, Rocka temporarily upgraded to this giant-sized body. At more than 11 in (29 cm) tall, Rocka XL was armed with a ball shooter and his double-blade claw combo tool.

At 174 pieces, Rocka XL had nearly six times the part count of the Rocka 3.0 figure.

2282 Rocka XL (2011)

Hero Factory: Breakout

HERO FACTORY doesn't just make heroes. It's also a prison for the most powerful and dangerous criminals from all across the galaxy—and at the beginning of 2012, the prisoners broke loose. It was up to the heroes to recapture them and stop the new villain Black Phantom from shutting the factory down for good ●

6203 Black Phantom (2012)

Black Phantom was armed with twin saber strikers, a double-ended staff, and a detachable arachnix drone.

BAGGED BOTS

2012 marked the first time since the beginning of the BIONICLE® universe that no "buildable figure" sets were sold in plastic canisters. Instead, many of the new Hero Factory heroes and villains came in two different sizes of heavy-duty resealable bags, or traditional boxes like Black Phantom.

Coming in at 39 pieces including his electricity shooter, plasma gun, and extra shoulder armor, Surge's latest upgrade was one of the smaller bagged sets.

6217 Surge (2012)

TOXIC FOE

Each of the heroes was paired up against a specific villain. Evo was sent to take on Toxic Reapa, whose toxic waste-spewing arms contaminated anything he touched. Online instructions showed how to combine both sets into a single super model.

6201 Toxic Reapa (2012)

Toxic Reapa hails from the planet Z'chaya. His sinister scheme was to infect the larvae on his home world and create an army of evil insects… unless Evo caught him first.

SOLO STYLE

With so many escaped villains on the loose, the factory's Mission Managers took the rare step of breaking up its teams and sending heroes out individually to round up the fugitives one by one. Each hero was given a shiny new set of hi-tech Hero Cuffs to use in catching the bad guys.

LAST LINE OF DEFENSE

With the other heroes scattered across the galaxy and Hero Factory locked down, Rocka—the only hero who hadn't yet been sent out on a mission—discovered that Black Phantom had stayed inside to destroy the hero-building Assembly Tower. Only he could save the factory… if he managed to survive the saboteur's booby traps.

6202 Rocka (2012)

Rocka was one of the larger-sized bagged sets. Built from 55 pieces, he was taller and more armored than his smaller teammates, like Evo and Surge. Of course, the 124-piece Black Phantom towered over him, too!

HEART OF A HERO

The most physically strong member of the Alpha 1 Team, though not the brightest, Dunkan Bulk helps to keep the task-oriented Stormer from getting too obsessed with rules and regulations. He's gone on many missions with his fellow veteran, the sonic-powered Jimi Stringer. This was his fourth design, counting a 2010 two-pack with exclusive villain Vapor.

During the year-long Breakout story, Bulk was armed with a laser-targeted missile launcher, a plasma shooter, and high-impact shoulder armor.

6223 Bulk (2012)

GAME POINTS

Each 2012 set included a Hero Core with a code printed on the back. Entering the code into the online *Hero Factory: Breakout* game earned points that could be used to upgrade the player's hero character. Bigger sets (like the deluxe-sized Breez) came with more points.

Natalie Breez is a nature-loving aerial ace. She can turn the blades of her hex shield sideways to act as a steering wing for her rocket boots.

6227 Breez (2012)

Razor spike

Plasma ball shooter

THE FACTORY

Rising like a silver shark's fin high above the buildings of Makuhero City—home to a million mechanical citizens—Hero Factory's Assembly Tower was the brainchild of Akiyama Makuro, the oldest known robot in the universe. In the real world, kids could tune in to the Hero Factory FM podcast and even call in with trouble reports for the heroes.

SPEEDY SLICER

Freed from prison, Speeda Demon didn't look back—he just burned rubber to the ice planet Kollix IV on his nitro rocket motorbike. It was up to Stormer XL to put the brakes on his getaway.

6231 Speeda Demon (2012)

Hero Core remover

6222 Core Hunter (2012)

Core Hunter's predatory pursuits were aided by his plasma shooter, six-eyed multi-vision mask, and armor covered with razor spikes, but most dangerous of all was the Hero Core remover tool on his left arm.

Stealthy armor plating

CORE COLLECTOR

Another former Hero Factory operative, the cruel Core Hunter waited a long time to strike back at his one-time allies. The breakout gave him just the opportunity he needed to return to his favorite hobby: stalking heroes and stealing their Hero Cores for his collection.

The lightning-fast Speeda Demon was double trouble for the heroes thanks to the wing-blades gripped in the extra hands on his shoulders.

Sets to Remember

8534 Tahu (2001)

8557 Exo-Toa (2002)

8525 Masks (2001)

8568 Pohatu Nuva (2002)

8596 Takanuva (2003)

8811 Toa Lhikan and Kikanalo (2004)

8759 Battle of Metru Nui (2005)

8755 Keetongu (2005)

8764 Vezon & Fenrakk (2006)

8723 Piruk (2006)

8918 Carapar (2007)

8943 Axalara T9 (2008)

8692 Vamprah (2008)

8998 Toa Mata Nui (2009)

8991 Tuma (2009)

7164 Preston Stormer (2010)

7116 Tahu (2010)

7148 Meltdown (2010)

2183 Stringer 3.0 (2011)

6203 Black Phantom (2012)

2282 Rock XL (2012)

6283 Voltix (2012)

LEGO® Creator

WHAT WILL YOU MAKE with a box full of bricks without any themes, characters, or stories? Just about anything! They've been called LEGO® Creator, Designer Sets, X-Pods, and Inventor. They may come with instructions and model ideas, but creative sets like these all represent the same thing: classic LEGO construction without rules or limitations ●

CREEPY CRAWLIES

If you liked scaring your little brother or sister, this was the LEGO Creator set for you. It could be assembled into a giant spider, a big bug, or a slithering cobra, each with multiple points of movement and pointy fangs.

4994 Fierce Creatures (2008)

Articulated spider legs

Flapping wings

POWER PACKED

Thanks to built-in gears and Power Functions motors, some LEGO Creator sets have the power to move, light up, and make noise on command. The Ferris Wheel model could spin around and around at the push of a switch.

4957 Ferris Wheel (2007)

CREATIVE CRUISING

LEGO construction never had more speed and style than with this convertible sports car with ninja sword windshield wipers, adjustable seats and mirrors, and 2 in (5 cm) rubber tires. It also had opening doors, a V8 engine under the hood, and bonus building instructions to convert it into a truck cab or a working mini-loader.

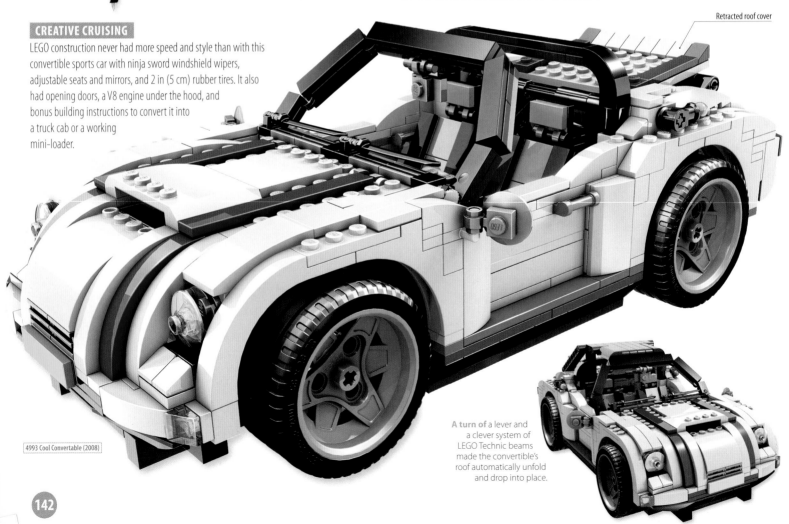

Retracted roof cover

4993 Cool Convertible (2008)

A turn of a lever and a clever system of LEGO Technic beams made the convertible's roof automatically unfold and drop into place.

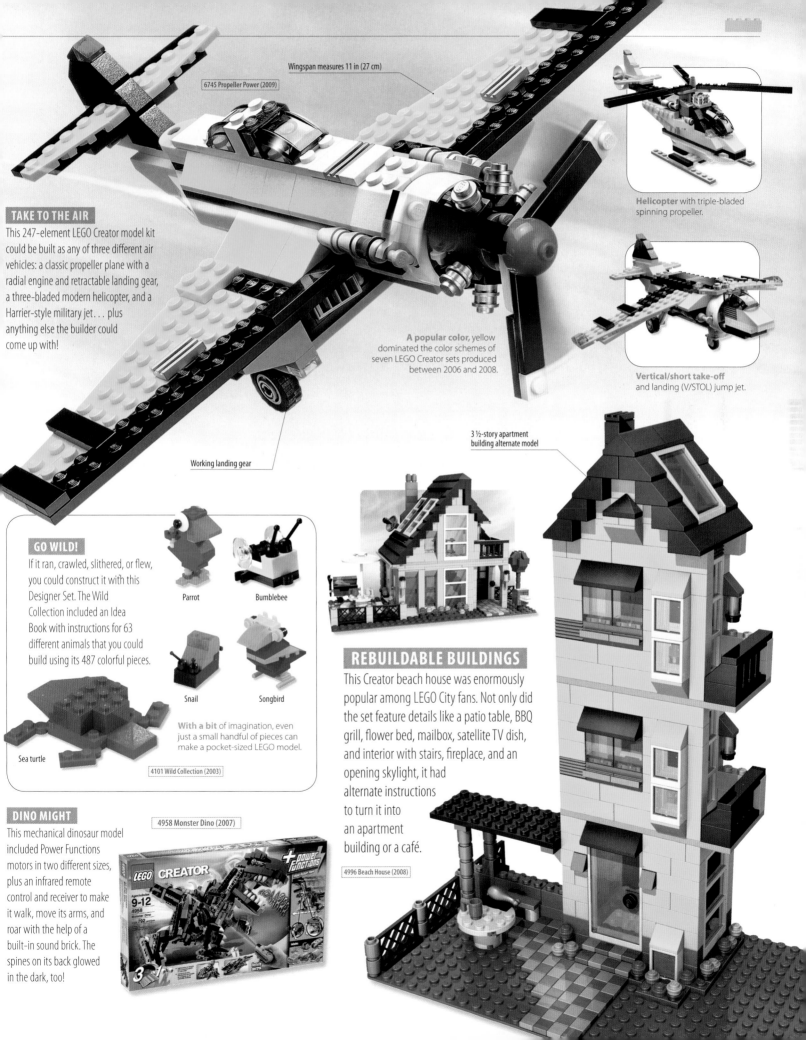

Wingspan measures 11 in (27 cm)

6745 Propeller Power (2009)

Helicopter with triple-bladed spinning propeller.

TAKE TO THE AIR

This 247-element LEGO Creator model kit could be built as any of three different air vehicles: a classic propeller plane with a radial engine and retractable landing gear, a three-bladed modern helicopter, and a Harrier-style military jet... plus anything else the builder could come up with!

A popular color, yellow dominated the color schemes of seven LEGO Creator sets produced between 2006 and 2008.

Vertical/short take-off and landing (V/STOL) jump jet.

Working landing gear

3 ½-story apartment building alternate model

GO WILD!

If it ran, crawled, slithered, or flew, you could construct it with this Designer Set. The Wild Collection included an Idea Book with instructions for 63 different animals that you could build using its 487 colorful pieces.

Parrot

Bumblebee

Snail

Songbird

Sea turtle

With a bit of imagination, even just a small handful of pieces can make a pocket-sized LEGO model.

4101 Wild Collection (2003)

REBUILDABLE BUILDINGS

This Creator beach house was enormously popular among LEGO City fans. Not only did the set feature details like a patio table, BBQ grill, flower bed, mailbox, satellite TV dish, and interior with stairs, fireplace, and an opening skylight, it had alternate instructions to turn it into an apartment building or a café.

4996 Beach House (2008)

DINO MIGHT

This mechanical dinosaur model included Power Functions motors in two different sizes, plus an infrared remote control and receiver to make it walk, move its arms, and roar with the help of a built-in sound brick. The spines on its back glowed in the dark, too!

4958 Monster Dino (2007)

LEGO CREATOR
Ages 9-12
4958
+Power Functions
792
3 1

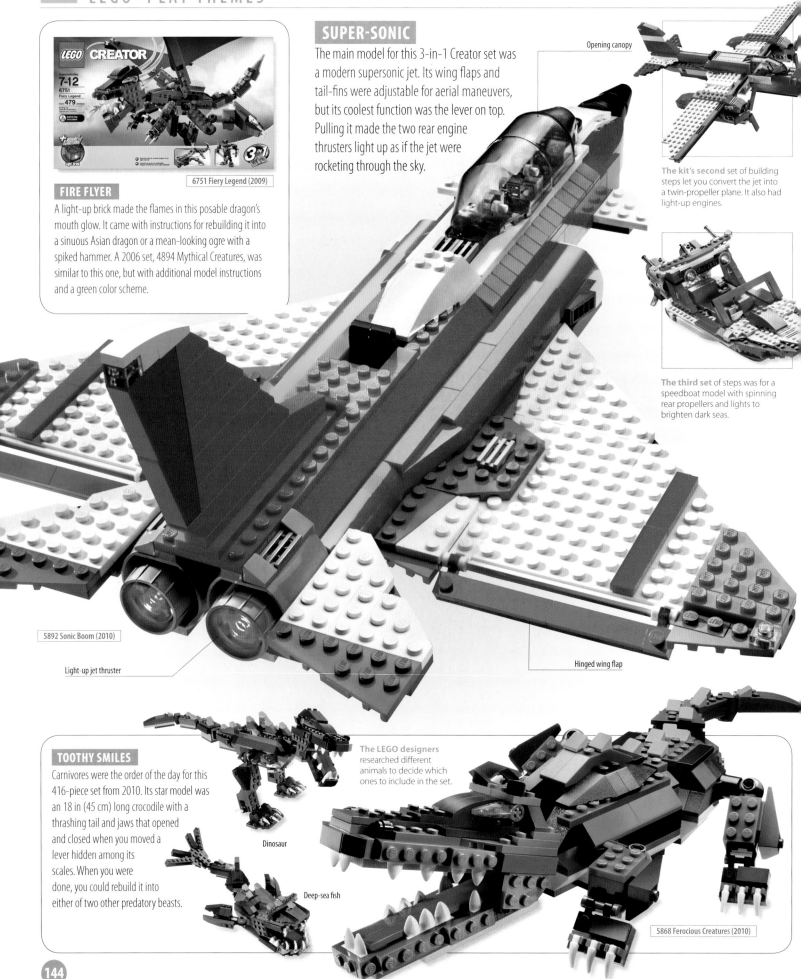

FIRE FLYER

A light-up brick made the flames in this posable dragon's mouth glow. It came with instructions for rebuilding it into a sinuous Asian dragon or a mean-looking ogre with a spiked hammer. A 2006 set, 4894 Mythical Creatures, was similar to this one, but with additional model instructions and a green color scheme.

6751 Fiery Legend (2009)

SUPER-SONIC

The main model for this 3-in-1 Creator set was a modern supersonic jet. Its wing flaps and tail-fins were adjustable for aerial maneuvers, but its coolest function was the lever on top. Pulling it made the two rear engine thrusters light up as if the jet were rocketing through the sky.

Opening canopy

The kit's second set of building steps let you convert the jet into a twin-propeller plane. It also had light-up engines.

The third set of steps was for a speedboat model with spinning rear propellers and lights to brighten dark seas.

5892 Sonic Boom (2010)

Light-up jet thruster

Hinged wing flap

TOOTHY SMILES

Carnivores were the order of the day for this 416-piece set from 2010. Its star model was an 18 in (45 cm) long crocodile with a thrashing tail and jaws that opened and closed when you moved a lever hidden among its scales. When you were done, you could rebuild it into either of two other predatory beasts.

The LEGO designers researched different animals to decide which ones to include in the set.

Dinosaur

Deep-sea fish

5868 Ferocious Creatures (2010)

FEATURES & FUNCTIONS

This LEGO Creator set was designed with Technic-style functions like working steering and suspension, a self-winding winch, and opening doors and tailgate panels. The main truck model's construction used an interesting method in which several bricks temporarily stabilized the chassis during the building process, and then came off to become part of the trailer.

Roof lights

Quad bike

Articulated trailer

5893 Offroad Power (2010)

Two of the set's models included extra vehicles for more play options. This transport truck carried a removable digger on its back.

Thanks to its big tires, the dune buggy alternate model was suited for driving over sandy beaches and other rough terrain.

Winch automatically retracts

TO THE RESCUE

A Power Functions light brick made the Rescue Robot's translucent yellow eye light up when it arrived to save the day. It co-starred with the LEGO City firefighters in a crossover *LEGO Club Magazine* comic in which it grew to a giant size and ran amok trying to help people.

An alternate model was a Robocat with a glowing nose.

5764 Rescue Robot (2011)

The first Creator set to come with a minifigure, the Log Cabin was a forest getaway with a kayak and campfire.

5766 Log Cabin (2011)

You could also build a riverside hut with a brook and bridge, or a country retreat with a duck pond.

A LIGHT IN THE DARK

This set let you build a striped lighthouse with a dock and the lighthouse-keeper's home on a small island. A crank on the side of the tower turned the mirror inside to rotate the light and warn passing ships away from the rocky shore. It even included buildable sea gulls!

5770 Lighthouse Island (2011)

The other models were a boathouse and a seafood restaurant with a light-up grill.

THE LEGO® WHEEL

● 2012 was the 50th anniversary of the release of the original LEGO® wheel ● The earliest known design drawings for the LEGO wheel date from 1958 ● The original LEGO wheel was a thin gray rubber tire around a red plastic hub with four studs and a connecting axle on the back. It could be built into models using a specially designed 2x4 brick with holes for the axle ● The first LEGO set with wheels was no. 400. Released in 1962, it was an accessory kit that included 4 wheels, 2 axle bricks, a tow-bar, and a base plate to let builders add rolling movement to their brick creations ● Until then, car models had to sit on square LEGO bricks ● The original wheel kit sold 820,400 sets in 1967 ● The first wheeled LEGO auto model was no. 315, a 40-piece black car released in 1963 ● The smallest LEGO wheel with a hub and tire was made in 1969. It was 0.57 in (1.44 cm) across ● The biggest LEGO wheel was made in 2000. It was 4.22 in (10.72 cm) across ● Today, the LEGO Group produces more than 300 million rubber tires per year, making it one of the biggest tire manufacturers in the world!

The larger wheel on the left was launched in 1963 with set no. 316 "Farm Tractor" and a new accessory kit, featuring large and small wheels, plus turntables.

On the Move

VEHICLES of all kinds have been part of the LEGO Group's success story since the very start. Having always wanted to be an auto mechanic, Godtfred Kirk Christiansen enjoyed designing toy cars for his father's workshop in the 1930s, and the tremendous sales of the Ferguson Tractor in the early 1950s led to the rise of the LEGO® brick and its unlimited possibilities for new transportation models. Rolling, floating, and flying, these are just a small sample of the amazing variety of LEGO vehicles out there ●

6743 Street Speeder (2009)

4893 Revvin' Riders (2006)

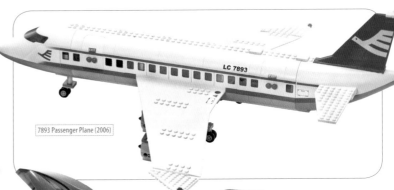

7893 Passenger Plane (2006)

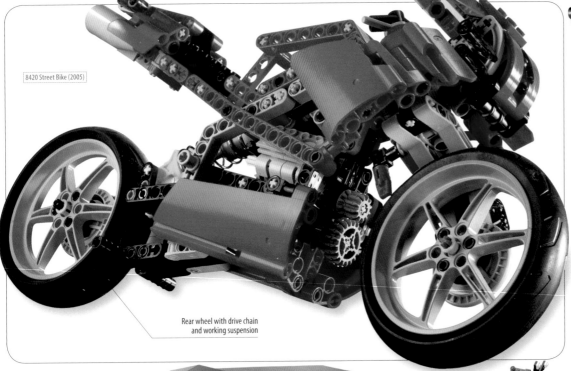

8420 Street Bike (2005)

Rear wheel with drive chain and working suspension

7990 Cement Mixer (2007)

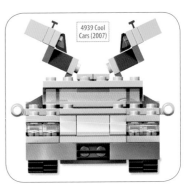

4939 Cool Cars (2007)

8635 Mission 6: Mobile Command Center (2008)

4995 Cargo Copter (2008)

7344 Dump Truck (2005)

7899 Police Boat (2006)

POLICE 7899

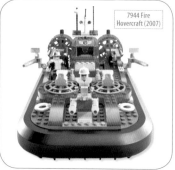

7944 Fire Hovercraft (2007)

7734 Cargo Plane (2008)

8292 Cherry Picker (2008)

7739 Coast Guard Patrol Boat & Tower (2008)

Opening gull-wing doors

Off-road tires with steering system and motorized suspension

8297 Off-Roader (2008)

Extending ladder for emergency rescue

7239 Fire Truck (2004)

4955 Big Rig (2007)

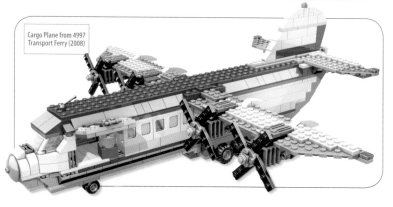

4896 Roaring Roadsters (2006)

7890 Ambulance (2006)

8434 Aircraft (2004)

Cargo Plane from 4997 Transport Ferry (2008)

Mini Loader from 4993 Cool Convertible (2008)

Hovercraft from 4953 Fast Flyers (2007)

Especially for Girls

OF COURSE, there's no rule that says that LEGO® construction is just for boys, and there are plenty of girls who play with exactly the same sets as the other half of the population. But some do prefer construction with a pinker tone, and so we present a sampling of LEGO sets specifically designed for girls ●

5808 The Enchanted Palace (1999)

Glittery, translucent tower

LEGO® BELVILLE™

Starting in 1994, LEGO BELVILLE introduced a new scale of bigger, multi-jointed figures. With sets that combine traditional LEGO bricks with decorative pink and purple pieces, shiny glitter and lots of horses to ride, the theme included both models of everyday life and scenes from fairy tales and fantasy. A 2005 series featured sets based on classic Hans Christian Andersen stories such as "The Little Mermaid," "The Snow Queen," "The Princess and the Pea," and "Thumbelina."

5585 LEGO® Pink Brick Box (2008)

THINKING PINK

A favorite among grandmothers at holiday time, this sturdy storage box came with fences, windows, doors, flowers, and lots of pink bricks mixed in with its 216 pieces for hours of building with a colorful twist.

6411 Sand Dollar Café (1992)

PARADISA

A sub-theme of LEGO Town that ran from 1992 to 1997, the seaside adventures of Paradisa took place at a tranquil tropical resort. In pastel-colored sets, Paradisa minifigures enjoyed sailing, windsurfing, beach-side barbecues, and playing with friendly dolphins. The color scheme and settings made Paradisa a very popular theme among girls.

6414 Dolphin Point (1995)

7538 Totally CLIKITS Fashion Bag and Accessories (2005)

This set included jewelry, school supplies, and a fashion bag to carry them.

CLIKITS™

A line of buildable, customizable jewelry and accessories, the CLIKITS™ theme featured sets with such fashionable items as photo frames, bracelets, and purses, each with connection points to let girls decorate and redesign them with a collection of hearts, stars, seashells, and other shapes.

Our website let girls decorate virtual rooms and build digital bracelets to send to their friends!

Each of the CLIKITS girls had her own color-coordinated pieces and unique decorations.

4307 Finger Rings (1980)

LEGO® SCALA™

CLIKITS wasn't the only line of buildable LEGO jewelry. In 1979, the first LEGO® SCALA™ series let girls use decorated tiles to create their own unique rings, necklaces, bracelets, and even a hand mirror. The theme was retired the following year, but it wouldn't be the last time the SCALA name appeared...

4336 Mirror (1980)

3149 Happy Home (2000)

HOUSE AND GARDEN

Unused since 1980, LEGO SCALA was brought back in 1997 as the name of a new dollhouse-style theme. Its characters, including Caroline, Christian, Marie, and Baby Thomas, were larger and more traditional fashion dolls than the stylized inhabitants of LEGO BELVILLE. Sets included fabric clothing packs and constructable scenes of gardens, homes, and neighborhood shops.

Foam foliage

4828 Princess Royal Stables (2007)

FAIRY-TALE FUN

With a princess, a prince, and three ponies with brushable hair, this LEGO® DUPLO® set was full of fun to spark the imagination of preschool girls.

LEGO® Friends

LAUNCHED IN 2012, the LEGO® Friends theme was designed to provide a fun play experience for girls who couldn't find a perfect match for their building interests in the rest of the LEGO assortment. Its new "mini-doll figures" are slightly taller than minifigures, but they can hold the same objects, connect to the same bricks, and even swap hairstyles ●

3061 City Park Café (2012)

OUT AT THE CAFÉ

The theme centers on the daily lives of five friends who live in the fictional Heartlake City. Its sets feature classic LEGO building, with lots of new elements, accessories, and colors. The City Park Café is a favorite hangout for all of the girls, and the only set to include Marie (in pink).

The café served everything from burgers to freshly-baked cupcakes and pie.

3187 Butterfly Beauty Shop (2012)

INVENTION LAB

3933 Olivia's Invention Workshop (2012)

Each of the friends has her own personality and interests. Olivia loves science, nature, and inventions, so her workshop is full of tools, collection jars, and even a microscope, not to mention her custom-built robot.

LEGO Friends mini-dolls have jointed heads, shoulders, and single-piece legs to let them sit or stand.

Emma (with black hair) wants to be a clothing and jewelry designer. She's also into interior decorating, horseback riding, and martial arts.

BEAUTY SHOP

This salon at the center of Heartlake City comes stocked with a variety of bows and clips that can be attached to mini-doll hair, as well as lipsticks, sunglasses, and a hairdryer. It even has a fashion head display with a spare hair piece for the ultimate makeover.

OLIVIA'S HOUSE

Along with her lab and tree house, Olivia comes in the biggest set in the theme's first year: the house where she lived with her parents and pet cat. Complete with a kitchen, bathroom, living room, bedroom, and rooftop patio, the house also included her mom Anna and dad Peter—the first male mini-doll figure.

Rooftop patio

Olivia keeps her diary in her bedroom drawer

Olivia's house is built in sections so that it can easily be taken apart and rearranged to make custom play-house creations.

The front yard had a mailbox, vegetable garden, lawnmower, swing set, and an outdoor grill for barbecues with friends and family.

Anna

Pete on turning chair

3315 Olivia's House (2012)

3932 Andrea's Stage (2012)

Boom box

Singer and song-writer Andrea is already on her way to being a star. Her music stage lets her put on a whole performance with the help of a microphone stand, a piano, a boom box, and an entrance with multicolored "lights".

Piano with bench and glass

Movable stage light

ROAD TRIP

Stephanie's car was built just like any other LEGO vehicle, but in colors that delivered on many girls' preferences. It came with her puppy Coco, a carwash stand with a lamp-post, faucet and bucket, and even a tiny MP3 player printed on a LEGO tile.

3183 Stephanie's Cool Convertible (2012)

3942 Heartlake Dog Show (2012)

PET PARADE

The Heartlake Dog Show featured a podium with a runway, a canine obstacle course with a see-saw and hurdle, a grooming station, prize ribbons, and a trophy for the winning pooch. It also had a plate of bones and a camera for snapping photos of well-trained pets.

Mia loves animals, whether training them or fixing them up when they're not feeling well.

Younger Builders

EVERY GREAT BUILDER has to start somewhere. Seeing the need for building play designed for young children, the LEGO Group has produced a number of toys over its history that are geared toward tots and toddlers. Since 1969, the most famous of these has been the wide range of LEGO® DUPLO® products: sets for kids aged 18 months and up that are full of big, rounded bricks suitable for small hands and big imaginations ●

It's a LEGO® DUPLO® World!

THE MOST WELL KNOWN and enduring of the LEGO® construction systems for younger builders, LEGO® DUPLO® sets have bigger pieces that are easy for small fingers to handle, assemble, and take apart. Designed for children between 1½ and 6 years old, these sets have been inspiring preschool creativity and helping children to develop early motor skills for more than 40 years ●

2940 Fire Truck (1992)

Standard 2x4 LEGO System brick

THE LEGO DUPLO BRICK

The LEGO DUPLO brick is twice as tall, twice as long, and twice as wide as a LEGO brick. The earliest DUPLO elements produced in 1969 had shorter studs and slightly different connectors underneath, but just like the modern version, they were fully compatible with standard LEGO pieces.

TOOLS FOR TOTS

For preschoolers who wanted to use tools just like their parents, the DUPLO TOOLO sets of the 1990s had vehicles with yellow connection joints that could be locked or unlocked with play tools that made satisfying clicking sounds when turned. In 2009, the building system returned with brand-new sets featuring the same beloved, child-safe screwdrivers and wrenches.

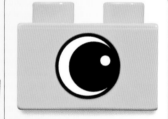

JUST IMAGINE...

DUPLO pieces with special shapes, colors, and painted decorations mean that toddlers can build just about anything they can imagine, from buildings to animals to vehicles that float, roll, and fly.

LOGO (1978)

LOGO

The DUPLO rabbit was first used on packaging in 1979. In 1997, it was redesigned with a friendlier appearance to match the new PRIMO elephant logo for infant toys. It disappeared in 2002, when DUPLO was merged into the new LEGO Explore theme for young children, but returned when the DUPLO name appeared once again in 2004.

duplo®

LOGO (1997)

The second rabbit logo was designed to be cute, colorful, and make eye contact with the viewer.

FIRST FIGURES

The DUPLO name did not always appear on young-builder packaging during the 1970s. Some boxes were labeled PreSchool, and others had no secondary title at all. This is when the first preschool human and animal figures were introduced, with decorated faces and simple, single-piece bodies.

537 Mary's House (1977)

Rooftop TV antenna

2770 Furnished Playhouse (1986)

By the mid-1980s, new DUPLO figures came in two sizes and could sit down and hold objects; however, the original-style figures continued to appear in sets into the next decade.

LEGO DUPLO PLAYHOUSE

In 1986, a DUPLO playhouse building set was released, featuring an assortment of family characters and furniture that could be used to assemble the interior of a rebuildable home. Separate accessory sets included parts for a bathroom, kitchen, living room, and extra wall and roof pieces. The concept would be visited again for several years during the 1990s.

One-piece wall with sliding door

A DAY AT THE ZOO

Everybody knows that kids love animals. That's why the DUPLO Zoo theme has returned over and over again with sets full of vehicles, environments, and lots of baby and grown-up animals.

A selection of animals and characters from various 1990s Zoo sets.

This stretched-out pooch doesn't just carry bricks. Thanks to its collar, it can connect to them too!

5503 DUPLO® Dog (2005)

BRICK COLLECTIONS

As a toddler grows, so does his or her DUPLO brick collection. Parents can get extra pieces in a variety of handy storage containers, from sturdy plastic buckets to this friendly dachshund storage tube that came with 32 bricks inside its see-through cylinder body.

All aboard for the big top!

LEGO DUPLO TRAINS

Another recurring favorite is DUPLO trains, which have their own track system and have been around since 2700 Preschool Freight Train in 1983. Built from 12 pieces, this circus train from the LEGO Ville daily life series had wheels with pistons that really moved when you pushed it forward, the latest style of DUPLO figure, and a baby elephant to ride in the back.

3770 My First Train (2005)

PICKING UP THE PIECES

"I eat blocks!" boasted this handy storage case and pick-up tool, which solved every parent's greatest sore-feet dilemma by gobbling up stray DUPLO pieces left lying on the floor. It also included a collection of extra bricks and had a studded plate on top that kids could use as a building surface.

Building plate

Carrying handle

Safe rubber brick scooper

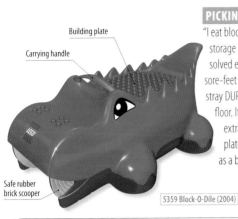

5359 Block-O-Dile (2004)

5593 Circus (2008)

PREHISTORIC PLAY

Dinosaurs and cave-people playing together? It could only happen in the DUPLO Dino Valley. This happy stone-age family had scaly friends to ride, a cozy cave with stackable cave-art bricks, fabric clothes, a canoe, a giant fish and a roasting steak with DUPLO studs for building.

5598 Dino Valley (2008)

BIG TOP, BIG BRICKS

When the circus train comes to LEGO Ville, here's where it arrives! The big top DUPLO circus was filled with friendly figures and features, including an acrobat with a horse and high-wire, a teeter-tottering elephant, a launching cannon, a monkey with a swing, a wheel-spinning, cake-throwing clown, and a ringmaster with a trained lion act.

BUCCANEERS AT BATHTIME

At a time when there hadn't been a single new LEGO Pirates set in years, preschoolers got to have all the fun with the DUPLO Pirates. This giant pirate ship not only floated, but also had wheels to roll across the floor. With a monkey in the rigging, a working winch for swinging from the sails, a firing cannon, a treasure chest and prison hold, and a plank for sending landlubbers to the deepest depths of the tub, plenty of big kids must have pined after this one.

7880 DUPLO Big Pirate Ship (2006)

WHAT'S A ZOOTER?

Goozle, Wazo, and Tez weren't only some of the weirdest-looking things in the LEGO DUPLO series—they were the Zooters, constructible creatures with a fabulous mix of claws, tentacles, and suction-cup feet. Kids aged three and up could disassemble and combine them to create a host of unique imaginary friends.

Goozle and Tez may have been your everyday aliens, but Wazo had a special feature: his head could record and play back speech and sounds!

3265 Wazo (2001)

3264 Tez (2001)

3263 Goozle (2001)

SORT AND BUILD

This sturdy storage box included blue, yellow, and red sorting plates that doubled as a lid. Young builders could use the plates to identify the color-coded bricks that they'd need to make an elephant, giraffe, or parrot model, and even see a picture of the right way to put them together.

6784 Creative Sorter (2012)

5506 LEGO DUPLO Large Brick Box (2010)

Boxes of basic DUPLO bricks can add new possibilities to a collection or just kick off some imaginative creative play. Many include inspirational building booklets.

LEGO VILLE

The busy LEGO Ville Supermarket was full of ways for kids to interact with their creations. They could pick out fruits, vegetables, and other foods, roll them over to the check-out counter, and help the clerk ring them up on a register that really made sounds.

LEGO City's younger cousin, LEGO Ville has been letting kids build fun everyday scenes since 2004.

5683 Market Place (2011)

5604 Supermarket (2008)

BAKING FUN

The 55 colorful DUPLO pieces in this set (including special meringue, muffin, and candle bricks) let young bakers prepare a buildable feast of delicious-looking desserts of all shapes and sizes. The box's lid even doubled as a serving tray.

6785 Creative Cakes (2012)

How's this for a fiery steed?

4776 Dragon Tower (2004)

Dragon with movable wings and jaws

LEGO DUPLO CASTLE

The DUPLO Castle series let kids build their own fortresses full of ferocious dragons, tough-looking knights, and hidden trap doors and treasures. The most impressive was 4785 Black Castle (2005), which, with 386 extra-large pieces, was one of the biggest DUPLO sets of all time. It included pictures that showed how to rebuild it into a 5½ ft (170 cm) tower.

Fire piece fits in dragon's mouth

A KNIGHTLY FIGURE

Unlike LEGO minifigures, DUPLO figures can't be taken apart. The modern figure has separated legs (which still move as a single piece), hands with visible fingers, rotating shoulders and head, and a little round bump for a nose. It often has a permanently-attached hat or hair and comes in three sizes: adult, child, and a new baby figure introduced in 2009.

This flail is perfect for gently bopping rival knights on the noggin.

The armor and helmet really come in handy when you fall off your dragon.

A mighty shield to block dragon flame… at least of the plastic sort.

ASSEMBLING ANIMALS

This series of animal-building sets featured unusual parts like accordion hinges for flexible necks and bodies, heads with opening mouths, and pull-string tails, designed to give young children a more physically interactive experience with their creations. Lots of extra bricks (some with painted-on eyes) were included to let kids make even more wild creatures than the ones on the box.

Originally released under the LEGO Explore "Explore Imagination" brand for children aged 1½ and up, these sets were re-packaged for 2–5-year-olds when DUPLO returned the next year.

3515 African Adventures (2003)

Sets to Remember

514 Pre-School Building Set (1972)

010 Building Set (1973)

524 LEGOVILLE Set (1977)

534 Passenger Boat (1978)

2623 Delivery Truck (1980)

2705 Play Train (1983)

2355 Basic Set "Vehicles" (1984)

2629 Tractor and Farm Tools (1985)

2770 Furnished Playhouse (1986)

2458 Barnyard (1990)

1583 Clown Bucket (1992)

2679 DUPLO Airport (1993)

2338 Kitty Cat's Building Set (1995)

2223 Spooky House (1998)

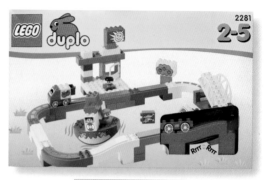
2281 Deluxe Harbor Highway (1999)

2400 Cute Vehicles (2000)

1403 Racing Leopard (2001)

4960 Giant Zoo (2006)

4973 Harvester (2007)

4683 Pony and Cart (2004)

2952 Marie (2001)

4864 Castle (2008)

2971 Action Police Bike (2001)

5604 Supermarket (2008)

4691 Police Station (2004)

5655 Caravan (2010)

6158 Animal Clinic (2012)

2024 Rattle (1983)

Bricks for Baby

THERE HAVE BEEN many LEGO® products designed for younger children, from infants and toddlers to preschoolers almost ready to start building with LEGO® DUPLO® bricks. Some of these baby-safe building and learning toys were experiments that came and went quickly, while others were popular enough to be revisited again and again with different names and colors. Here are just a few of the LEGO items that the smallest builders have played and developed creativity with over the years ●

SHAKE, RATTLE, AND CHEW

This duck rattle may look simple, but it was the result of years of research on how babies play and learn. Because infants instinctively react to a moving eye, the duck's eyes bounced when the rattle was shaken, and the ball in the middle could spin and make sounds. The two grips were added on the advice of a panel of mothers. Studs on top and openings on the bottom allowed the rattle to be attached to a child's DUPLO or LEGO bricks later on.

LEGO PRIMO & LEGO BABY

In 1995, the company unveiled LEGO PRIMO, a line of building toys with big, teething-proof pieces for babies between the ages of six and 24 months. In 1997, it became its own brand as LEGO PRIMO, with a yellow elephant logo and sets that included a shape sorter, a music-making boat, a buildable mouse, and lots of colorful, durable, stackable pieces. PRIMO was renamed LEGO Baby in 2000, merged into LEGO Explore in 2002, became Baby again with a new teddy bear logo in 2004, and was officially discontinued in 2006.

BABY BRICKS

Colorful LEGO PRIMO and LEGO Baby pieces were made to be safe, sturdy, and simple enough for the smallest builders to stack up and take apart.

Pieces from 5461 Shape Sorter House (2005)

2503 Musical Apple (2000)

Pushing down on the worm in the apple made it pop up and play music.

BOUNCING BUG

A favorite of children aged six to 18 months all over the world, the Bendy Caterpillar would flatten out when pushed down, then spring up again when released for a guaranteed baby laugh. It could also roll around on the floor and came with bug friends that could be stacked up on the bumps on its back.

The caterpillar was also made in dark green and red for LEGO PRIMO in 1997 and yellow and dark green for LEGO Baby in 2001 and LEGO Explore in 2002.

5443 Hanging Rattle (2003)

FOR THE YOUNGEST

This smiling-faced LEGO Explore rattle with fabric, string, and soft plastic parts could hang from the railing of a crib or playpen. It was made for newborns under the "Explore Being Me" label.

5465 Bendy Caterpillar (2005)

5470 My First QUATRO Figure Set (2006)

Less than a dozen sets were released between 2004 and 2006, making this not just the first, but the only QUATRO figure ever made.

LEGO® QUATRO™ THEME

As DUPLO bricks were to System bricks, so LEGO® QUATRO™ was to LEGO DUPLO. Made for children aged one to three, its teething-friendly pieces were more rounded and twice as long, wide, and tall as the DUPLO versions. Emblazoned with a blue version of the original PRIMO elephant logo, QUATRO sets were mostly brick collections that focused more on building giant free-form towers than assembling models.

MUSICAL CUTHBERT AND FRIEND

A LEGO PRIMO set for babies aged 0 to 2, Cuthbert the Camel was a music box that children could twist around to wind up and release to make him play a happy, soothing tune. His feet could attach to PRIMO pieces, and his hump was a stud that other compatible elements, including his round-bodied PRIMO figure friend, could stack on top of.

2007 Musical Cuthbert and Friend (1998)

SHAPES & COLORS

Released in the first year of the PRIMO brand after it was split off from the DUPLO one, this set helped babies aged eight to 24 months learn shapes and colors by discovering which pieces fit into which cubes. The cubes could be stacked on top of each other as well as on the green baseplate that served as the packaging lid.

2099 Shape Sorter (1997)

Train cars with bumps for stacking

2974 Play Train (2001)

BABY TRAINS

Made from seven pieces for babies six months and up, this train toy was, like the caterpillar, produced in several different colors for different LEGO Baby brands between 2000 and 2005. It made sounds when you pushed down on the locomotive's smokestack.

LEGO® FABULAND™

FROM THE MOMENT its first sets arrived in 1979, LEGO® FABULAND™ was something different and special. Its simple-to-build models and friendly, funny animal-headed figures filled the gap between LEGO® DUPLO® play and LEGO System, and appealed to boys and girls. FABULAND was also the first LEGO theme to feature storybooks, children's clothing, and even an animated TV series ●

This sturdy paddle steamer was captained by Wilfred Walrus. Mike Monkey swept the deck, and another monkey crew member worked on the engine.

3673 Steamboat (1985)

350 Town Hall with Leonard Lion and Friends (1979)

A WORLD OF MAKE-BELIEVE

LEGO FABULAND was the perfect theme for children who loved to pretend. Its colorful, charming buildings and vehicles were built from large pieces for fast construction, and its houses had rooms that were large enough to play with figures inside.

Lionel Lion (sometimes called Leonard Lion) was the mayor of FABULAND. His Town Hall set also came with his friends Buster Bulldog the fire-fighter and the trouble-making but good-hearted Freddy Fox.

Boat from 3660 Fisherman's Cottage (1985)

FUZZY FRIENDS

Halfway between minifigures and DUPLO figures in scale, the creature cast of FABULAND all had their own names, accessories, and sometimes even hats and uniforms related to particular jobs. Edward Elephant arrived with a rowboat and fisherman's cottage in 1985, while Charlie Cat just tagged along with his friend for a fun fishing trip far from town.

Bernhard Bear drops in on Billy Bear at the service station, which included a gas pump and car-fixing tools.

3670 Service Station (1984)

> Welcome aboard, Miss Hippopotamus!

3662 Bus (1987)

STORY BUILDING

Children from the age of 3 and up could use their FABULAND sets to create houses, boats, fairground rides, police and fire stations, and much more. Larger sets included easy-to-follow building guides with stories for parents to read aloud while their children built.

PICTURE BOOKS

"Lionel Lion, mayor of Fabuland, had invited all his friends to a fancy dress party. All the invitations had been delivered and everyone was very excited—there was going to be a competition for the best fancy dress costume. 'I'll go as a car,' said Max. He found an old cardboard box and painted some wheels on the sides". . . and the adventure continued in one of the many FABULAND storybooks!

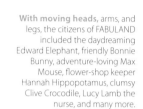

I like to help all my friends, even the ones who haven't asked yet!

With moving heads, arms, and legs, the citizens of FABULAND included the daydreaming Edward Elephant, friendly Bonnie Bunny, adventure-loving Max Mouse, flower-shop keeper Hannah Hippopotamus, clumsy Clive Crocodile, Lucy Lamb the nurse, and many more.

Bonnie Bunny

Max Mouse

Mike Monkey

A LAND OF DREAMS

After a decade of fun and imagination, the FABULAND theme finally came to an end in 1989. The last sets released were a school room, a carousel, and a park with a slide and swing. But the children who grew up with high-flying Joe Crow and all his friends remember them fondly, and the happy world of LEGO FABULAND still has many fans and collectors today.

Plane from 3671
Airport (1984)

How do you get to FABULAND?
"It's not far away—just a little to the left as you go north, or a little to the right as you go south. Edward Elephant lives there, and so do all his friends."

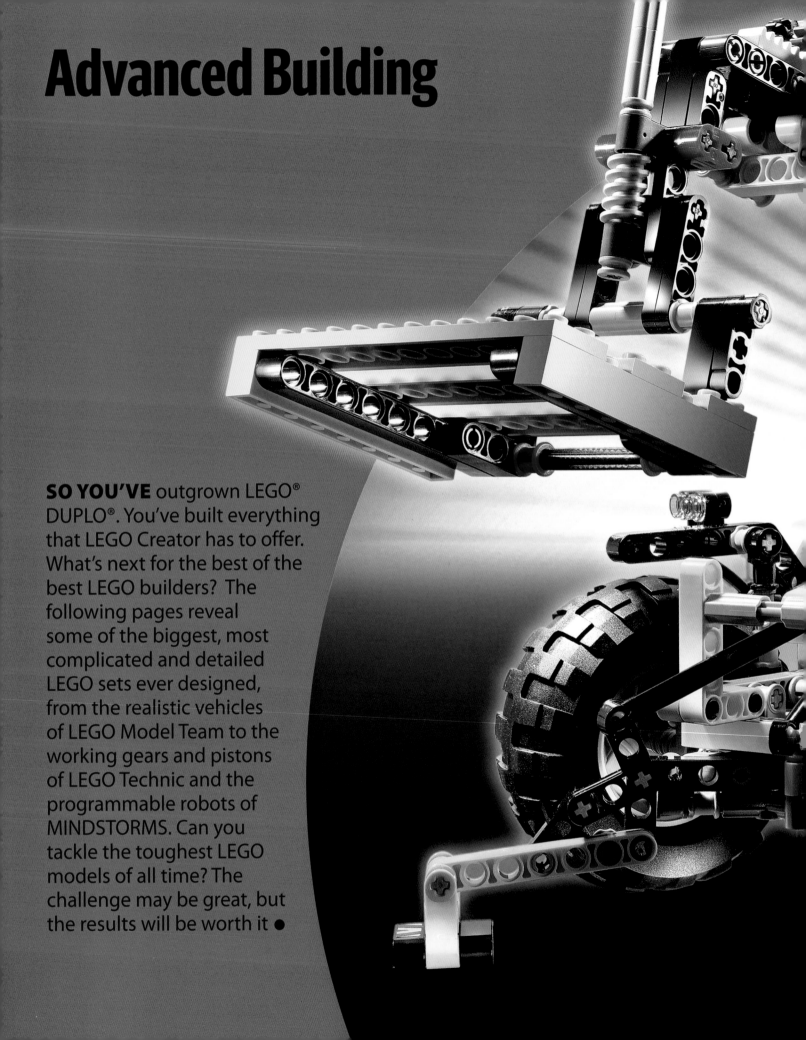

Advanced Building

SO YOU'VE outgrown LEGO®
DUPLO®. You've built everything
that LEGO Creator has to offer.
What's next for the best of the
best LEGO builders? The
following pages reveal
some of the biggest, most
complicated and detailed
LEGO sets ever designed,
from the realistic vehicles
of LEGO Model Team to the
working gears and pistons
of LEGO Technic and the
programmable robots of
MINDSTORMS. Can you
tackle the toughest LEGO
models of all time? The
challenge may be great, but
the results will be worth it ●

LEGO® Technic

DEVELOPED FROM special gear sets and the Expert Builder series of the 1970s, LEGO® Technic adds mechanical motion to LEGO models. By building in gears, axles, and motors, builders can bring their LEGO creations to life with extending crane booms, wheel-linked steering systems, adjustable suspensions, and other realistic functions ●

8300 Action Figures (2000)

LEGO® TECHNIC FIGURES

From 1986 to 2001, many LEGO Technic sets included figures with highly-posable limbs to serve as drivers for large-scale vehicles. Although they had the traditional yellow hands and faces of LEGO minifigures, they towered over their smaller cousins. In true LEGO construction style, they could also be attached to bricks and Technic pieces.

Mechanical actuators raise, lower, and extend articulated arm

857 Motorcycle (1979)

Switch-activated bucket scoop extends and retracts for digging

FORM AND FUNCTION

This bike with sidecar had the brick-built appearance of a classic Model Team set, but the functionality of a Technic model. It featured big rubber wheels, front-wheel steering, a working piston, and an engine with a drive-chain assembled from 26 tiny link elements.

Gear extends crane arm when wheel at base is spun

Early LEGO Technic models had traditional studded pieces, making them resemble LEGO System vehicles more closely than today's streamlined Technic sets.

855 Mobile Crane (1978)

WHEELS & GEARS

Thanks to a clever combination of spinning gears and revolving axles, a trio of wheels built into this Technic crane model could be turned by hand to raise and lower the crane's arm, extend its boom, and drop or retract its lifting cable.

5571 Giant Truck (1996)

LEGO MODEL TEAM

Technic wasn't the only LEGO theme for experienced builders. In 1986, the company launched LEGO Model Team, a series of vehicles built to be as realistic as possible. Made from 1,743 pieces, the super-detailed, large-scale Model Team Giant Truck was until recently the all-time biggest LEGO set.

LEGO TECHNIC TITAN

This 1,884-piece construction vehicle bore little resemblance to its 1978 ancestor. Its functions included six-wheel steering, retractable side outriggers, and an arm lifted by a working pneumatic cylinder and powered by a motor that could extend the crane's length to 18 in (46 cm).

8421 Mobile Crane (2005)

MODERN CONSTRUCTION

Thanks to their heavy-duty appearance and a multitude of moving parts and mechanisms, construction vehicles are some of the most popular Technic sets. Along with a variety of cranes, excavators, and dump trucks, recent years' models have included a motorized bulldozer, a telehandler, and backhoe, front-end, and wheel loaders.

The 8293 Power Functions Motor Set could be added for motorized functions.

9394 Jet Plane (2012)

SMOOTH FLYING

Most modern Technic sets are made from a combination of smooth, non-studded support beams and angled, decorative plates with gearing and other functions built into the middle. This largely brick-less construction system gives Technic models a more realistic shape than other LEGO kits.

Rotating treads built from individual link segments

KING OF THE ROAD

Stretching 26 in (66 cm) long and built out of 1,877 pieces, this monster of a Technic tow truck had working rack-and-pinion steering, a V6 engine with moving pistons and a spinning radiator fan, metallic-finished bricks and custom decals, and a telescopic towing crane with a ratchet-regulated winch.

8285 Tow Truck (2006)

The truck could elevate its crane, extend its boom, and lower its metal hook with controls hidden in the cab's side panels. It had a deployable towing platform with pneumatic lift, and rear stabilizers for heavy loads.

8294 Excavator (2008)

8110 Mercedes-Benz Unimog U 400 (2011)

UNIMOG

The Unimog's 2,048 pieces made it the largest Technic set so far. It had a working suspension system and a switch that let you provide pneumatic Power Functions control to either the grapple crane in back or the recovery winch in front.

Cab platform rotates 360°

Super Models

3723 LEGO Minifigure (2000)

THEY'RE HUGE! They're realistic! They're made from lots and lots of bricks! These are the ultimate LEGO® models, chosen from among the most amazing (and expensive!) official sets ever made. Behold—the LEGO Super Models ●

At a 1:300 scale, the LEGO Eiffel Tower set stood an impressive 42½ in (108 cm) tall. Designed using blueprints of the real tower in Paris and assembled from 3,428 pieces, it was accurate from the lifts at the base to the French flag on top.

10181 Eiffel Tower (2007)

One of the first official LEGO sculptures, this friendly fellow took 1,850 pieces to build and stood 20 in (51 cm) tall, 12 times the size of a regular minifigure. More than just a statue, he had rotating shoulders and hands and a removable cap.

33 in (84 cm) tall from her base to the top of her burning torch, the LEGO model of New York's famous "Lady Liberty" was built from 2,882 bricks, almost entirely colored sand green.

10187 VW Beetle™ (2008)

Based on the iconic "Charlotte" model of 1960, this VW Beetle was picked by LEGO fans as the classic car that they'd most like to have as a set. At 16 in (41 cm) long and 1,626 pieces, it had a movable stick shift, opening doors, hood, trunk, and glove compartment, folding seats, rear engine, spare tire, and windshield wipers.

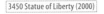

3450 Statue of Liberty (2000)

10177 Boeing 787 Dreamliner™ (2006)

3451 Sopwith Camel (2001

This licensed LEGO version of Boeing Commercial Airplanes' next-generation jet airliner was made from 1,197 pieces and included a display stand and information card. Designed using specifications from Boeing, the model was 26 in (66 cm) long, with a 27 in (69 cm) wingspan.

The Sopwith Camel was that rarest of things: a LEGO "war" model. Built from 577 pieces and complete with strings for tension wires, it was a replica of the British World War I fighter plane. It was followed the next year by an arch-rival: the Red Baron's Fokker Dr.I triplane.

This incredibly detailed model of the world-famous "Jewel of India," with an equally incredible piece count of 5,922, was built from the most elements of any LEGO set created so far. Its intricate architecture and decorations required advanced building techniques to construct and incorporated many rare and unusual pieces that were found in few other sets. The model was 20 in (51 cm) wide and 16 in (41 cm) tall.

10189 Taj Mahal (2008)

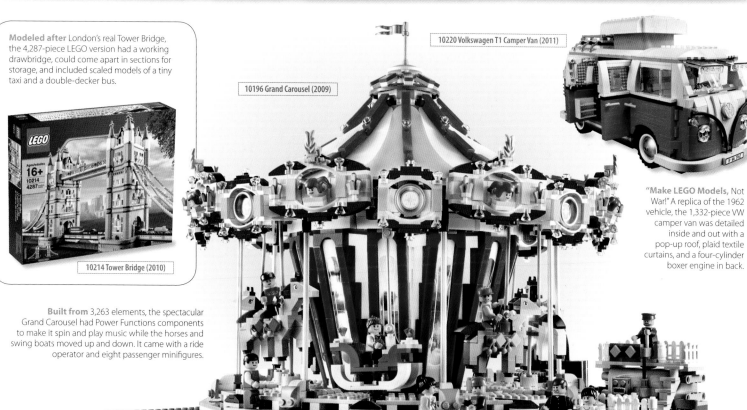

Modeled after London's real Tower Bridge, the 4,287-piece LEGO version had a working drawbridge, could come apart in sections for storage, and included scaled models of a tiny taxi and a double-decker bus.

10214 Tower Bridge (2010)

10220 Volkswagen T1 Camper Van (2011)

10196 Grand Carousel (2009)

"Make LEGO Models, Not War!" A replica of the 1962 vehicle, the 1,332-piece VW camper van was detailed inside and out with a pop-up roof, plaid textile curtains, and a four-cylinder boxer engine in back.

Built from 3,263 elements, the spectacular Grand Carousel had Power Functions components to make it spin and play music while the horses and swing boats moved up and down. It came with a ride operator and eight passenger minifigures.

Modular Buildings

LEGO® MODULAR BUILDINGS models give experienced fans the chance to assemble highly detailed and realistic buildings, created by expert designers using advanced building techniques. Built with detachable levels for easy customization and access to interiors, the models can be connected together side-by-side to create a street scene, complete with busy minifigure inhabitants ●

10197 Fire Brigade (2009)

FIRE BRIGADE

This model was styled after the vintage fire stations of the 1930s. It had a garage with an opening door for the old-time fire truck, a water tower and bell on the roof, a ping-pong table for the times between emergencies, and even a loyal fire dog.

Four-level townhouse

Rooftop terrace

10211 Grand Emporium (2010)

The Grand Emporium was a three-story department store with a clothing department, housewares section, and top-floor toy shop. Its details included revolving doors, an escalator, and a window washer working outside.

Boy on push-scooter

IN THE BEGINNING

The Modular Buildings series started in 2007 with Café Corner, a 2,056-piece hotel and café. It was followed by Market Street, a LEGO Factory exclusive (see pp.224–25) created by talented fan Eric Brok. The next addition was Green Grocer, which featured apartments built above a neighborhood grocery store.

10190 Market Street (2007)

10185 Green Grocer (2008)

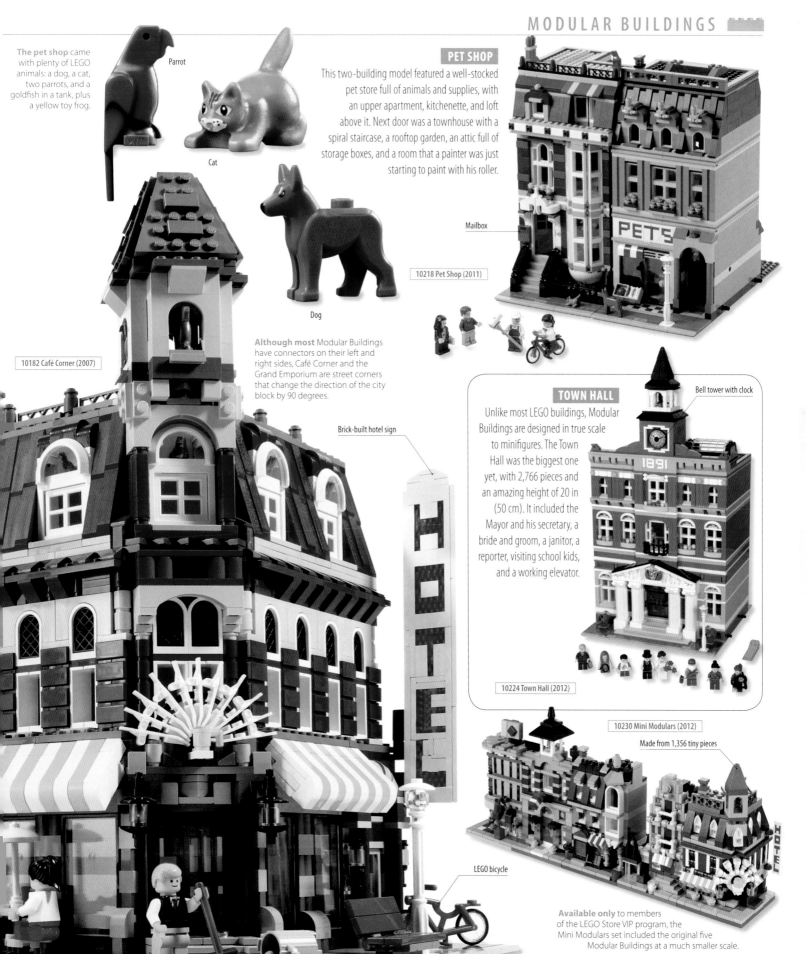

The pet shop came with plenty of LEGO animals: a dog, a cat, two parrots, and a goldfish in a tank, plus a yellow toy frog.

Parrot

Cat

Dog

PET SHOP

This two-building model featured a well-stocked pet store full of animals and supplies, with an upper apartment, kitchenette, and loft above it. Next door was a townhouse with a spiral staircase, a rooftop garden, an attic full of storage boxes, and a room that a painter was just starting to paint with his roller.

Mailbox

10218 Pet Shop (2011)

10182 Café Corner (2007)

Although most Modular Buildings have connectors on their left and right sides, Café Corner and the Grand Emporium are street corners that change the direction of the city block by 90 degrees.

Brick-built hotel sign

TOWN HALL

Bell tower with clock

Unlike most LEGO buildings, Modular Buildings are designed in true scale to minifigures. The Town Hall was the biggest one yet, with 2,766 pieces and an amazing height of 20 in (50 cm). It included the Mayor and his secretary, a bride and groom, a janitor, a reporter, visiting school kids, and a working elevator.

10224 Town Hall (2012)

10230 Mini Modulars (2012)

Made from 1,356 tiny pieces

LEGO bicycle

Available only to members of the LEGO Store VIP program, the Mini Modulars set included the original five Modular Buildings at a much smaller scale.

Spilled rubbish

173

LEGO® MINDSTORMS®

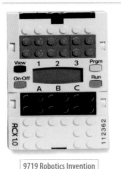

9719 Robotics Invention System 1.0 (1998)

IN 1984, THE LEGO GROUP formed a unique partnership with the Media Laboratory at the US-based Massachusetts Institute of Technology (MIT). One of the first results was the LEGO® Technic Computer Control for educational products in 1986, but it was in 1998 that the cooperation of research lab and building toy led to a truly revolutionary product: the LEGO® MINDSTORMS® RCX computer brick, which could be used to construct and program moving, working robots ●

THE FIRST GENERATION

The first RCX (Robotic Command System) programmable brick contained an 8-bit microcontroller CPU and 32K of RAM. Users could "build" a program on their home computer and download it to the RCX using an infrared interface. The program told the motors and sensors plugged into the computer brick how to move and bring a robot to life.

UPGRADES

9747 Robotics Invention System 1.5 (1999) and 3804 Robotics Invention System 2.0 (2001) updated the previous versions of LEGO robot technology.

Decorative LEGO element eyes

CUSTOM CREATIONS

By combining Robotics Invention System sensors, motors and the RCX brick with the beams and gears from their LEGO Technic collections, builders could create robots with a virtually endless variety of looks and functions.

9731 Vision Command (2000) camera

Rubber tire for mouth

RCX 1.0 brick

Gear rotates torso

This bartender robot was built for the Nuremberg Toy Fair in 2001. It is programmed to recognize green and red cards and serve a BIONICLE® or Jack Stone themed drink depending on which card is presented.

LEGO Technic gear

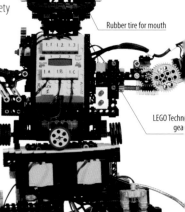

Robotics Invention System robot

3801 Ultimate Accessory Set (2000)

EXPANDING HORIZONS

How do you make a LEGO robot even better? With expansion sets that add even more sensors, motors, elements, and programming possibilities, like this one with a rotational sensor, a glowing lamp and the first LEGO MINDSTORMS remote control.

SPORT-BOTS

The RoboSports expansion let you build sports-playing robots, such as this rolling, dunking basketball star. It came with a Challenge CD, a mat to serve as a sports field, an extra motor, and useful elements, including balls and pucks.

Ball-dunking claw

Basketball hoop

9730 RoboSports (1998)

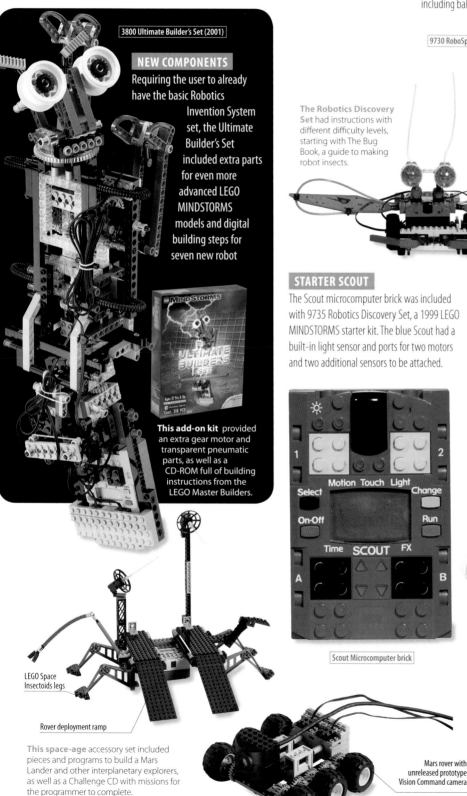

3800 Ultimate Builder's Set (2001)

NEW COMPONENTS

Requiring the user to already have the basic Robotics Invention System set, the Ultimate Builder's Set included extra parts for even more advanced LEGO MINDSTORMS models and digital building steps for seven new robot

This add-on kit provided an extra gear motor and transparent pneumatic parts, as well as a CD-ROM full of building instructions from the LEGO Master Builders.

The Robotics Discovery Set had instructions with different difficulty levels, starting with The Bug Book, a guide to making robot insects.

9735 Robotics Discovery Set (1999)

STARTER SCOUT

The Scout microcomputer brick was included with 9735 Robotics Discovery Set, a 1999 LEGO MINDSTORMS starter kit. The blue Scout had a built-in light sensor and ports for two motors and two additional sensors to be attached.

1   2

Motion Touch Light

Select   Change

On-Off   Run

Time SCOUT FX

A   B

Scout Microcomputer brick

9748 Droid Developer Kit (1999)

MicroScout controller

ON-OFF   SELECT

RUN

LEGO Space Insectoids legs

Rover deployment ramp

This space-age accessory set included pieces and programs to build a Mars Lander and other interplanetary explorers, as well as a Challenge CD with missions for the programmer to complete.

9736 Exploration Mars (2000)

Mars rover with unreleased prototype Vision Command camera

DESIGNING DROIDS

LEGO MINDSTORMS products entered a galaxy far, far away with expansion sets based on the *Star Wars*™ movies. The Droid Developer Kit let you make your own rolling R2-D2™ and other droids, while 9754 Dark Side Developer Kit (2000) had parts and instructions for building a walking Imperial AT-AT, a marching Destroyer Droid, and more. Both came with a new MicroScout controller with a built-in motor and light sensor.

"NXT" Generation

EIGHT YEARS after the Robotics Invention System was launched, 8527 LEGO® MINDSTORMS® NXT arrived with the goal of making robot creation simple enough for someone to build and program one in half an hour. The RCX was replaced by the NXT Intelligent Brick, and new motors and sensors were designed to give the latest robots even more capabilities, as well as a sleek, futuristic look ●

Ultrasonic sensor

NXT Intelligent Brick

ALPHA REX

The signature LEGO MINDSTORMS NXT robot, Alpha Rex could walk with built-in rotation sensors in his leg motors, and feel and hear with the sensors on the ends of his arms. He could see using his ultrasonic-sensor eyes, and even be programmed to display a virtual heartbeat on the NXT screen in his chest.

Touch sensor "stinger"

Claws made from BIONICLE® pieces

Technic beam legs with motors

Another robot that could be built from the MINDSTORMS NXT set was Spike the scorpion, which crawled on six legs and "stung" targets with its spring-out tail.

8527 Spike

8527 MINDSTORMS NXT (2006)

The original NXT set included instructions for building the robots Alpha Rex, Spike, TriBot, and the T-56 mechanical arm.

NXT INTELLIGENT BRICK

The NXT is the new generation of programmable bricks, with an ARM 32-bit microprocessor, 256 KB memory, USB 2.0 and Bluetooth support, and a whole array of new and enhanced sensors and motors.

Interactive Servo Motor: built-in rotation sensor for precision movement

Touch Sensor: detects touch and release to let robot "feel" its environment

8527 NXT Intelligent Brick

Users drag and drop "blocks" on their computer screens to program their robot's behavior.

Sound Sensor: lets robot hear and react to sounds, including voice commands

Light Sensor: allows robot to detect different colors and light intensities

Ultrasonic Sensor: enables robot to "see," measure distance, and react to movement

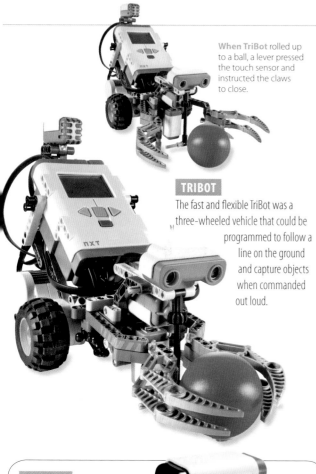

When TriBot rolled up to a ball, a lever pressed the touch sensor and instructed the claws to close.

TRIBOT

The fast and flexible TriBot was a three-wheeled vehicle that could be programmed to follow a line on the ground and capture objects when commanded out loud.

FIRST LEGO® LEAGUE

Created with the non-profit organization FIRST (For Inspiration and Recognition of Science and Technology), the *FIRST* LEGO® League is an annual program that culminates in a robotic technology tournament for elementary and middle school students from around the world.

Teams are judged based on teamwork, robot design, research presentations, and the performance of their robots on the playing field.

Teams of 5 to 10 players design robots using LEGO MINDSTORMS kits and compete to solve scientific and technical challenges based on real-world issues ranging from alternative energy to space exploration—learning life skills along the way.

ADD-ONS

Additional components, some made by licensed second-party developers, are available at the LEGO online shop, including sensors that measure rotation, detect infrared light, and even tell a robot which way is up or how fast it is accelerating.

MS1034 Compass sensor

The compass sensor measures the Earth's magnetic field to determine which direction a robot is facing.

MS1048 RF ID Sensor

The RF ID sensor uses a key transponder to unlock and activate NXT programs.

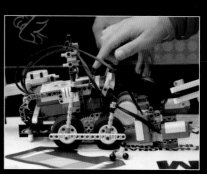

More than 137,000 children in 50 countries have taken part in the FLL program in recent years.

WHAT'S NXT?

Meet the next version of LEGO MINDSTORMS NXT. The 2009 edition of the state-of-the-art LEGO robotics kit came with more customizable programming options, instructions for making even more robots, and all-new technology, including its own color sensor!

8547 MINDSTORMS NXT 2.0 (2009)

The all-new, all-different Alpha Rex was bigger, sturdier, and had even more built-in and programmed options.

FIRST also runs a *FIRST* Robotics Competition and a *FIRST* Tech Challenge for high schoolers, and the Junior *FIRST* LEGO League for kids aged 6–9.

FIRST Championship photography by Adriana Groisman. Other photography courtesy of students, volunteers, and sponsors.

Licensed Themes

WHO WOULDN'T want to build the characters, vehicles, and worlds from their favorite TV shows and movies? It was only a matter of time before LEGO® sets started to branch out into some of the biggest licenses around. As early as the 1970s, the company was making branded gas station models and airlines were selling LEGO kits of their jets. However, in 1999, with the release of LEGO® *Star Wars*™, licensed LEGO themes really took off. Since then, we've seen LEGO® Batman™, LEGO® Mickey Mouse™, LEGO® SpongeBob SquarePants™, LEGO® Spider-Man™, and many more ●

LEGO® *Star Wars*™

7961 Darth Maul's Sith Infiltrator™ (2011) was the third minifigure-scale version of the ship. It introduced a soft-plastic cap to give Darth Maul his fierce Zabrak horns.

THE LEGO GROUP'S first licensed property in more than 40 years, LEGO® *Star Wars*™ launched in 1999. With constructible classic vehicles and the whole cast of famous heroes, villains, aliens, and droids rendered in minifigure style for the first time ever, the theme was an immediate success with builders of all ages—and it's still proving very popular ●

STAR WARS: EPISODE I *THE PHANTOM MENACE*

RACE FOR FREEDOM

One of the first sets released from the *Star Wars* prequel trilogy, Mos Espa Podrace let builders pit young Anakin Skywalker and his custom Podracer against rivals Sebulba and Gasgano in a race for his freedom in the perilous Boonta Eve Classic Podrace. With lots of unusual elements and colors, it remains a popular set among LEGO fans. Just like in the movie, Sebulba's orange Podracer was equipped with sneaky gadgets to sabotage his opponents' vehicles.

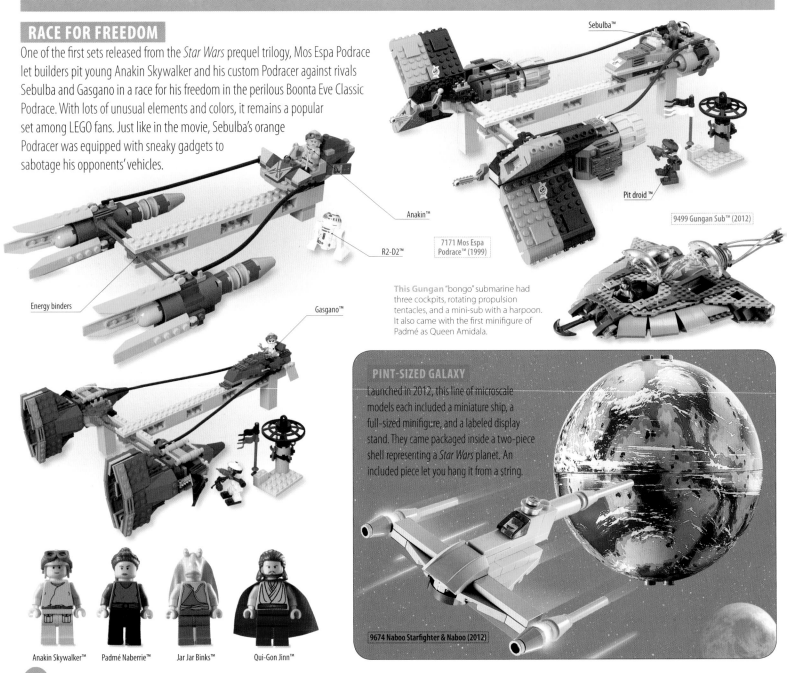

Sebulba™

Anakin™

R2-D2™

Energy binders

Gasgano™

Pit droid™

7171 Mos Espa Podrace™ (1999)

9499 Gungan Sub™ (2012)

This Gungan "bongo" submarine had three cockpits, rotating propulsion tentacles, and a mini-sub with a harpoon. It also came with the first minifigure of Padmé as Queen Amidala.

PINT-SIZED GALAXY

Launched in 2012, this line of microscale models each included a miniature ship, a full-sized minifigure, and a labeled display stand. They came packaged inside a two-piece shell representing a *Star Wars* planet. An included piece let you hang it from a string.

9674 Naboo Starfighter & Naboo (2012)

Anakin Skywalker™   Padmé Naberrie™   Jar Jar Binks™   Qui-Gon Jinn™

STAR WARS: EPISODE II *ATTACK OF THE CLONES*

7153 Jango Fett's *Slave I*™ (2002)

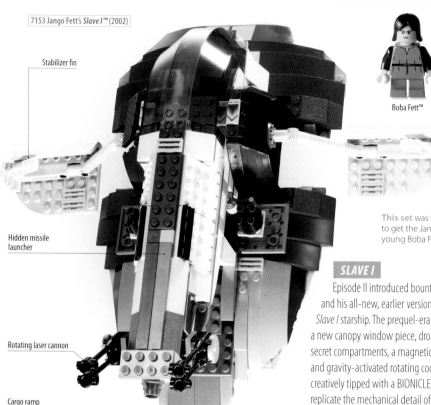

- Stabilizer fin
- Hidden missile launcher
- Rotating laser cannon
- Cargo ramp

Boba Fett™

Jango Fett™

This set was the only place to get the Jango Fett and young Boba Fett minifigures.

7163 Republic Gunship™ (2002)

Super battle droids and destroyer droid

SLAVE I

Episode II introduced bounty hunter Jango Fett and his all-new, earlier version of the familiar *Slave I* starship. The prequel-era LEGO *Slave I* had a new canopy window piece, dropping bombs, secret compartments, a magnetic cargo container, and gravity-activated rotating cockpit and wings, creatively tipped with a BIONICLE® foot piece to replicate the mechanical detail of the movie ship.

REPUBLIC GUNSHIP

Straight from the final battle on the planet Geonosis, the LEGO Republic Gunship had a 15 in (38 cm) wingspan, movable side laser turrets, a detachable top section, a magnetic tool-box, opening troop bay doors, and hidden compartments. Popular for its many features and a high count of droid and clone trooper minifigures, it also included a mysterious unnamed Jedi Knight to help battle the Separatists. A new, even bigger version of the Republic Gunship was made in 2008 for *The Clone Wars* line.

STAR WARS: EPISODE III *REVENGE OF THE SITH*

SPACE BATTLE

The Jedi Knight who would soon become Darth Vader blasted off one last time as a good guy aboard Anakin Skywalker's new Eta-2 interceptor, closely pursued by a Separatist vulture droid that could convert from flight to walking mode. With both hero and villain vehicles included, this set let builders reenact the blazing battle in the skies above Coruscant from the opening scenes of Episode III.

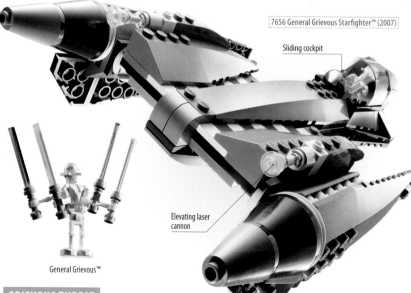

7656 General Grievous Starfighter™ (2007)

- Sliding cockpit
- Elevating laser cannon

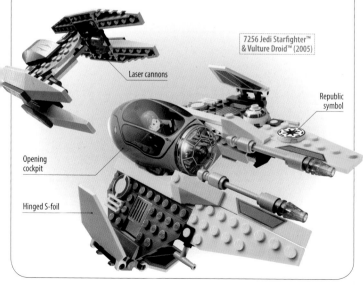

7256 Jedi Starfighter™ & Vulture Droid™ (2005)

- Laser cannons
- Republic symbol
- Opening cockpit
- Hinged S-foil

General Grievous™

GRIEVOUS THREAT

General Grievous, the cyborg commander of the Separatist droid army, piloted this modified Belbullab-22 starfighter during the Clone Wars, but it was Obi-Wan Kenobi who flew away with it after their final battle on Utapau. The model had a slide-open cockpit, flip-up laser cannons, and a tail fin that folded down for landing. A new version was released for *The Clone Wars* in 2010.

Storage clips on the bottom of the model held the four-armed general's four stolen Jedi lightsabers.

STAR WARS: EPISODE IV *A NEW HOPE*

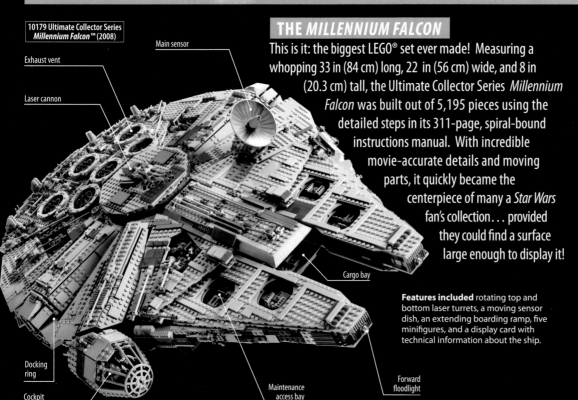

10179 Ultimate Collector Series *Millennium Falcon™* (2008)

- Main sensor
- Exhaust vent
- Laser cannon
- Cargo bay
- Docking ring
- Cockpit
- Maintenance access bay
- Forward floodlight

THE *MILLENNIUM FALCON*

This is it: the biggest LEGO® set ever made! Measuring a whopping 33 in (84 cm) long, 22 in (56 cm) wide, and 8 in (20.3 cm) tall, the Ultimate Collector Series *Millennium Falcon* was built out of 5,195 pieces using the detailed steps in its 311-page, spiral-bound instructions manual. With incredible movie-accurate details and moving parts, it quickly became the centerpiece of many a *Star Wars* fan's collection… provided they could find a surface large enough to display it!

Features included rotating top and bottom laser turrets, a moving sensor dish, an extending boarding ramp, five minifigures, and a display card with technical information about the ship.

9492 TIE Fighter™ (2012) included detailed wing panels, flick-firing missiles, an exclusive droid, and a new helmet for its Death Star Trooper.

Chewbacca™   Han Solo™

Luke Skywalker™   Princess Leia™   Obi-Wan Kenobi™

TATOOINE

You'll never build a more wretched hive of scum and villainy. 2004's Mos Eisley Cantina set provided lots of LEGO firsts: the first-ever Dewback riding lizard, the first-ever sandtrooper, and the first-ever Greedo minifigure. The desert planet grew with 2012's Droid Escape set, which updated a model from 11 years earlier with new versions of the escape pod, fugitive droids R2-D2 and C-3PO, and a pair of Sandtroopers with a swoop bike.

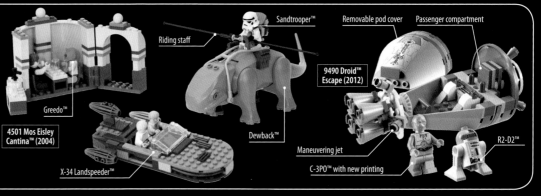

- Greedo™
- 4501 Mos Eisley Cantina™ (2004)
- Riding staff
- Sandtrooper™
- Dewback™
- X-34 Landspeeder™
- Removable pod cover
- Passenger compartment
- 9490 Droid™ Escape (2012)
- Maneuvering jet
- C-3PO™ with new printing
- R2-D2™

STAR DESTROYER

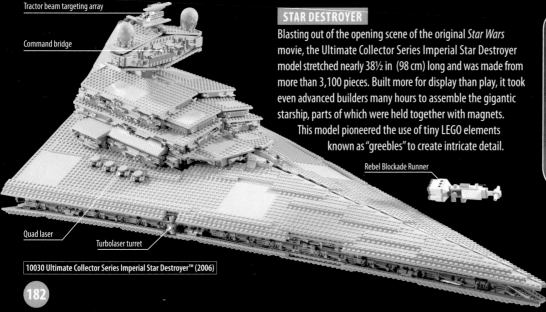

- Tractor beam targeting array
- Command bridge
- Quad laser
- Turbolaser turret

10030 Ultimate Collector Series Imperial Star Destroyer™ (2006)

Blasting out of the opening scene of the original *Star Wars* movie, the Ultimate Collector Series Imperial Star Destroyer model stretched nearly 38½ in (98 cm) long and was made from more than 3,100 pieces. Built more for display than play, it took even advanced builders many hours to assemble the gigantic starship, parts of which were held together with magnets. This model pioneered the use of tiny LEGO elements known as "greebles" to create intricate detail.

Rebel Blockade Runner

The MINI collection brought a whole new scale to LEGO *Star Wars*. The first series, including 4484 MINI X-wing vs. TIE Advanced (2003), came with pieces to make two pocket-sized models, plus part of a bonus TIE Bomber that could be fully assembled when you collected all 4 sets.

STAR WARS: EPISODE V *THE EMPIRE STRIKES BACK*

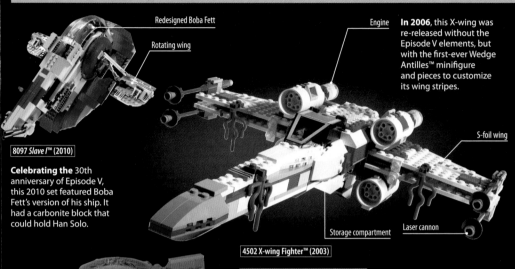

Redesigned Boba Fett

Rotating wing

8097 *Slave I*™ (2010)

Celebrating the 30th anniversary of Episode V, this 2010 set featured Boba Fett's version of his ship. It had a carbonite block that could hold Han Solo.

Engine

In 2006, this X-wing was re-released without the Episode V elements, but with the first-ever Wedge Antilles™ minifigure and pieces to customize its wing stripes.

S-foil wing

Storage compartment

Laser cannon

4502 X-wing Fighter™ (2003)

X-WING FIGHTER

A LEGO X-wing fighter set was released with the first wave of *Star Wars* sets in 1999, but the new 2003 version was a major improvement. It was bigger, had better colors, and was more accurate to the movies, plus it came with detachable swamp muck and Yoda's Dagobah hut. The wings were even geared to open and close when you turned a piece on the back of the model!

Luke Skywalker™

Yoda™

Yoda's hut opened up to reveal his bed, stew pot, and a secret compartment for his lightsaber.

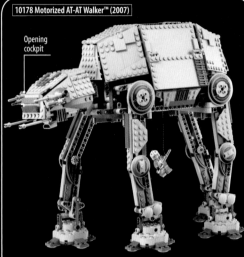

10178 Motorized AT-AT Walker™ (2007)

Opening cockpit

IMPERIAL WALKER

The winner of a 2006 fan vote to decide the next exclusive LEGO *Star Wars* set, the second minifigure-scale AT-AT (All Terrain Armored Transport) included a LEGO Power Functions motor and battery box. The flip of a switch enabled it to walk forward or back and move its head. Clever builders added an infrared receiver to make their walkers remote-controlled.

STAR WARS: EPISODE VI *RETURN OF THE JEDI*

10143 Death Star II™ (2005)

RETURN TO TATOOINE

The LEGO version of Jabba's sail barge was packed with fun play features. You could move the blaster cannon and sails, use the mini-catapult to launch Boba Fett into the air, extend the skiff's gangplank to feed pesky Rebels to the hungry Sarlacc, and open the sides to reveal Jabba the Hutt himself, complete with throne room, prison, and even a well-stocked kitchen.

Jabba's 2012 palace included (among others) majordomo Bib Fortuna, dancing girl Oola, monkey-lizard Salacious Crumb, and an all-new Jabba on his throne above the Rancor pit.

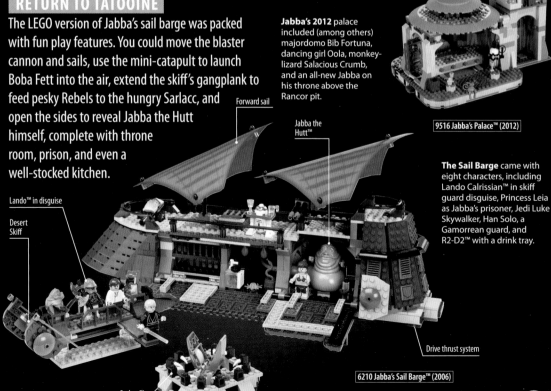

Forward sail

Jabba the Hutt™

9516 Jabba's Palace™ (2012)

The Sail Barge came with eight characters, including Lando Calrissian™ in skiff guard disguise, Princess Leia as Jabba's prisoner, Jedi Luke Skywalker, Han Solo, a Gamorrean guard, and R2-D2™ with a drink tray.

Lando™ in disguise

Desert Skiff

THE SECOND DEATH STAR

An Ultimate Collector Series model designed for assembly by advanced builders 16 and up, the *Death Star II* was made from 3,449 pieces and measured 19 in (48 cm) across and 25 in (63.5 cm) high on its display stand. It included translucent pieces to create a firing superlaser beam and a tiny Star Destroyer built to scale with the giant battle station.

Drive thrust system

6210 Jabba's Sail Barge™ (2006)

Sarlacc™

STAR WARS: THE CLONE WARS™

In 2008, *Star Wars*™ hit both big and small screens with *The Clone Wars*, an action-packed new computer-animated series that took place between the events of Episode II and Episode III. Naturally, the LEGO Group followed suit with buildable versions of the new vehicles and characters!

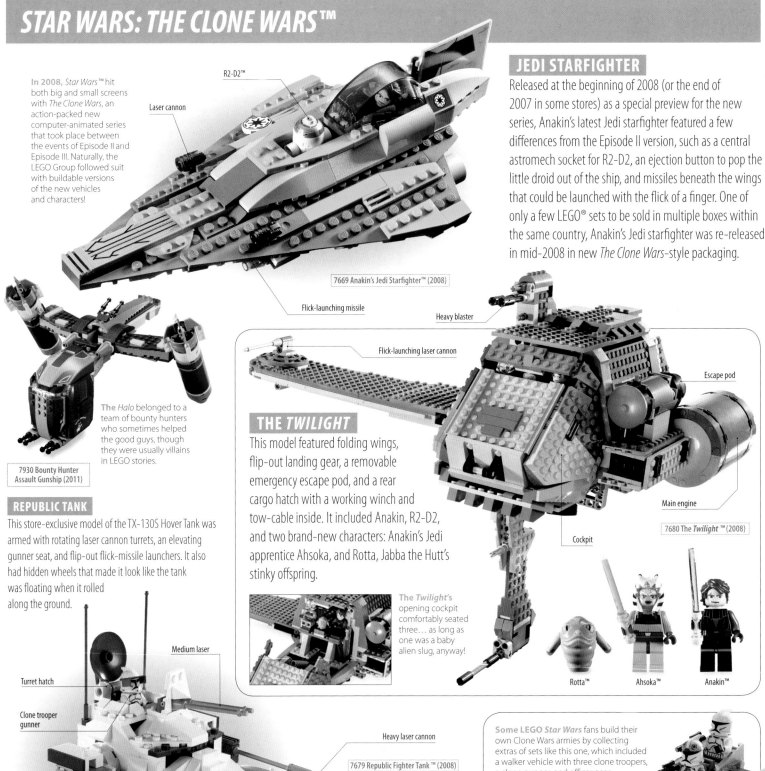

R2-D2™

Laser cannon

Flick-launching missile

7669 Anakin's Jedi Starfighter™ (2008)

JEDI STARFIGHTER

Released at the beginning of 2008 (or the end of 2007 in some stores) as a special preview for the new series, Anakin's latest Jedi starfighter featured a few differences from the Episode II version, such as a central astromech socket for R2-D2, an ejection button to pop the little droid out of the ship, and missiles beneath the wings that could be launched with the flick of a finger. One of only a few LEGO® sets to be sold in multiple boxes within the same country, Anakin's Jedi starfighter was re-released in mid-2008 in new *The Clone Wars*-style packaging.

The *Halo* belonged to a team of bounty hunters who sometimes helped the good guys, though they were usually villains in LEGO stories.

7930 Bounty Hunter Assault Gunship (2011)

REPUBLIC TANK

This store-exclusive model of the TX-130S Hover Tank was armed with rotating laser cannon turrets, an elevating gunner seat, and flip-out flick-missile launchers. It also had hidden wheels that made it look like the tank was floating when it rolled along the ground.

Heavy blaster

Flick-launching laser cannon

Escape pod

THE *TWILIGHT*

This model featured folding wings, flip-out landing gear, a removable emergency escape pod, and a rear cargo hatch with a working winch and tow-cable inside. It included Anakin, R2-D2, and two brand-new characters: Anakin's Jedi apprentice Ahsoka, and Rotta, Jabba the Hutt's stinky offspring.

Main engine

Cockpit

7680 The *Twilight*™ (2008)

The *Twilight*'s opening cockpit comfortably seated three… as long as one was a baby alien slug, anyway!

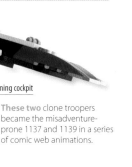

Rotta™   Ahsoka™   Anakin™

Turret hatch

Medium laser

Clone trooper gunner

Heavy laser cannon

7679 Republic Fighter Tank™ (2008)

Opening cockpit

Clone trooper

These two clone troopers became the misadventure-prone 1137 and 1139 in a series of comic web animations.

Some LEGO *Star Wars* fans build their own Clone Wars armies by collecting extras of sets like this one, which included a walker vehicle with three clone troopers, a clone gunner, and officer gear.

8014 Clone Walker Battle Pack (2009)

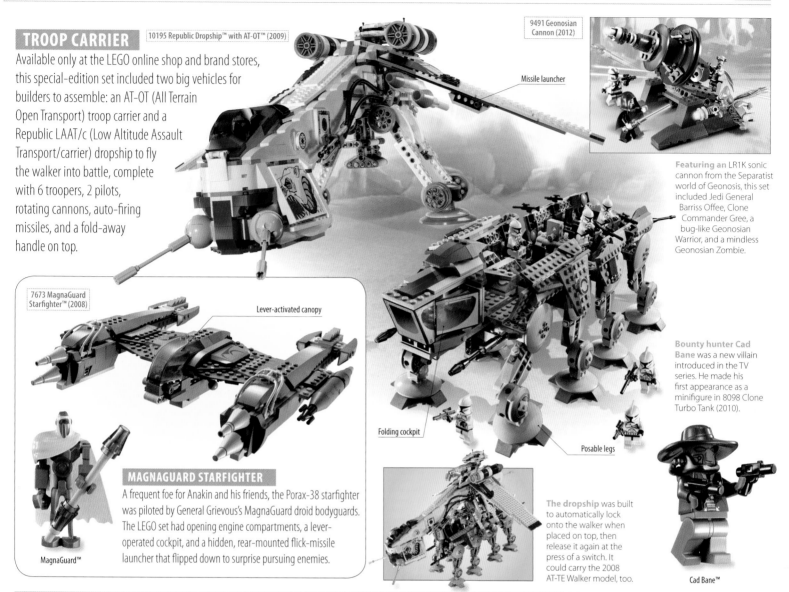

TROOP CARRIER

10195 Republic Dropship™ with AT-OT™ (2009)

Available only at the LEGO online shop and brand stores, this special-edition set included two big vehicles for builders to assemble: an AT-OT (All Terrain Open Transport) troop carrier and a Republic LAAT/c (Low Altitude Assault Transport/carrier) dropship to fly the walker into battle, complete with 6 troopers, 2 pilots, rotating cannons, auto-firing missiles, and a fold-away handle on top.

Missile launcher

9491 Geonosian Cannon (2012)

Featuring an LR1K sonic cannon from the Separatist world of Geonosis, this set included Jedi General Barriss Offee, Clone Commander Gree, a bug-like Geonosian Warrior, and a mindless Geonosian Zombie.

7673 MagnaGuard Starfighter™ (2008)

Lever-activated canopy

MAGNAGUARD STARFIGHTER

A frequent foe for Anakin and his friends, the Porax-38 starfighter was piloted by General Grievous's MagnaGuard droid bodyguards. The LEGO set had opening engine compartments, a lever-operated cockpit, and a hidden, rear-mounted flick-missile launcher that flipped down to surprise pursuing enemies.

MagnaGuard™

Folding cockpit

Bounty hunter Cad Bane was a new villain introduced in the TV series. He made his first appearance as a minifigure in 8098 Clone Turbo Tank (2010).

Posable legs

The dropship was built to automatically lock onto the walker when placed on top, then release it again at the press of a switch. It could carry the 2008 AT-TE Walker model, too.

Cad Bane™

CHARACTER MODELS

JEDI MASTER

This Ultimate Collector Series model let you build the diminutive Jedi Master himself out of more than 1,000 LEGO pieces. Standing 14 in (36 cm) tall from the tips of his toes to the top of his head when completed, the LEGO Yoda had a rotating head and wore his blissl flute around his neck. Mastery of the Force not included!

7194 Yoda™ (2002)

DARING DROID

Plucky astromech R2-D2 joined the ranks of the Ultimate Collector Series with this 2012 model. Built from a whopping 2,127 pieces, the 12 in (31 cm) high droid featured opening body panels with hidden tools, a swiveling dome, and a retractable third leg, plus a data plaque and his own minifigure.

Photoreceptor eye

Holographic projector

Spacecraft linkage control arms

Fold-out circular saw (hidden behind panel)

Adjustable legs

10225 R2-D2™ (2012)

SITH APPRENTICE

Looming more than 17 in (43 cm) tall, this life-sized bust of the deadly Darth Maul took 1,860 LEGO pieces to complete, almost all of them black or red. Detailed down to the tiny silver stud in one ear, the sinister Sith Lord came packaged in a black and white box as a LEGO Store exclusive. This is the set that paved the way for all Ultimate Collector Series *Star Wars* models to come!

10018 Darth Maul™ (2001)

STAR WARS™: THE EXPANDED UNIVERSE

THE OLD REPUBLIC

There's much more to *Star Wars* than just what you see on the screen. Beyond the movies and television series, there's a whole expanded universe full of video games, comic books, novels, and other tales. Blasting out of the *Star Wars: The Old Republic* online role-playing game, the *Fury*-class Interceptor transported the Sith Lord Darth Malgus and his Sith troopers in their war against the original Republic more than 3,000 years before the events of the *Star Wars* films.

Opening cockpit

9497 Republic *Striker*-class Starfighter™ (2012)

Wings sweep forward for cruising

9500 Sith™ *Fury*-class Interceptor™ (2012)

HEROES OF THE PAST

A distant ancestor of the X-wing, the *Striker*-class starfighter flew for the Old Republic during the Great Galactic War. The LEGO® model had wings that repositioned for flight or attack, flick-fire missiles, and a spot for lightsaber storage.

The set included Jedi Master Satele Shan, an armored Republic Trooper, and old-time astromech droid T7-O1.

Like Darth Vader long after him, Darth Malgus was a mighty dark side warrior kept alive by a cybernetic respirator.

Rotating wings

Vader's broken helmet was a black Aquazone mask flipped on its side!

The player's character was Galen Marek, code-named Starkiller. Also included were pilot (and love interest) Juno Eclipse and a battle-damaged Darth Vader.

Blaster cannon

VADER'S SECRET

The *Star Wars: The Force Unleashed* video game series let you play as Darth Vader's secret apprentice, and ultimately choose between the light and dark sides of the Force. The *Rogue Shadow* was the stealthy ship that carried the apprentice on his missions across the galaxy. Its wings and engines rotated together for flight and landing modes.

7672 *Rogue Shadow*™ (2008)

IMPERIAL ARMADA

The *Star Wars* movies are full of TIE (twin ion engine) variations: Darth Vader's TIE Advanced, the twin-hulled TIE Bomber, the speedy TIE Interceptor, and the standard TIE starfighter that makes up most of the Empire's squadrons. The Expanded Universe also had the powerful three-winged TIE Defender that first appeared in the *Star Wars: TIE Fighter* video game.

The TIE Defender included a TIE Pilot with a new helmet to sit in the fighter's spinning cockpit, plus a Stormtrooper to stand guard outside.

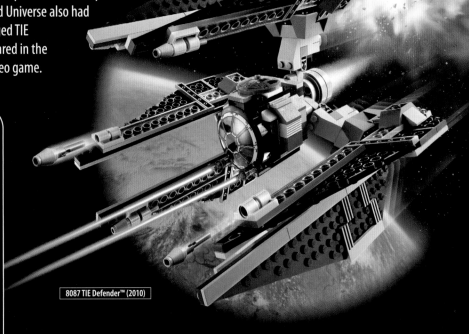

7664 TIE Crawler™ (2007)

8087 TIE Defender™ (2010)

TIE CRAWLER

Another unusual variant was the TIE Crawler, which traded in its wings for giant treads to become a land-roving century tank. It included flip-out blasters, a pair of black-armored Shadow Stormtroopers, and the ability to stand up on its treads to get a higher view of the battlefield.

Maintenance hatch

DROPSHIP

With a squad of three Stormtroopers and a Shadow Stormtrooper, the Imperial Dropship used its detachable troop platform to get the Empire's forces into combat quickly. Rather than a comic or game, it came straight from the minds of the LEGO designers.

Solar wing array

Laser cannon

TIE/D from 10131 TIE™ Collection (2004)

The TIE/D was a unique type of TIE fighter— it didn't have a pilot! Instead, it was controlled by an internal (and removable) droid brain.

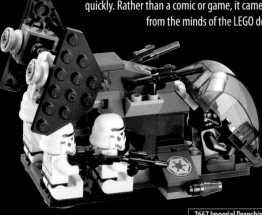

7667 Imperial Dropship™ (2008)

SCOUT SPEEDER

The Rebel Scout Speeder was a battle pack set including four Rebel Troopers and a removable heavy blaster cannon. Like the Dropship, it was an original LEGO design.

7668 Rebel Scout Speeder™ (2008)

MERRY SITH-MAS!

A holiday tradition that started in 2011, LEGO *Star Wars* advent calendars let builders count down to Christmas with 24 buildable micro-vehicles, accessories and minifigures— including 2012's exclusive Santa-garbed Darth Maul and snow-droid R2-D2!

9509 LEGO® *Star Wars*™ Advent Calendar (2012)

LEGO® *Indiana Jones*™

Indiana Jones (2008)

IN 2008, adventure got a new name: LEGO® *Indiana Jones*! With the release of a long-awaited fourth Indy movie, the whip-wielding, globe-trotting, all-action archeologist hero finally arrived in minifigure form ●

Pilot Jock and his pet snake weren't originally planned for this set, but the LEGO designers and Lucasfilm agreed that he was an important addition to

Flexible plastic pipes let the giant boulder roll down after Indy, just like in the movie!

Rolling boulder

Seaplane

Skull carving

René Belloq

Golden idol

Skeleton

7623 Temple Escape (2008)

Booby traps included collapsing walls, shooting spears, slashing swords, tumbling rocks, a pit to swing over, and a spider web.

Satipo

THRILLING ESCAPE

Straight from the opening scene of the first Indiana Jones film, *Raiders of the Lost Ark*™, the Temple Escape set stretched 21 in (53 cm) long and let builders construct and play with all of the deadly traps and daring escapes from the famous adventurer's debut. Actors Harrison Ford (Indiana Jones) and Alfred Molina (Indy's guide Satipo) both got their second minifigure characters with this set. Upside-down baby dinosaur elements were used to decorate the temple entrance.

A piece that you won't find in any other LEGO set: the golden Chachapoyan fertility idol of Peru!

Russian vehicle

Obelisk tower

7627 Temple of the Crystal Skull (2008)

TEMPLE OF AKATOR

From *Indiana Jones and the Kingdom of the Crystal Skull*™, the peril-filled Temple of Akator included a whirling circle of crystal skeletons to enable you to reenact the exciting ending of the movie.

Indiana Jones™ — Mutt Williams — Irina Spalko — Russian soldier — Ugha Warrior™

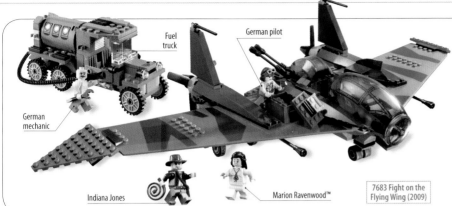

Fuel truck

German pilot

German mechanic

Indiana Jones

Marion Ravenwood™

FLYING WING

As German soldiers prepare to leave Egypt with the Ark of the Covenant, Indiana Jones and Marion try to keep their experimental plane from taking off. The LEGO version had a 23 in (58 cm) wingspan, spinning propellers, an opening cockpit, and a hidden cargo hold.

7683 Fight on the Flying Wing (2009)

JONES & SON

This small set from *Indiana Jones and the Last Crusade*™ was the only one from the third movie in the theme's first year. It included a German checkpoint, two motorcycles, and the first-ever minifigure of Indy's dad, Professor Henry Jones, Sr.

7620 Motorcycle Chase (2008)

Prof. Jones's Grail diary

Falling rocks

Booby-trapped altar

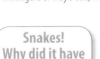

Snakes! Why did it have to be snakes?

FINDING THE ARK

"Why did it have to be snakes?" Trapped underground in the Well of Souls, Indy and Marion have to find a way to escape and recover the Ark. Fortunately, there's a handy statue that they can tip over to break the wall and get away!

Look closely and you may notice a few *Star Wars* characters hidden among the wall carvings (they were there in the movie, too).

7621 The Lost Tomb (2008)

The Ark of the Covenant

MINE CART CHASE

The first year of LEGO *Indiana Jones* had no models from the second movie, *Indiana Jones and the Temple of Doom*™. Fortunately, 2009 more than made up for it with this set, which used all-new LEGO track elements to re-create the film's thrilling roller-coaster mine cart chase.

Pull the lever to drop "rocks" on the Thuggee guards below!

Sankara Stones

Rock bin trap

Sloped track

Lava plume

7199 The Temple of Doom (2009)

Mine cart

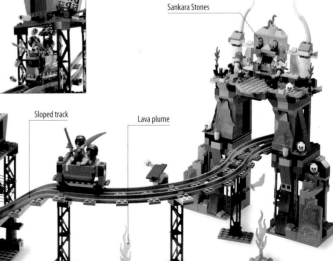

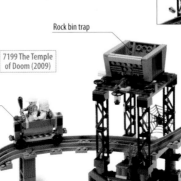

Indiana Jones™

Willie Scott

Short Round

Mola Ram

LEGO® Batman™

IN 2006, the Dark Knight™ arrived in the world of LEGO® construction. LEGO® Batman™ brought all of his famous vehicles and gadgets with him for the battle against crime. His toughest foes also came along for the ride through 13 sets, a video game, and even a computer-animated TV mini-movie ●

Batman (2008)

THE BATMOBILE™

Almost as big as life, this super-sleek, super-detailed version of Batman's most classic vehicle took 1,045 elements to build and stretched over 17½ in (45 cm) long and 6 in (15 cm) wide. Its black-on-black-on-black design made it challenging to keep track of pieces while putting it together.

Turning the steering wheel raised the front bat-shield, revealing hidden intakes for an extra burst of speed!

Angled bat-wing fins

Opening cockpit

Bat-shield battering ram

Built with jet technology, the Batmobile's fiery turbines spun as it rolled forward!

Headlights

Gold Bat-symbol hubcaps

Low-riding chassis

7784 The Batmobile™: Ultimate Collectors' Edition (2006)

ARKHAM ASYLUM™

This special-edition set included three of Batman's most fearsome foes, plus high-security prison cells to contain them until the next big breakout. Fortunately, the Dark Knight had help in the form of Nightwing, the grown-up original Robin.

7785 Arkham Asylum™: (2006)

The fright-faced Scarecrow's head was made of a special translucent plastic that really glowed in the dark!

Guard   The Riddler™   Batman™   Nightwing™   Poison Ivy™   Scarecrow™

7886 The Batcycle™: Harley Quinn's Hammer Truck (2006)

THE BATCYCLE™

With a giant-sized crush on The Joker, prank-playing Harley Quinn™ is more a pest than a super villain… but when she went on a crime spree in her big-wheeled hammer-slammer truck, it was still up to Batman and his speedy cycle to bring the mischievous jester to justice.

Batcomputer™
Net/rocket launcher
Bat-Signal™

Costume transformation chamber

Bruce Wayne   Robin   Alfred

Mr. Freeze™   The Penguin™   Henchman

Mr. Freeze came with an ice block to capture enemies, while The Penguin included special legs to make him shorter than other minifigures... and a trio of penguin sidekicks to help him commit his crimes!

Bat-blade ice vehicle

The Penguin's mini-sub   Hench-penguins

7783 The Batcave™: The Penguin™ and Mr. Freeze's Invasion (2006)

THE BATCAVE™

Built from 1,075 pieces, Batman's secret underground lair contained everything a caped crime-fighter needed to battle evil, from a detective lab filled with captured clues to training weights, a costume quick-change chamber, and a rotating vehicle repair bay. This was also the only set to include minifigures of Bruce Wayne (Batman's billionaire secret identity) and his faithful butler Alfred.

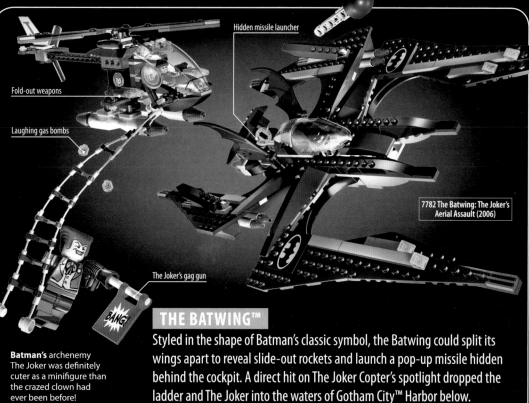

Hidden missile launcher

Fold-out weapons

Laughing gas bombs

The Joker's gag gun

7782 The Batwing: The Joker's Aerial Assault (2006)

Batman's archenemy The Joker was definitely cuter as a minifigure than the crazed clown had ever been before!

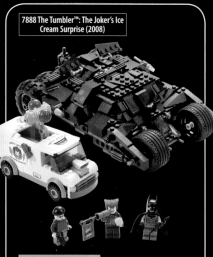

7888 The Tumbler™: The Joker's Ice Cream Surprise (2008)

THE TUMBLER™

The only movie-based model in the line, the armored Tumbler looked like it drove right off the screen of *Batman Begins* and *The Dark Knight*. Included was The Joker's Ice Cream Van, which launched a surprise missile out of the back doors when you pushed the cone on the roof.

THE BATWING™

Styled in the shape of Batman's classic symbol, the Batwing could split its wings apart to reveal slide-out rockets and launch a pop-up missile hidden behind the cockpit. A direct hit on The Joker Copter's spotlight dropped the ladder and The Joker into the waters of Gotham City™ Harbor below.

Batman has worn a few different costumes over the years. The LEGO minifigures followed suit with multiple comic and movie-styled versions.

Batman's special crime-fighting equipment included Batarangs and Bat-cuffs for catching the bad guys.

LEGO®DC Universe™ Super Heroes

LEGO® BATMAN™ returned in 2012, but he was not alone. The LEGO DC Universe Super Heroes theme gave the LEGO designers license to create sets featuring superpowered heroes and villains from all across the DC Universe, starting with some of the biggest names around. Most of the boxes included pack-in comics that provided a story for the models inside ●

4528 Green Lantern (2012)

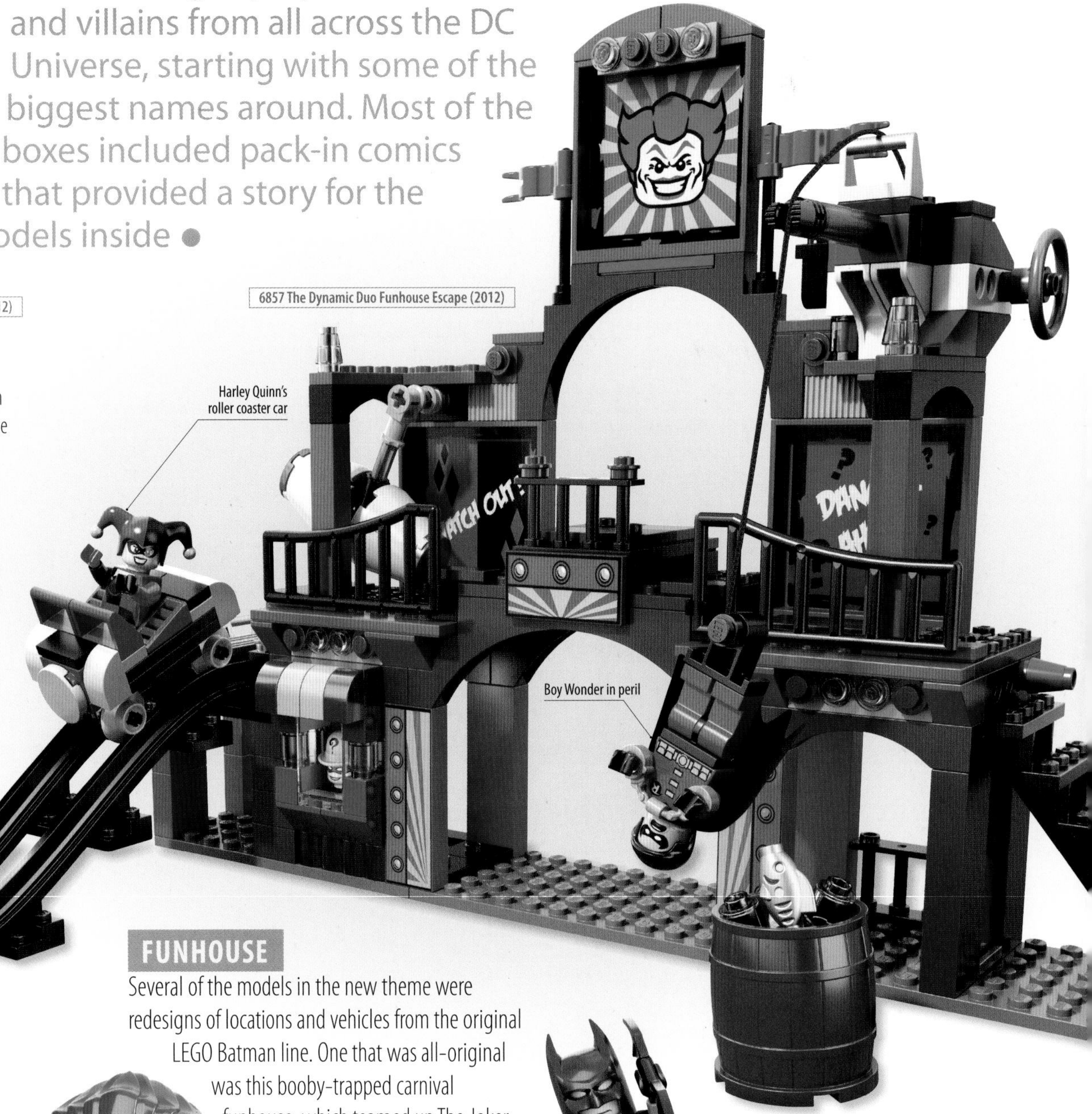

6857 The Dynamic Duo Funhouse Escape (2012)

BUILDABLE CHARACTERS

Drawing on the action figure construction style pioneered for the BIONICLE® universe and LEGO® Hero Factory, these large characters were built out of armor plates snapped onto a posable ball-jointed skeleton. Online instructions let you upgrade Green Lantern, Batman, and The Joker with pieces from each other's kits.

Harley Quinn's roller coaster car

Boy Wonder in peril

FUNHOUSE

Several of the models in the new theme were redesigns of locations and vehicles from the original LEGO Batman line. One that was all-original was this booby-trapped carnival funhouse, which teamed up The Joker, The Riddler, and Harley Quinn in an attempt to defeat the Dynamic Duo once and for all.

The Riddler's new (but classic) costume included a bowler hat and a crowbar for his question-mark cane.

The Joker had a new look, too—along with a double-sided face with a toothy grin on the other side.

Rubber tires

Batman had to reach Robin on his Batcycle before his sidekick was dunked in a barrel full of Joker toxin.

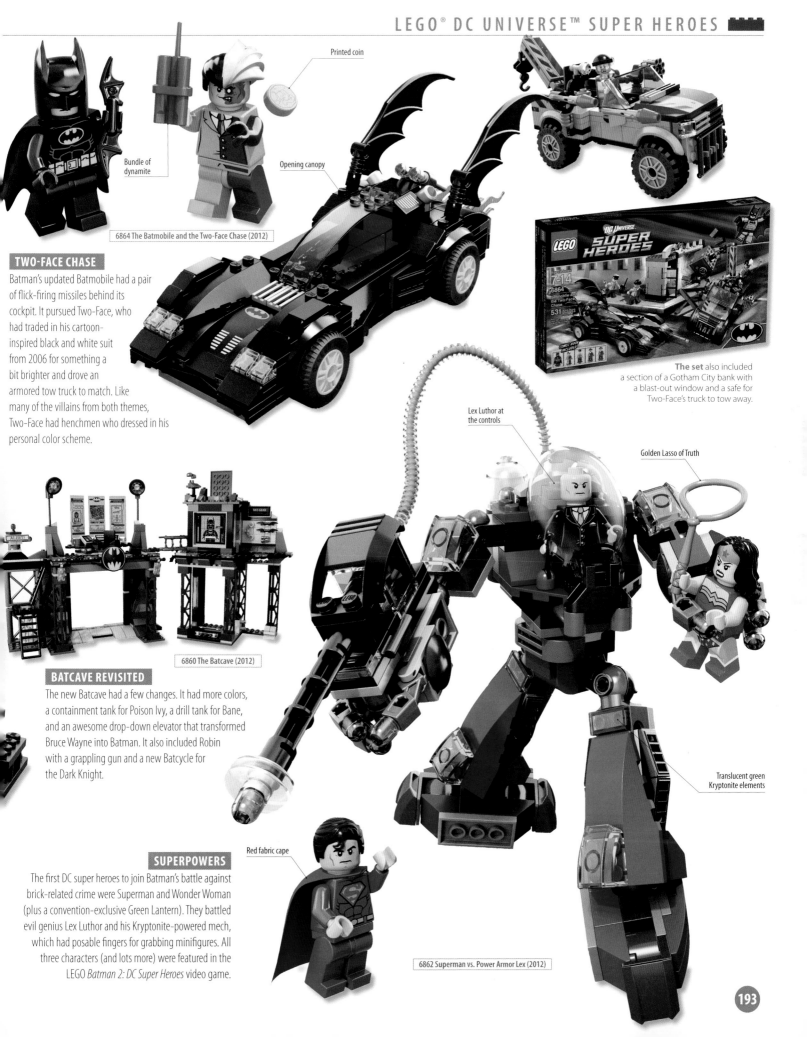

Printed coin

Bundle of
dynamite

6864 The Batmobile and the Two-Face Chase (2012)

Opening canopy

TWO-FACE CHASE

Batman's updated Batmobile had a pair
of flick-firing missiles behind its
cockpit. It pursued Two-Face, who
had traded in his cartoon-
inspired black and white suit
from 2006 for something a
bit brighter and drove an
armored tow truck to match. Like
many of the villains from both themes,
Two-Face had henchmen who dressed in his
personal color scheme.

The set also included
a section of a Gotham City bank with
a blast-out window and a safe for
Two-Face's truck to tow away.

Lex Luthor at
the controls

Golden Lasso of Truth

6860 The Batcave (2012)

BATCAVE REVISITED

The new Batcave had a few changes. It had more colors,
a containment tank for Poison Ivy, a drill tank for Bane,
and an awesome drop-down elevator that transformed
Bruce Wayne into Batman. It also included Robin
with a grappling gun and a new Batcycle for
the Dark Knight.

Translucent green
Kryptonite elements

Red fabric cape

SUPERPOWERS

The first DC super heroes to join Batman's battle against
brick-related crime were Superman and Wonder Woman
(plus a convention-exclusive Green Lantern). They battled
evil genius Lex Luthor and his Kryptonite-powered mech,
which had posable fingers for grabbing minifigures. All
three characters (and lots more) were featured in the
LEGO *Batman 2: DC Super Heroes* video game.

6862 Superman vs. Power Armor Lex (2012)

LEGO® Marvel Super Heroes

2012 WAS CERTAINLY a super-powered year, featuring not just one giant comic-book license for the LEGO Group, but two. The LEGO® Marvel Universe Super Heroes theme opened up the action-packed worlds of Marvel comics and movies to LEGO building, starting with sets based on *The Avengers* film, the *Ultimate Spider-Man* TV series, and the comic book adventures of the uncanny X-Men ●

6869 Quinjet Aerial Battle (2012)

Thor

Black Widow

Loki's scepter

Iron Man

Mini-jet drone

Detachable repulsor ray elements

Alien chariot

4529 Iron Man™ (2012) and 4597 Captain America™ (2012)

BUILDABLE CHARACTERS

The Marvel Super Heroes buildable characters line kicked off with three mighty sets: the invincible Iron Man, the star-studded Captain America, and the incredible Hulk. Instructions for super-model combinations could be downloaded from the LEGO website.

The Hulk figure could move at the shoulders and wrists.

AVENGERS ASSEMBLE!

Most of the first-year Marvel sets were inspired by the blockbuster *The Avengers* movie. The heroes' iconic vehicle was the Quinjet, a supersonic transport with adjustable wing-tips, firing flick-missiles, and a prison pod for arch-enemy Loki or his alien foot soldier. It was the only 2012 set to include superspy team member Black Widow.

6868 Hulk's Helicarrier Breakout (2012)

HULK SMASH

This interior section of S.H.I.E.L.D.'s flying helicarrier base featured an exploding containment cell for the captured Loki to escape from, launching fuel canisters, and a small jet piloted by Avengers archer Hawkeye. The star of the show, though, was the giant-sized Hulk figure!

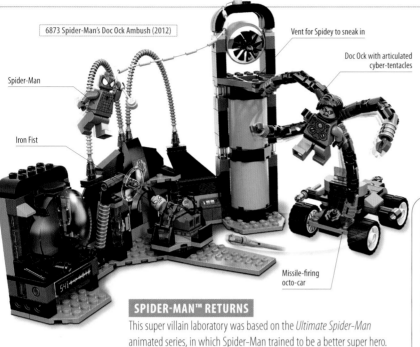

6873 Spider-Man's Doc Ock Ambush (2012)

Spider-Man

Iron Fist

Vent for Spidey to sneak in

Doc Ock with articulated cyber-tentacles

Missile-firing octo-car

SPIDER-MAN™ RETURNS

This super villain laboratory was based on the *Ultimate Spider-Man* animated series, in which Spider-Man trained to be a better super hero. It came with new versions of Spider-Man and Doctor Octopus, and the first-ever minifigure of Spidey's fellow rookie, Iron Fist.

CAPTAIN AMERICA™

Un-frozen World War II hero Captain America raced into action on his patriotic motorcycle. The small set also included two aliens and their invasion equipment. Although there had been many LEGO shields before, Cap's decorated shield was a brand-new piece.

6865 Captain America's Avenging Cycle (2012)

X-MEN

Marvel's most famous band of mutants was represented by lone member Wolverine in this set, which pitted the quick-healing, metal-clawed hero against the master of magnetism Magneto and Deadpool, a mentally-unhinged mercenary flying his own helicopter into battle.

6866 Wolverine's Chopper Showdown (2012)

As part of the new LEGO Group policy for licensed characters, the *Spider-Man 2* minifigures had realistic skin colors instead of the classic universal yellow.

 Mary Jane

Peter Parker

 Spider-Man™

Aunt May

  Doc Ock™

SPIDER-MAN™

The first LEGO® Spider-Man™ movie theme in 2002 was part of LEGO® Studios, with models that were designed both to build scenes from the film and to act out movie-making action stunts. One announced set, 1375 Wrestling Scene, was mysteriously never released.

1374 Green Goblin™ (2002)

Spider-Copter from 4858 Doc Ock's Crime Spree (2004)

Several *Spider-Man 2* sets were made as part of the LEGO 4 plus series for younger builders, with larger-scale "mid-figures" and construction based on bigger and fewer elements.

SPIDER-MAN™ 2

Although the LEGO Studios theme had come to an end by the time the sequel was in theaters, models based on *Spider-Man 2* were produced as their own stand-alone sets.

Not all of the *Spider-Man 2* sets came directly from scenes in the movie. This one, in which Spider-Man foils a heist by cycle-riding robbers, could happen on any day in the life of the friendly neighborhood web-slinger.

Spidey's web-line— a re-colored LEGO vine!

VARICK ST.

DIAMONDS

Cycle-jumping ramp

4853 Spider-Man's Street Chase (2004)

LEGO® Harry Potter™

THE LEGO® HARRY POTTER™ theme began in 2001 with the theatrical release of *Harry Potter and the Sorcerer's Stone* and featured sets based on the entire *Harry Potter* film series. Starring the movies' characters, the models conjured an enchanted world of moving staircases, hidden rooms, and magical creatures ●

HOGWARTS™ EXPRESS

The second LEGO® model of the magic locomotive that carried Harry and his friends to school at Hogwarts was produced for the third movie, *Harry Potter and the Prisoner of Azkaban*. It was almost identical to 2001's 4708 Hogwarts Express, but had slightly fewer pieces, a smaller Hogsmeade™ train station, and minifigures with the new flesh-toned hands and faces required for licensed LEGO characters.

A motorized version with a larger station and tracks was available the same year.

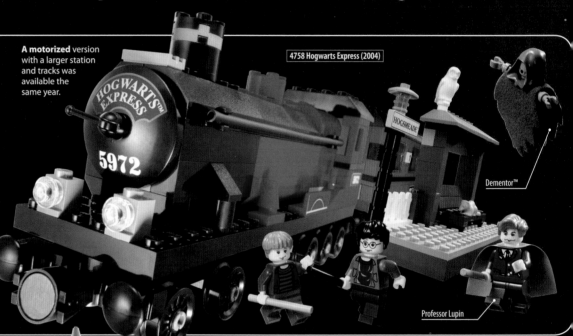

4758 Hogwarts Express (2004)

Dementor™

Professor Lupin

The winged Thestral made use of a skeleton horse designed earlier by the company but never before used in sets.

Thestral

5378 Hogwarts™ Castle (2007)

HOGWARTS™ CASTLE

The buildable star of the LEGO Harry Potter theme was unquestionably Hogwarts Castle, with over a dozen different castle and classroom sets produced over the course of the series. The 2007 version was the only LEGO model released for the fifth film, *Harry Potter and the Order of the Phoenix*.

Greenhouse

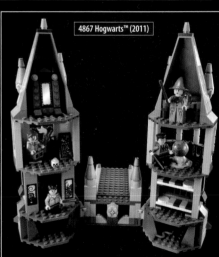

4867 Hogwarts™ (2011)

The latest brick incarnation of the famous school of wizardry included two castle towers and an exploding bridge in between.

The Mandrakes in the castle's greenhouse included their own unique minifigure heads.

TRIWIZARD TOURNAMENT™

When Harry took part in the Triwizard Tournament in 2005's *Harry Potter and the Goblet of Fire*, he was given the dangerous task of stealing a golden egg from a fire-breathing dragon. The LEGO version of the scene gave Harry a magnet to scoop up the egg in a flash, a catapult to "magically" launch his flying broom to him, and a spectator stand that collapsed when the enraged Hungarian Horntail pulled on its chain.

Hungarian Horntail's body parts were new, it included two classic LEGO elements: a pair of tan bananas for the claws on its wings!

Toppling spectator stand

4767 Harry and the Hungarian Horntail (2005)

Magnetic golden egg

4755 Knight Bus (2004)

KNIGHT BUS™

Thinking he was being stalked by the mysterious Grim, Harry caught an emergency ride to Hogwarts aboard the Knight Bus. The set's rare purple pieces were prized among collectors. A new version of the bus was released in 2011.

A **roof** of LEGO plates replaced the original 2001 hut's printed plastic sheet and rubber band.

4754 Hagrid's Hut (2004)

HAGRID'S HUT

The friendly half-giant Hagrid lived in the groundskeeper's hut near Hogwarts Castle. Three LEGO versions of his home were made, including this second model with a pumpkin patch outside and hinges so it could open up into a cozy interior playset.

10217 Diagon Alley (2011)

DIAGON ALLEY™

The biggest set in the theme, the special-edition Diagon Alley featured highly detailed versions of Ollivanders Wand Shop, Borgin and Burkes, and Gringotts Wizarding Bank. It was built from 2,025 pieces and came with 11 minifigures.

YOU-KNOW-WHO

When Lord Voldemort™ made his long-awaited return to the land of the living in *Harry Potter and the Goblet of Fire*, the 548-piece LEGO Graveyard Duel model captured the fateful scene of the evil wizard's resurrection and confrontation with Harry. The set had opening graves, secret compartments, snakes, skeletons, tombstones, a spooky bat-filled tree, a crypt with an underground tomb, caretaker's tools, and even a garbage can.

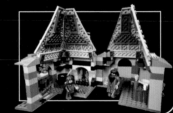

Tom Riddle's tomb

Opening grave

Pop-up skeleton

The resurrected, snake-eyed Lord Voldemort had a glow-in-the-dark head.

Lucius Malfoy with reversible Death Eater face

4766 Graveyard Duel (2005)

Nickelodeon™ Sets

IN THE US AND ABROAD, Nickelodeon™ is one of the most popular children's television networks. With its imaginative shows and world-famous original characters, "Nick" proved the perfect partner for the LEGO Group. Their team-up has led to a series of themes for fun-loving builders ●

SpongeBob (2006)

The LEGO® SpongeBob™ minifigure's pants were even squarer than usual!

SPONGEBOB SQUAREPANTS™

When the evil Plankton took over SpongeBob's brain, wacky adventures were in store for Bikini Bottom's silliest citizen. The only LEGO® SpongeBob set not in minifigure scale, this buildable version stood over 11.5 in (29 cm) tall. He could spin his eyes, launch jellyfish bubbles from his mouth, and change expression from happy to sad.

Antenna eyelashes

Spinning eyes

Changeable mouth

Square pants

Posable arms

3826 Build-a-Bob (2006)

Gears, controls, and a picture on the wall… it looks like Plankton's planning on staying!

HOWDY, NEIGHBORS!

3834 Good Neighbors at Bikini Bottom (2009)

Like his television namesake, LEGO SpongeBob lives in a big orange pineapple under the sea. The second of two LEGO models of SpongeBob's house, this one includes a reef blower for SpongeBob, a boat with a marshmallow launcher for Patrick, and yet another headache for poor old Squidward—but at least his head is a brand-new piece this time!

LEGO SpongeBob characters come in all shapes and sizes. Gary is built out of tiny LEGO pieces, including an upside-down pair of green cherries for his eyes.

Gary the snail   SpongeBob   Patrick   Squidward

KRUSTY BUT NEVER RUSTY

SpongeBob works here at the Krusty Krab, where his boss Mr. Krabs fiercely guards the secret formula for Krabby Patties from his rival Plankton. The LEGO version had a safe for the formula, a trash bin out back, and a patty-flipping grill to toss burgers at SpongeBob's long-suffering neighbor and fellow employee, Squidward.

Krabby Patty

Plankton

THE KRUSTY KRAB

ENTER

Mr. Krabs

3825 The Krusty Krab (2006)

THE MANY FACES OF SPONGEBOB

The animated SpongeBob is one expressive fellow, so the minifigures followed suit with a whole range of zany faces. Can you spot the robot imposter?

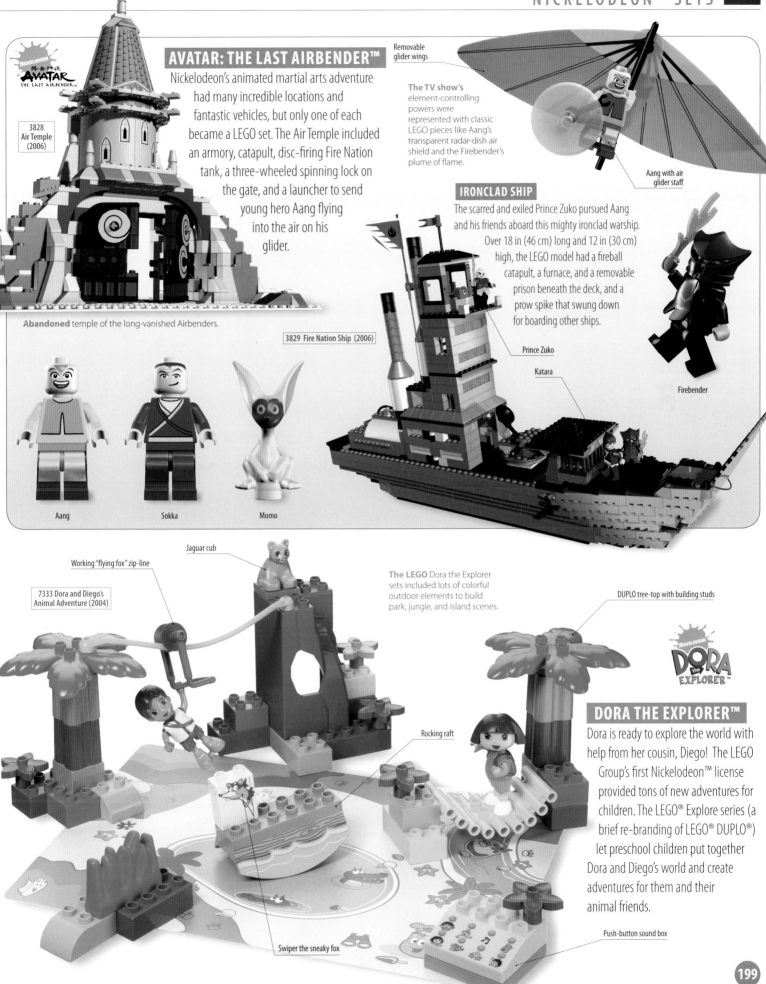

AVATAR: THE LAST AIRBENDER™

Nickelodeon's animated martial arts adventure had many incredible locations and fantastic vehicles, but only one of each became a LEGO set. The Air Temple included an armory, catapult, disc-firing Fire Nation tank, a three-wheeled spinning lock on the gate, and a launcher to send young hero Aang flying into the air on his glider.

3828 Air Temple (2006)

Abandoned temple of the long-vanished Airbenders.

Removable glider wings

The TV show's element-controlling powers were represented with classic LEGO pieces like Aang's transparent radar-dish air shield and the Firebender's plume of flame.

Aang with air glider staff

IRONCLAD SHIP

The scarred and exiled Prince Zuko pursued Aang and his friends aboard this mighty ironclad warship. Over 18 in (46 cm) long and 12 in (30 cm) high, the LEGO model had a fireball catapult, a furnace, and a removable prison beneath the deck, and a prow spike that swung down for boarding other ships.

3829 Fire Nation Ship (2006)

Prince Zuko

Katara

Firebender

Aang

Sokka

Momo

Jaguar cub

Working "flying fox" zip-line

7333 Dora and Diego's Animal Adventure (2004)

The LEGO Dora the Explorer sets included lots of colorful outdoor elements to build park, jungle, and island scenes.

DUPLO tree-top with building studs

Rocking raft

Swiper the sneaky fox

DORA THE EXPLORER™

Dora is ready to explore the world with help from her cousin, Diego! The LEGO Group's first Nickelodeon™ license provided tons of new adventures for children. The LEGO® Explore series (a brief re-branding of LEGO® DUPLO®) let preschool children put together Dora and Diego's world and create adventures for them and their animal friends.

Push-button sound box

199

The LEGO Group & Disney

LEGO Mickey Mouse (2000)

IN 1999, the LEGO Group joined with the Walt Disney Company to produce construction toys for younger builders based on some of Disney's classic characters. But those sets featuring Mickey Mouse™ and Winnie the Pooh™ were not the first team-up between the two companies, nor would they be the last: in 2010, the partnership resumed with new sets based on some of Disney's biggest action and adventure properties ●

THE FIRST EVER TOYS

The LEGO Group's very first licensed Disney products were a set of inflatable bathing rings released in 1956, featuring characters like Mickey Mouse and Lady from Lady and the Tramp. That same year, a painted wooden pull-toy of Mickey's faithful pooch Pluto was manufactured by the company's wooden toy department, along with a rifle, musket, and cabin based on Disney's new Davy Crockett film.

Pull-string attached to collar

427 Pluto pull-toy (1956)

Classic LEGO® logo

Pluto's legs moved when the wheels rolled.

The fully painted Mickey and Minnie figures could sit, stand, and move their heads and arms.

MICKEY & FRIENDS

Five LEGO® sets were produced in 2000 for Disney's Mickey Mouse theme, making use of large pieces so that young builders could put them together quickly and easily. Each included a Mickey figure and one or more classic cartoon-styled vehicles. In this set, decorative stickers transformed bricks into letters, animal friends, and even a slice of birthday

4178 Mickey's Fishing Adventure (2000)

4165 Minnie's Birthday Party (2000)

Extra pieces

Mickey's jalopy

FISHY TALE

This bucket set included Mickey, Minnie, a shark, and about 100 elements for plenty of water-themed adventures. One of the suggested models was a paddleboat that might have been inspired by the 1928 Disney cartoon *Steamboat Willie*, Mickey Mouse's very first with sound.

2594 Disney's Baby Mickey & Minnie (2000)

Three sets were produced under the LEGO® Baby brand for infants aged six to 24 months. They featured one-piece baby versions of Mickey and Minnie and big, simple, stackable bricks.

2979 Winnie the Pooh Build and Play (2001)

This unique set included a Pooh figure and a circular pop-up playset with dividers that recreated four different parts of the Hundred Acre Wood.

WINNIE THE POOH™

With 15 sets released between 1999 and 2001, the LEGO® DUPLO® Winnie the Pooh™ series was the longest-lasting line produced under the original Disney license. The sets for toddlers aged two and up (plus one for 18-month-olds) included posable Winnie the Pooh figures and stationary versions of his friends Piglet, Eeyore, and Tigger. In 2011, three new DUPLO sets were released, featuring a redesigned Pooh along with his house, a picnic, and a fishing expedition for the newly-articulated Tigger and Piglet.

Treetop elements

As everyone knows, Winnie the Pooh lives under the name of Mr. Sanders—literally! This 2011 set had an opening door, a slide, plenty of honey, and even a clear yellow DUPLO brick with a bee printed on it.

Bee brick

Piglet can sit and move his arms

DUPLO brick table

Front door

5947 Winnie the Pooh's House (2011)

Eeyore with DUPLO stud for building or riding

Pot of honey

6151 Sleeping Beauty's Room (2012)

DISNEY PRINCESS

2012 saw the release of LEGO DUPLO sets based on the Disney Princesses. Snow White and Cinderella joined Sleeping Beauty, whose fairy-tale room came with a bed so she could get plenty of rest.

TOY STORY™ & CARS™

Little kids could get in on the big-screen adventure with these DUPLO sets based on the worlds of the *Toy Story* and *Cars* movies. They included many of the same characters and locations as the models for bigger builders, but with all the fun and chunky charm of LEGO DUPLO bricks and building.

Sheriff's office

5657 Jessie's Round-Up (2010)

5817 Agent Mater (2011)

Heroic horse Bullseye had a big stud on his back to let DUPLO figures ride him around.

Agent Mater came apart for extra building fun. His child-safe firing cannon could knock over the included target bricks.

Disney Action

FROM THE DESERTS of ancient Persia to the stormy seas of the Caribbean, these LEGO® themes captured some of the most exciting moments of movie action ever shown on screen. They also provided fans with new parts, and new minifigures of many of their favorite movie stars and monsters ●

YO HO, YO HO!

Disney, action, and pirates—could there be a more classic combination for a new LEGO theme? First teased with a Jack Sparrow minifigure hidden in a *Prince of Persia* display at San Diego Comic-Con 2010, the LEGO *Pirates of the Caribbean*™ line of ships and playsets sailed into port the next year in time for the fourth film in the blockbuster series. Also released were a video game and a series of animations detailing Captain Jack's tall tales.

FAMOUS FIEND

The *Queen Anne's Revenge*™ was the infamous real-world pirate Blackbeard's ship. Of course, the real Blackbeard probably couldn't turn pirates into zombies, or control his ship's rigging with a magic sword.

Blackbeard's pirate flag

Main mast

Fearsome crimson sails

Firing cannon

Several different **costume** variations for Captain Jack were made. This one had cannibal king paint on both faces of his reversible head.

4182 The Cannibal Escape (2011)

A PIRATE'S LIFE

Full of action features like runaway mill wheels, launching nets, rotating cave walls, and collapsing lighthouse towers, the LEGO *Pirates of the Caribbean* theme packed as much of the thrills and fun of the celebrated movies as possible into its models. Printed and painted elements abounded, from Captain Jack Sparrow's elaborate hat and hair pieces to his ever-present compass.

A colorful collection of characters included pirates, zombie pirates, and mutated sea-life pirates.

Hadras from 4183 The Mill (2011)

Removable captain's cabin

4195 *Queen Anne's Revenge*™ (2011)

The ship featured three brick-firing cannons, a working anchor, and seven minifigures including Blackbeard™ and his daughter Angelica (who has a bone to pick with Jack), plus a tiny Jack Sparrow voodoo doll!

Skeleton ship details

PAINT IT BLACK

The latest set created for the theme was the long-awaited *Black Pearl*, Captain Jack's beloved (and frequently misplaced) pirate ship. Released in November 2011, it was built from 804 pieces.

4184 *The Black Pearl* (2011)

The set included Jack Sparrow, Will Turner, Joshamee Gibbs, and exclusive figures of Davy Jones, Bootstrap Bill, and the shark-headed Maccus, plus the black figurehead on its prow.

THE ROGUE RETURNS

Accompanying sets based on the original movie trilogy were models for the new *Pirates of the Caribbean: On Stranger Tides*. One depicted Captain Jack's attempt to escape from King George's soldiers in a frantic chase through the streets of London.

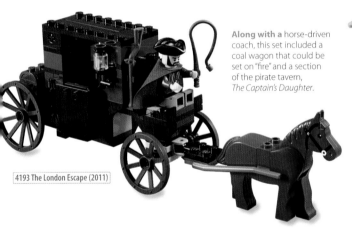

4193 The London Escape (2011)

Along with a horse-driven coach, this set included a coal wagon that could be set on "fire" and a section of the pirate tavern, *The Captain's Daughter*.

FINAL BATTLE

The Fountain of Youth model let you recreate the climactic duel between Blackbeard and Jack's sometimes-foe, sometimes-ally Captain Barbossa, who had gained a new peg-leg since his last minifigure appearance.

An interesting piece was the reverse-flowing waterfall that hid the fountain's sanctuary, printed on a curtain-like plastic sheet.

4192 Fountain of Youth (2011)

PRINCE OF PERSIA™

The first action theme produced under the partnership was for the 2010 film *Prince of Persia: The Sands of Time*. Based on the best-selling series of video games, the movie chronicled the quest of Prince Dastan to clear his name and save his empire from a plot to use the fabled Sands of Time to rewrite

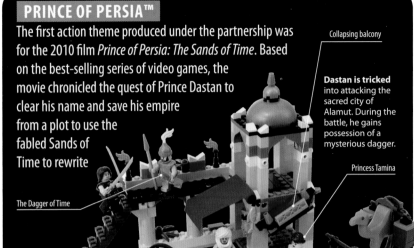

Collapsing balcony

Dastan is tricked into attacking the sacred city of Alamut. During the battle, he gains possession of a mysterious dagger.

Princess Tamina

The Dagger of Time

7571 The Fight for the Dagger (2010)

WILD RACE

Sets were based on scenes from throughout the movie. In this one, Dastan takes part in a chaotic, high-speed ostrich race. The model also included the wily Sheik Amar, a spectator stand, and a weapons rack.

7570 The Ostrich Race (2010)

7572 Quest Against Time (2010)

NO TIME TO LOSE

In the catacombs beneath Alamut, Dastan has to run a gauntlet of traps to reach the Sandglass of Time before his treacherous uncle Nizam.

ALAMUT CITY

The largest set in the theme depicted the walled city and palace of Alamut, where several of the movie's major battle scenes took place. The gate was defended by catapults and barrels of boiling oil. Studs on the sides of the walls helped builders recreate Dastan's unique parkour-based fighting style by letting him run and jump on vertical surfaces.

7573 Battle of Alamut (2010)

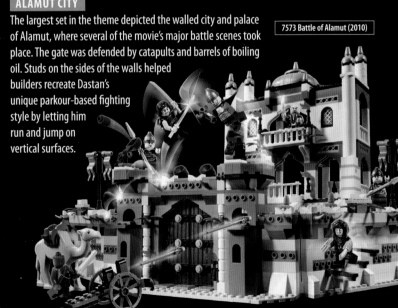

Buzz Lightyear minifigure
fits inside cockpit

7593 Buzz's Star Command
Spaceship (2010)

Disney Adventure

THE WALT DISNEY COMPANY is traditionally known for its all-ages animated movies and family adventures, and its modern partnership with computer animation studio Pixar has produced more than a dozen beloved feature films. At the top of the list are the *Toy Story*™ and *Cars*™ movies, some of the most popular and successful animated pictures of all time ●

OFF-SCREEN ADVENTURES

Not all of the *Toy Story* sets depicted events directly from the movies. Buzz's spaceship was based on the outer-space adventures of the "real" Buzz Lightyear, Space Ranger, while Woody's western town represented the world of the fictional old-time *Woody's Roundup* TV series, complete with co-stars Jessie, Bullseye, and Stinky Pete the Prospector.

TOY STORY™

In the world of the *Toy Story* movies, your playthings are secretly alive, and have their own adventures whenever you're out of the room. Woody, Buzz, and many of their friends (and foes) starred in LEGO® sets based on the first two films at the beginning of 2010.

Gold mine

SHE RIFF

GOLD MINE JAIL

JAIL

WANTED

7594 Woody's
Roundup! (2010)

Stinky Pete

Jessie and Woody
had extra-long
arms and legs

PIZZA PLANET

The Pizza Planet restaurant chain's delivery truck cameos in almost every Pixar movie. The exclusive pizza-launching LEGO version recreated the scene from *Toy Story 2* when the toy heroes try to drive the human-scaled vehicle, with comic results.

7598 Pizza Planet
Truck Rescue (2010)

7591 Construct-a-
Zurg (2010)

BUILDABLE FIGURES

For kids who wanted something bigger to play with, there were constructable action figures of Buzz Lightyear and his arch-nemesis, the Evil Emperor Zurg. Both included a green alien sidekick.

7595 Army
Men on Patrol
(2010)

7592
Construct-a-
Buzz (2010)

ARMY OF FUN

The minifigure Army Men were much more posable than the classic toys they were based on. Containing a medic, a minesweeper, two riflemen, and a Jeep, this set was small and inexpensive enough that you could buy extras and build your own toy army.

Buzz had moving wings, a retractable visor, and a flick-fire missile to simulate his laser.

At 9 in (23 cm) tall, the special-edition Zurg had a rotating waist and a sphere-shooting cannon.

BAD BEAR

Toy Story 3 sets were released in the summer of 2010. To avoid spoiling secret villain Lotso's true role, his minifigure's official description made him sound like a new friend for Buzz and Woody.

7789 Lotso's Dump
Truck (2010)

TRAIN CHASE

Recreating the thrilling opening sequence of *Toy Story 3*, this 584-piece set let you build a toy steam locomotive with three magnetically-linked cars. It included an exclusive version of piggy bank pal Hamm play-acting as the evil Dr. Porkchop. His hat and cork were both removable.

One-piece head and hat

7597 Western Train Chase (2010)

Evil Dr. Porkchop

Rex the friendly dinosaur

Slammer-powered car launcher

Bulleye's legs are posable

Buzz Lightyear to the rescue!

Combination gas station/carwash

CARS™

First launched as a line of LEGO® DUPLO® sets in 2010, the *Cars* movies made their System-scale debut in 2011. Models were based on characters and locations from both films, including Radiator Springs's V8 Café, which came with a whopping six characters from the original movie: Lightning McQueen, Mater, Sarge, Fillmore, Sally, and café owner Flo.

SPY GAMES

In *Cars™ 2*, tow truck Mater is mistakenly recruited as a spy to help take down a globe-spanning plot. The LEGO theme echoed the movie's international flavor with models set in Japan and England, where the Big Bentley clock tower had a flying-car launcher.

8639 Big Bentley Bust Out (2011)

8487 Flo's V8 Café (2011)

COOL CARS

To reflect the hi-tech gear and gadgets used by the characters in the sequel, sets included a variety of equipment built into their car models, from Agent Mater's jet thrusters to superspy Finn McMissile's propeller-powered submarine mode. Other sets let you assemble McMissile in standard, hydrofoil, flight, weaponized, and police car disguise configurations.

8426 Escape at Sea (2011)

LEGO
7-12
8639

BIG WHEELS

Several detailed, larger-scale character sets were released, too. The 242-piece Ultimate Build Lightning McQueen gave the starring race car gold wheel hubs and his World Grand Prix decorations. Mater and rival F-1 racer Francesco were also made in Ultimate Build scale. Lightning and Francesco included pit crew forklift helpers, while Mater had removable spy gear.

8484 Ultimate Build Lightning McQueen (2011)

LEGO® *The Lord of the Rings*™

FANS ALL OVER the world had demanded it for years, and in 2012 they finally got their wish with the first LEGO® sets based on the epic *The Lord of the Rings* movie trilogy. From Gandalf's arrival in the Shire to the battle of *Helm's Deep*, you could collect the entire Fellowship of the Ring and take them on adventures through *Middle-earth*. And that was only the beginning, because LEGO® *The Hobbit: An Unexpected Journey* sets were just behind ●

Rohan™ soldier

Éomer™

9472 Attack on Weathertop™ (2012)

WORLD OF MIDDLE-EARTH

The LEGO® *The Lord of the Rings*™ theme featured many new elements, including weapons, armor, and horses that could rear up on their hind legs… not to mention the golden One Ring itself, which could fit around the top of a minifigure's hand. Its brick-built locations were full of bold heroes, savage enemies, and interactive details that really captured the action and atmosphere of the movies.

THE RING AND THE WRAITHS

Entrusted with the legendary One Ring, *Frodo* is menaced by fearsome, faceless *Ringwraiths* among the ruins of *Weathertop*. Only the blazing torch and sword of the ranger *Aragorn* can save him. This set's model of an ancient stone fortress included fellow hobbit Merry and opened on hinges so you could explore its interior.

9471 Uruk-hai™ Army (2012)

Armored hook-launching ballista

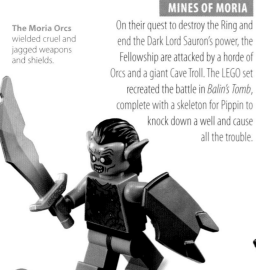

The Moria Orcs wielded cruel and jagged weapons and shields.

MINES OF MORIA

On their quest to destroy the Ring and end the Dark Lord Sauron's power, the Fellowship are attacked by a horde of Orcs and a giant Cave Troll. The LEGO set recreated the battle in *Balin's Tomb*, complete with a skeleton for Pippin to knock down a well and cause all the trouble.

Cave Troll with club

Book of Mazarbul

9473 The Mines of Moria™ (2012)

The Hornburg tower

9474 The Battle of Helm's Deep™ (2012)

Siege ladder hooks onto wall

Besieged by an army of ferocious *Uruk-hai* warriors, the defenders of *Helm's Deep* fight back in *The Two Towers*. An additional set let you add to the model's walls and armies.

Uruk-hai bomb in culvert

Fearless Dwarf Gimli

Haldir the Wood Elf

Berserker Uruk-hai™

Gollum was an entirely new minifigure with a unique crouching body and jointed arms. A levered catapult let you fling him into action.

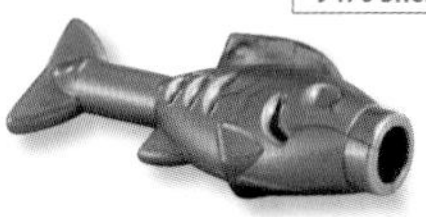

Crank under abdomen extends or retracts web-line

Halberd weapon

Uruk-hai™ helm

9470 Shelob™ Attacks (2012)

9471 Uruk-hai™ Army (2012)

FRIEND OR FOE?
Desperate to get his hands on the Ring, the treacherous *Gollum* leads *Frodo* and his companion *Samwise Gamgee* into a deadly trap in *The Return of the King*. The giant spider *Shelob* had eight posable legs and a web-line that could wrap around poor Frodo, whose minifigure included an alternate face to show him paralyzed by her sting.

ARMY OF EVIL
Created in the Orc Forge (which was released as an exclusive LEGO set), *Uruk-hai* are tougher than normal Orcs and have no fear of daylight. Several varieties of Uruk-hai minifigures were made, including warriors, a berserker, and their general, *Lurtz*.

LEGOLAND®

LEGO® FANS have always constructed their own LEGO worlds, but until the first LEGOLAND® theme park opened in Billund, Denmark, in 1968, they never had one big enough to walk around in! Today, LEGOLAND Parks, Discovery Centers, water parks, and hotels can be found all around the world. Filled with the miniature cities and monuments of MINILAND, thrilling LEGO themed rides, enormous brick-built sculptures, and spectacular, specially built models, they're both a fan and a family's dream come true ●

A 2012 map of LEGOLAND® Billund
guides visitors to all of the theme park's areas and attractions, including MINILAND, Pirate Land, Adventure Land, the Imagination Zone, LEGOREDO® Town, the new Polar Land, and much more.

Park Design

AS THE LEGO® BRICK'S fame grew in the 1960s, so did the number of visitors to the company's Billund headquarters. When Godtfred Kirk Christiansen realized that more than 20,000 people a year were coming to admire the elaborate LEGO sculptures that decorated the factories, he decided to create an outdoor display. Envisioned as a small garden, it became the first ever LEGOLAND® Park ●

THE FIRST PARK

The original LEGOLAND Park opened on June 7, 1968 and quickly became Denmark's most popular tourist attraction outside its capital city, Copenhagen. It originally took up nearly 125,000 sq ft (38,100 sq m), but doubled in size over the next 30 years.

PARKS AROUND THE WORLD

With the success of LEGOLAND® Billund came the idea to create more parks in other countries. LEGOLAND Parks opened in Windsor, UK, in 1996, followed by California, USA, in 1999, Günzburg, Germany, in 2002, Florida, USA, in 2011, and Malaysia in 2012.

Based on a LEGOLAND® Windsor model, these concept sketches depict a moving, water-shooting dinosaur sculpture designed for the main entrance at LEGOLAND® California.

Brick-built dinosaur sculpture

water

The final display closely resembles the concept artwork, except that the dinosaur construction worker has changed from green to red.

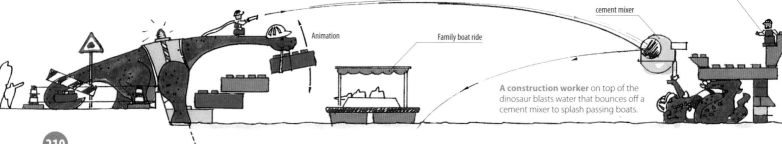

Large-scale "minifigure"

cement mixer

Animation

Family boat ride

A construction worker on top of the dinosaur blasts water that bounces off a cement mixer to splash passing boats.

RIDES AND ATTRACTIONS

The LEGOLAND Parks are filled with constantly changing themed areas, interactive rides, and seasonal events, from LEGOLAND Windsor's transport-themed Traffic section with its Driving School and Fire Academy rides, and the wild rides and coasters of LEGOLAND® California's Dino Island and Castle Hill, to LEGOLAND® Deutschland's Imagination area featuring the Build & Test Center, Kids' Power Tower, and Pedal-A-Car ride.

Each car of the Pedal-A-Car attraction at LEGOLAND Deutschland holds four passengers.

LEGOLAND® Malaysia is the sixth LEGOLAND Park and the first to be built in Asia. Divided into seven themed areas, its 76 acres of adventure are packed full of more than 40 rides, shows, and attractions.

Under construction (left), the elevated ride track circles around LEGOLAND Deutschland's Imagination section, giving riders a spectacular view of the Park.

As they pass over MINILAND, Pedal-A-Car passengers can look down over a scale model of Bavaria's Neuschwanstein Castle built from more than 300,000 LEGO bricks.

LEGOLAND® Florida, the world's largest LEGOLAND Park, incorporates the gardens from the former Cypress Gardens amusement park. A water park was added in 2012.

MAKING MODEL MAGIC

Around every corner of a LEGOLAND Park is an amazing LEGO sculpture. The Parks are home to thousands of models of buildings, people, and animals, built from millions of LEGO bricks. Each LEGOLAND Park has its own team of model designers and builders who take care of the Park's existing sculptures and create all-new ones.

LEGOLAND Deutschland model builders built a scale replica of Munich Airport entirely out of LEGO bricks!

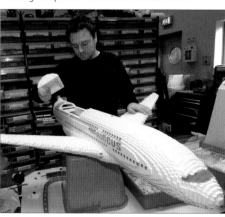

A LEGOLAND model builder assembles a 1:20-scale model of an Airbus A380 passenger airliner in the German Park's workshop.

Finishing touches are added on-site to LEGOLAND Deutschland's MINILAND Munich Airport display. Every morning, the model builders tour the Park to check, repair, and clean all of its models.

MINILAND Areas

The heart of every LEGOLAND® Park is its unique MINILAND display. Constructed out of millions of bricks by the LEGOLAND Master Model Builders and populated by brick-built citizens, these constantly evolving and expanding 1:20-scale dioramas let visitors explore famous landmarks from their home countries and around the world, all in one amazing place ●

BILLUND

At the original MINILAND in LEGOLAND® Billund, 20 million bricks have been used to create scenes of European life, with sections representing Denmark, Sweden, Germany, Norway, Finland, and more. Passengers on the Miniboat ride sail past Thailand's Wat Phra Keo Temple, and Park guests can take in the entire amazing display from the top of a rotating panoramic tower.

WINDSOR

Almost 40 million bricks went into building LEGOLAND® Windsor's MINILAND, which features city scenes from London and across Europe and the US, complete with traffic noises and moving cars, buses, and trains. A newer addition is a space exploration section with a 1:20 scale version of America's Cape Canaveral and the John F. Kennedy Space Center.

Famous London landmarks at MINILAND UK include Canary Wharf, 30 St. Mary's Axe, the Lloyd's Building, City Hall, and the Millennium Bridge.

Copenhagen Nyhavn Harbor's red roofs are perfectly reproduced in LEGO® bricks.

The largest part of MINILAND Billund is the Port of Copenhagen, with moving miniature ships that travel 8,500 nautical miles a year.

MALAYSIA

The centerpiece of the new LEGOLAND® Malaysia is its spectacular MINILAND display, which features scaled replicas of famous Asian towns and landscapes, assembled from over 25 million LEGO bricks with great care and detail.

Motion technology lets the people, animals, cars, ships, trains, and airplanes of LEGOLAND Malaysia's MINILAND move at the touch of a button, together with location-appropriate background sounds.

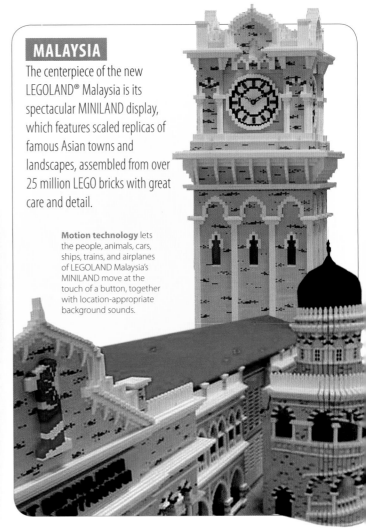

GÜNZBURG

MINILAND at LEGOLAND® Deutschland includes miniature models of Berlin (like the Reichstag), the financial district of Frankfurt, a church and dairy from a Swabian village, Neuschwanstein Castle, and Munich's famous airport and Allianz Arena. The Park's Venice display contains St. Mark's Cathedral and the Doge's Palace, while canals, drawbridges, and turning windmills adorn the Netherlands area. Attendees can interact with the 25-million-brick world by pressing buttons and moving joysticks to bring its intricate scenes to life.

An evening stroll in the Swiss city of Lucerne reveals glowing electric lights inside the miniature buildings and street lamps.

Miniature divers are captured in mid-leap (and mid-cannonball) at a Berlin swimming pool in MINILAND Deutschland. The swimmers and sunbathers may be plastic, but the water is real.

FLORIDA

LEGOLAND® Florida's display, known as MINILAND USA, includes models of Daytona International Speedway; a pirate battle at Pirate Shores; and sections of Florida, California, Las Vegas, Washington DC, and New York City, with such sights as Times Square, the Empire State Building, and the Bronx Zoo.

The Capitol Building and the Statue of Liberty together? Only at MINILAND USA!

CARLSBAD

At LEGOLAND® California, mini-ice skaters enjoy a New York winter in Central Park, and New Orleans comes alive at Halloween with a cemetery filled with spooky skeletons. MINILAND Las Vegas has hotels, a wedding chapel, and a working monorail, and giant miniature crowds gather on the steps of the Capitol Building in Washington DC every four years for the inauguration of the next President of the 23 million bricks of MINILAND.

Watch out for the moving cable cars! A LEGOLAND Master Model Builder works on a street scene in the MINILAND San Francisco display.

500 photos from every angle were taken to get the details of San Francisco's famous Steiner Street houses exactly right.

Realistically decorated gabled roof

Victorian clapboard architecture

LEGO® *Star Wars*™ MINILAND

MINILAND areas usually represent locations from the real world, but that all changed in 2011 when the California, Billund, and Deutschland LEGOLAND® Parks opened the world's first Star Wars™ MINILAND displays! Built out of more than 1.5 million LEGO® bricks, each attraction features seven different scenes from the Star Wars™ movies and The Clone Wars TV series ●

It took the LEGOLAND® Model Builders 143 hours and 19,200 pieces to design and build the MINILAND *Millennium Falcon*™.

TATOOINE™

In the *Star Wars* Episode IV display set on the desert planet of Tatooine, visitors can tour the Mos Eisley spaceport and watch the animated band play inside the Cantina where Luke Skywalker and Obi-Wan Kenobi first met Han Solo — currently being cornered by the bounty hunter Greedo — and his loyal co-pilot Chewbacca.

The *Star Wars* MINILAND models were initially developed by eight model designers and two animation electricians at LEGOLAND® Deutschland.

The Theed Royal Palace is built out of more than 15,000 LEGO bricks

Cliff-side tower

Statues of famous Naboo philosophers

Green tile roof

Theed Hangar

In a climactic scene from *Star Wars* Episode I, the battle droid forces of the Trade Federation march into battle against the *Gungan* army on Naboo, with the capital city of Theed in the background.

Anakin Skywalker, Obi-Wan Kenobi, Qui-Gon Jinn, and Darth Maul can all be found inside the Theed Hangar.

Fambaa with deflector shield generator

Gungan battle wagon

Gungan "bongo" sub

I was expecting someone… a little taller

NEW ARRIVALS

The original California *Star Wars* MINILAND display was updated in 2012 when new models were added to each of the seven scenes, including a Jawa sandcrawler on Tatooine, a Rebel ion cannon in the Episode V Hoth diorama, and an immense Opee Sea Killer from Naboo's aquatic core.

The Opee's prey-catching tongue has snared a fleeing Gungan sub, which was built with multicolored lights in front.

Darth Vader came face to helmeted face with himself at the new MINILAND *Star Wars* Gallery, which features 3 foot (0.9 m) tall LEGO brick minifigures of famous characters from the saga.

AROUND THE GALAXY

A fourth LEGO® Star Wars™ MINILAND was added in 2012 at LEGOLAND Windsor Resort in the UK. As the first indoor MINILAND at a LEGOLAND Park, it features 2,000 LEGO models built at a 1:20 scale and takes visitors on a chronological tour of the Star Wars™ saga with immersive special effects like sound, climate changes, and video.

Battle droids deploy from a Trade Federation MTT

Repulsorlift AATs reinforce the droid army

The displays come to life with button-activated movement, lights, and sound effects straight from the movies.

OPENING DAY

Actress Carrie Fisher (Princess Leia) made a special appearance at the grand opening of LEGOLAND California's *Star Wars* MINILAND on March 31, 2011. Costumed characters and voice actors from *The Clone Wars* also attended.

A young fan used a lightsaber to break the ribbon and officially open the attraction.

Allianz Arena

No pressure... I'm only being watched by 30,000 fans!

PROUDLY DISPLAYED in MINILAND at LEGOLAND® Deutschland in Günzburg, Germany, is the Allianz Arena, one of the biggest LEGO® buildings in the world. Constructed from more than a million LEGO bricks, the 1: 50-scale model of Munich's famous soccer stadium is 16.5 ft (5 m) long, 15 ft (4.5 m) wide, and 3.3 ft (1 m) high, and weighs in at 1.5 tons ●

Special semi-translucent bricks let exterior glow

Even at its smaller than MINILAND-standard minifigure scale, the arena model is enormous next to a pair of LEGOLAND Deutschland's smaller visitors. Button controls on the nearby columns activate special moving features inside the model.

When the sun sets and night falls, 5,000 LEDs (Light-Emitting Diodes) illuminate the MINILAND Allianz Arena in red or blue to represent the colors of the Bayern Munich and 1860 Munich soccer teams—just like the real thing!

30,000 minifigure spectators

Luxury VIP suite

Stadium

Soccer fans above the four parking g

MAKING A STADIUM

Each minifigure in the bleachers and on the playing field was posed and placed by hand before the model's first appearance on May 12th, 2005. Park visitors received an exclusive LEGO brick to commemorate the occasion.

A LEGO Master Model Builder adds finishing touches to the pitch in the LEGOLAND workshop.

217

Discovery Centers

VISITING A LEGOLAND® Discovery Center is like jumping into the world's biggest box of LEGO® bricks. With locations open in Germany, the USA, the UK, and Japan, plus even more on the way, these big indoor attractions feature plenty of LEGO themed fun, including MINILAND displays, 4D cinemas, interactive rides, party rooms, school workshops, and much more.

A giraffe built out of LEGO bricks welcomes visitors to the USA's first Discovery Center just outside of Chicago. They'll find more wildlife like snakes, parrots, and monkeys at the Jungle Adventure Trail inside, along with other curious characters and a quiz to unlock the jungle's hidden secrets.

PICTURE THIS...

The first LEGOLAND Discovery Center opened in Berlin, Germany, in 2007. But before a Discovery Center can be built, it first has to be designed. Concept images help to create the latest additions to the LEGOLAND family.

Concepts show the development of the Factory Tour and LEGO Friends areas at the Chicago Discovery Center. A visit will reveal the difference between ideas and reality!

DRAGON RIDE

At the Berlin Discovery Center, kids can climb aboard a giant green dragon for a twisting, turning ride through a medieval castle full of moving LEGO characters and models. Try to spot the red dragon hidden somewhere along the way.

I didn't keep my hands inside the dragon ride, so the King and Queen sent me to the tickle torture room!

MODEL WORKSHOP

A real live LEGOLAND Master Model Builder hosts the Discovery Center's Model Builders Workshop, where young LEGO fans can get a hands-on tutorial from the experts and learn how to create their very own brick masterpieces.

Today's new generation of LEGO builders might just become tomorrow's new generation of LEGO Master Builders!

MINILAND AREAS

Every good LEGOLAND experience needs its iconic MINILAND! At the Chicago/Schaumburg Discovery Center, the main attraction is a miniature scale model of Chicago built from nearly 1.5 million LEGO bricks. Filled with lights and sound, the city is made up of models ranging from a parking meter constructed from only three tiny pieces to the gigantic Willis Tower, built from 190,000 bricks and weighing in at over 200 lbs (90.7 kg).

Chicago's Navy Pier shoreline on Lake Michigan, complete with its famous Ferris wheel and carousel, is captured in bricks of all shapes and colors.

4D MOVIES

Hold on tight, because four-dimensional LEGO films pop right off the screen at the LEGOLAND Discovery Center four-dimensional Cinema, with state-of-the-art 3D special effects and an interactive theater environment guaranteed to keep audiences on the edge of their seats.

SOFT PLAY ZONE

Need to let off some steam? Kids can get physical in the Soft Play Zone, full of stackable, oversized LEGO bricks, a multi-colored jungle gym, and a big climbing wall. It's excitement, entertainment, and exercise all rolled into one.

You've never played with LEGO bricks like these ones before!

Safety helmet

Every stage of manufacturing is on display on the LEGO Factory Tour.

Quality control worker

Factory brick

FACTORY TOUR

At the Factory Tour, visitors get a close-up look at the process by which LEGO bricks are made, from the raw materials all the way to the colorful finished product. You can even get an exclusive LEGO Factory brick to take home as a special souvenir!

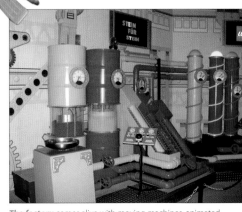

The factory comes alive with moving machines, animated workers, and authentic sound effects.

A LEGO® World

FROM INTERNATIONAL fan clubs
to action-packed video games, from
minifigure movies to artists' studios, the
LEGO® brick has definitely made the leap
from simple plastic construction toy to
global phenomenon. Every day, people
around the world are finding new
ways to move beyond the instruction
booklets and make their passion for
LEGO building a part of their lives. Read
on to discover how some of them show
off and share their love of imagination,
creativity, and that famous little brick ●

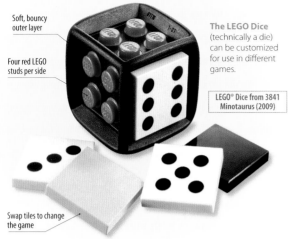

Soft, bouncy outer layer

Four red LEGO studs per side

The LEGO Dice (technically a die) can be customized for use in different games.

LEGO® Dice from 3841 Minotaurus (2009)

Swap tiles to change the game

LEGO® Games

ALTHOUGH LICENSED LEGO® games have existed for years, it wasn't until 2009 that game-playing was able to fully capture the fun and imagination of LEGO building. That's when the company launched LEGO Games, a line of tabletop games that players can assemble out of LEGO bricks, play together with their friends and family, and then—if they want to—change the pieces around to make up completely new games of their own ●

MICROFIGURES

With the new gaming system came a new type of LEGO character: the microfigure! Standing a miniscule two bricks tall, microfigures are single-piece game tokens with printed details to give them personality. They can connect to LEGO bricks on the top and bottom.

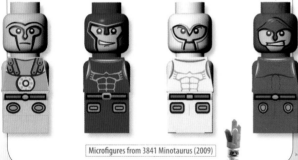

Microfigures from 3841 Minotaurus (2009)

LEGO® WORLDS

Some LEGO Games take place inside the familiar worlds of the LEGO play themes. In the City Alarm game, players become LEGO City Police officers or robbers in a chase through a micro-sized LEGO City that includes a lighthouse, a coffee shop, and even a pizzeria.

3865 City Alarm (2012)

GUESS THE MODEL

In Creationary, you roll the LEGO Dice to select a category of vehicles, buildings, nature, or things, and then build your assigned object from a randomly picked card using a collection of 338 LEGO pieces... all while your fellow players try to guess what you are making. A 2011 booster pack added more cards, categories, and pieces.

3844 Creationary (2009)

The funny thing with Creationary is that if you are really good, people will guess your model before you get to finish building it!

3843 Ramses Pyramid (2009)

Created by famous board game designer Reiner Knizia, Ramses Pyramid won a Toy Innovation 2009 award. A sequel, Ramses Return, came out in 2011.

PYRAMID OF PERIL

The heroes of LEGO Pharaoh's Quest and the Adventurers aren't the only ones who have to deal with troublesome mummy kings. In 2009's Ramses Pyramid, groups of two to four players compete to unlock crystal-coded layers and climb to the top of the pyramid to defeat Ramses and take his golden crown.

3845 Shave A Sheep (2010)

WILD AND WOOLY

Released as Wild Wool in the USA, Shave A Sheep is an addictively simple game in which players roll the LEGO Dice to grow wool on their sheep, shave the wool that has already grown, swap sheep with another player, or send the wolf to scare off all of an opponent's wool.

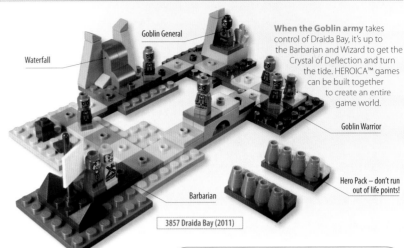

Goblin General

Waterfall

Goblin Warrior

When the Goblin army takes control of Draida Bay, it's up to the Barbarian and Wizard to get the Crystal of Deflection and turn the tide. HEROICA™ games can be built together to create an entire game world.

Hero Pack – don't run out of life points!

Barbarian

3857 Draida Bay (2011)

3848 Pirate Plank (2010)

LEGO plate sail

Micro-sized pirates for a micro-sized ship

WALK THE PLANK

Forced to walk the plank by the big-hatted captain, your job is to make your fellow buccaneers hop into the shark-filled water first and end up the last pirate standing. The LEGO designers had a lot of fun creating the game's miniature-scale pirate ship. It even has a tiny cannon!

Players are encouraged to change the rules each time they play. For example, you can let pirates hop across planks, or take the extra skull-and-crossbones tile off the sail to use on the LEGO Dice.

HEROICA™

Introduced in 2011, HEROICA is designed to make board games that can be played like video games and role-playing games. Each game pits player heroes like the Knight, Ranger, Druid, and Rogue against evil warriors and monsters in a quest to capture relics and free the world of HEROICA from darkness.

3860 Castle Fortaan (2011)

TEAM UP TO WIN

Not all LEGO Games call for head-to-head competition. In the LEGO Ninjago game, groups of two to four players can play individually as they look for hidden golden weapons, swing on ropes, and battle guards with the help of a buildable spinner— and if they find all four before the Skeleton General can steal any away, everybody wins the game at the same time!

Time to roll the bones!

3856 Ninjago (2012)

LEGO® HARRY POTTER™

The Harry Potter Hogwarts game lets you take on the role of a student wizard and race around moving staircases and secret passages, searching the classrooms to collect your homework. The first student to get back to their common room wins.

3862 Harry Potter™ Hogwarts™ (2010)

Although you play as a nameless student from one of Hogwarts' four houses, the game also comes with microfigures of Harry Potter, Hermione, Ron, Draco, and Dumbledore.

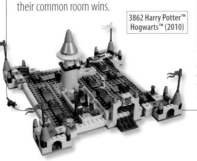

LEGO® Digital Designer

IT'S THE ULTIMATE DREAM of the LEGO® fan: to get to see your creation transformed into a real LEGO set. On the LEGO Factory and LEGO Design byME websites, builders could use a program called LEGO Digital Designer to build models on their computers, upload them to inspire other fans, and order the pieces online to build their creations in person. A few lucky fans even had their models produced and sold as official LEGO Factory sets ●

THE CONTEST

In 2005, the LEGO Group offered a challenge to the fan community: to construct micro-scale models using LEGO Digital Designer, with weekly rounds of voting to decide the winners. The highest-scoring models became the very first LEGO Factory sets.

5524 Airport (2005)

5526 Skyline (2005)

The 10 winning fan-created models were combined into three LEGO Factory sets. They were sold online and in LEGO Brand Stores.

Detail from 5525 Amusement Park (2005)

FACTORY ORIGINALS

Every model released under the LEGO Factory brand was created by talented LEGO fans, working together with professional model designers to make sure that their creations had the stability and ease of building of all official LEGO sets.

10200 Custom Car Garage (2008)

The set included both printed instructions and a CD to help builders get started with LEGO Digital Designer.

Browse each step or animate the entire process

Fan expertise helped the Custom Car Garage make use of special building techniques seen in few other LEGO models.

Removable V8 racing engine

Current piece selection

Custom decals

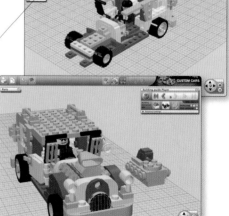

Rotating view to see every angle

The complete set included three custom hot rod cars with drivers, a mechanic with tools, a racing garage with a removable roof and working repair lift, and six modular engines that could be swapped from car to car.

Classic hot rod styling

MAKING TRAINS

With few LEGO Train sets released to stores these days, LEGO Factory became a haven for train builders around the world. The website featured train-building tips, fan files, and a timeline of LEGO train models from 1964 to the present, while LEGO Digital Designer included parts to help hobbyists build their perfect engines and rolling stock cars.

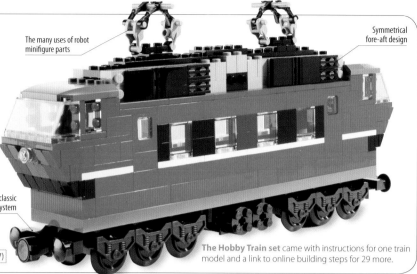

The many uses of robot minifigure parts

Symmetrical fore-aft design

Designed with the help of many fans, the Hobby Train included more than 1,000 pieces.

Compatible with classic 9V electric train system

10183 Hobby Train Set (2007)

The Hobby Train set came with instructions for one train model and a link to online building steps for 29 more.

SPACE MODELS

Fans of LEGO Space blasted off again with these LEGO Factory sets inspired by the classic era of the theme. Featuring the heroic Star Justice team and the evil Space Skulls, the multi-model collections were designed by a pair of adult builders.

10192 Space Skulls (2008)

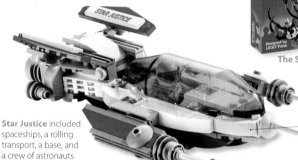

The Space Skulls were skull-faced space villains with a singular technological theme.

Star Justice included spaceships, a rolling transport, a base, and a crew of astronauts and robots.

"Studs Not On Top" construction style

Spaceship from 10191 Star Justice (2008)

LEGO® DESIGN BYME

In 2009, LEGO Factory became LEGO Design byME. As before, builders could use Digital Designer to design models online, create names, packaging, and auto-generated building steps, and then purchase their creations. In 2011, Design byME added Hero Recon Team, which let you do the same with Hero Factory parts. In 2012, both ordering services closed down, although LEGO Digital Designer remained available for online use.

DESIGNING YOUR OWN MODEL

At LEGOfactory.com, users can download the free LEGO Digital Designer program and use its pre-programmed modules and a large palette of LEGO elements and colors to drag, drop, and rotate pieces as they build new models on their computer screens. When they are done, they can upload the digital model to an online gallery, design a custom box for their creation, and mail-order the pieces to be delivered to their homes.

With a huge variety of current LEGO pieces, the possibilities for what you could make in LDD are quite literally endless.

Don't see the car you want? Go online and build it yourself!

LEGO Factory packaging featured a computer-rendered image of the model with options for different backgrounds, special effects, and even comic speech balloons.

Hosted by team leader Merrick Fortis, Hero Recon Team recruited the best and the brightest fan-designed heroes. Its parts included a black and silver chest plate that could not be found in retail sets.

LEGO Island (1997)

The one that started it all, 1997's LEGO Island introduced the world to pizza delivery boy Pepper Roni, the deconstructing Brickster, and an island full of fun missions.

LEGO® Video Games

FROM LEGO® ISLAND to famous licenses like *Star Wars*™ and Batman™, LEGO video games have been letting fans race, adventure, and play in the worlds of LEGO bricks for over 15 years. Here are some of the growing number of video game titles that have been produced so far ●

STARTING SMALL

The earliest LEGO video games had simple concepts. LEGO Chess gave you the option of playing chess with a Western or a Pirates theme, LEGO Creator let you build with standard pieces or special "Action Bricks" and then bring your models to animated life, and in LEGO Loco you could build a town and railway system.

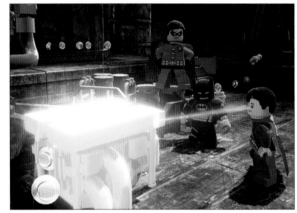

LEGO Batman 2: DC Super Heroes (2012)

BIG NAME GAMES

The LEGO Group's biggest successes in the video games field have definitely been its games based on licensed properties. With four LEGO *Star Wars* titles and other familiar names including Batman, Indiana Jones™, Harry Potter™, and Pirates of the Caribbean™, they present well-known stories and characters with a uniquely silly LEGO twist.

The whole minifigure Justice League teamed up to battle Lex Luthor and the Joker in LEGO Batman 2: DC Super Heroes.

LEGO Chess (1998)   LEGO Creator (1998)

LEGO Loco (1998)   LEGO Friends (1999)

Although it had little to do with bricks or building, in LEGO Friends (no relation to the play theme) you arranged music and dance routines for a band of teenaged friends.

ROCK RAIDERS

Different games inspired by the LEGO Rock Raiders theme were produced for the PC and PlayStation platforms. Both gave you control of the expedition's mining team and provided you with the objective of collecting energy crystals, surviving in a hostile alien environment, and finally making your way home.

LEGO Rock Raiders (1999)

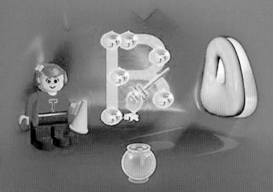

LEGO My Style Kindergarten (2000)

LEGO My Style Kindergarten used learning buddies to introduce concepts of music, math, language, and art to younger children who were just discovering those subjects in school.

LEGO Creator Knights' Kingdom (2000)

The second LEGO Creator game let kids create a medieval kingdom—or bring it tumbling down with a Destructa Brick.

LEGO Stunt Rally (2000)

In this racing game, you could collect power-ups to help you win, or unlock elements to build your own tracks.

SECRET AGENT ACTION

LEGO Alpha Team had you take on the role of Dash Justice as you solved puzzles, rescued your teammates, and thwarted the world-domination plans of the evil Ogel with the help of special items like chutes, trampolines, lasers, and anti-gravity generators.

LEGO Alpha Team (2001)

No minifigures were injured in the playing of this video game, though a few Ogel-controlled drones may have been lightly singed.

Galidor: Defenders of the Outer Dimension (2002)

GALIDOR

Based on the TV series, the Galidor game let you play as hero Nick Bluetooth and travel between the worlds of the Outer Dimension, using your limb-morphing "glinching" power to help your friends and battle the evil tyrant Gorm. The game could also interact with the Kek Powerizer toy.

BIONICLE® GAMES

BIONICLE® has been the company's most prolific video game franchise to date. Its epic storyline and biomechanical heroes came to life in five different titles released between 2001 and 2006. It also had two popular online games that let players explore the island and mysteries of Mata Nui on their web browsers.

The first BIONICLE game, Tales of the Tohunga (later renamed Quest for the Toa) was produced exclusively for the Game Boy Advance in 2001. You played as a Mata Nui villager on a mission to summon the mighty Toa and save your island.

BIONICLE: Tales of the Tohunga (2001)

BIONICLE Heroes (2006)

A third-person action game, BIONICLE Heroes let you play as different Toa and use their element-controlling powers to battle the Piraka and other classic BIONICLE foes.

SEQUELS

A number of LEGO video games proved popular enough to earn follow-ups. In addition to the four LEGO Creator and five BIONICLE games, there have been three LEGO Island Games and two LEGO Battles games, including a Ninjago-themed sequel.

LEGO Racers 2 (2001)

LEGO Racers 2 had courses from the Adventurers, Arctic, and Life on Mars themes.

LEGO Island 2: The Brickster's Revenge (2001)

Pepper and the Brickster returned in LEGO Island 2 and again in Island Xtreme Stunts.

LEGO UNIVERSE

Launched in late 2010, LEGO Universe was a multiplayer online game that let LEGO fans from around the globe create their own minifigure characters and team up to quest their way through different worlds of brick-based adventures. However, lower than expected sales led to the game's demise in early 2012.

LEGO Universe (2010)

Making a LEGO® Video Game

WHAT GOES IN THE MIX? It all starts when the game developers work together with the LEGO Group to find the characters and worlds that would work best for a new game. They boil the chosen LEGO® theme down to its most important elements, and then the development and publishing teams meet to discuss the best way to blend them together ●

Every frame of character movement is created by professional animators. Sometimes they do it twice!

Each **character**, vehicle, or object made of LEGO elements in the game is built on a computer using a digital library of every LEGO piece ever made.

Suddenly, an alarm bell sounds and Catwoman is caught in a spotlight. She looks startled.

Catwoman runs to the end of the ledge and leaps off...

Catwoman makes her escape by leaping and somersaulting across the rooftops.

Illustrated storyboards set up the visual story and the timing of action and jokes for the game's programmers to animate later on.

EARLY CONCEPTS

Once the game's key features are decided, it's time to create a concept framework. A small team of programmers and designers works on new abilities and functions for the game, while the art and animation teams work up ideas for the characters, the environments they'll inhabit, and the game's storyline.

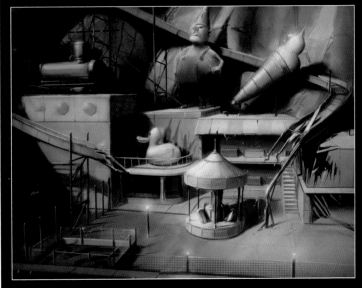

Early in the design process, concept paintings are created to help establish the mood and locations for the final game.

FROM PAPER TO PIXELS

Some of the initial illustrated designs make it into the game, while others are changed or removed if they don't seem quite right. The result is a "First Playable" prototype that lets the designers test their ideas in a simpler version of the game.

KID TESTING

Now it's time for the biggest test of all: will kids like it? Kid testing is important because new players may notice problems with gameplay that the designers have missed. Thanks to their feedback, the team can create a better game for everybody.

Nearly finished character and vehicle models are tested in a simplified game world before the final details are added.

A 3-D "wire-frame" game environment.

The wire-frame filled in, with shading added.

The final rendered version has light, color, and detailed textures.

Rough wire-frame rendering

Two-Face™ and the rest of Batman's cast of characters are scripted and animated to be true to their comic selves... plus a bit of uniquely brick-ified LEGO humor.

Two faces, two personalities

FILLING IN THE DETAILS

With the overall design in place, even more animators, artists, and programmers join the team. They help create the rest of the game's environments, characters, story events, levels, and puzzles.

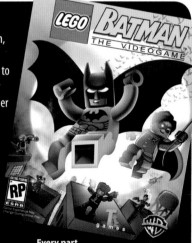

This LEGO® Batman™: The Videogame cake was created for the game's big 2008 launch party in New York City. Complete with edible sugar dough minifigures, it weighed a whopping 300 lbs!

THE PUBLICITY MACHINE

Now the game is in full production, and it's up to the marketing and promotional teams to decide how to introduce it to the world, whether through magazines, online, or other media. Screenshots, trailers, interviews, and playable demos are released in the months leading up to the game's debut to whet the public's appetite.

Every part of the game, even early packaging concepts, has to be approved by the LEGO Group and other partners.

More than 30 LEGO video games have been released since the original *LEGO Island* in 1997.

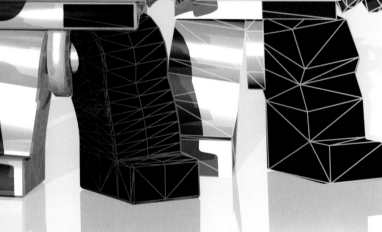

Bricks on Film

BRICKS... CAMERA... ACTION! From official LEGO® movies to themed sets that enable builders to create animations of their own, and on to an entire industry of amazing fan-made films, LEGO building and the world of movie-making have forged a beautiful friendship destined to last for years to come ●

The main LEGO Studios set included a real camera, actors, a rampaging dinosaur, special effects props, a city street stage, and a minifigure film-making crew. More sets could be added to create new stunts and action scenes.

LEGO® STUDIOS

In 2000, the LEGO Group teamed up with the world-famous director Steven Spielberg to create a new kind of LEGO theme. LEGO Studios wouldn't just be about construction and play, but making video stories using the principle of stop-motion animation. In this process, a camera takes a single picture of a model or scene, which is then moved slightly and photographed again. By repeating this over and over and then playing back the shots in sequence, the many still pictures blend together to make an animated LEGO movie.

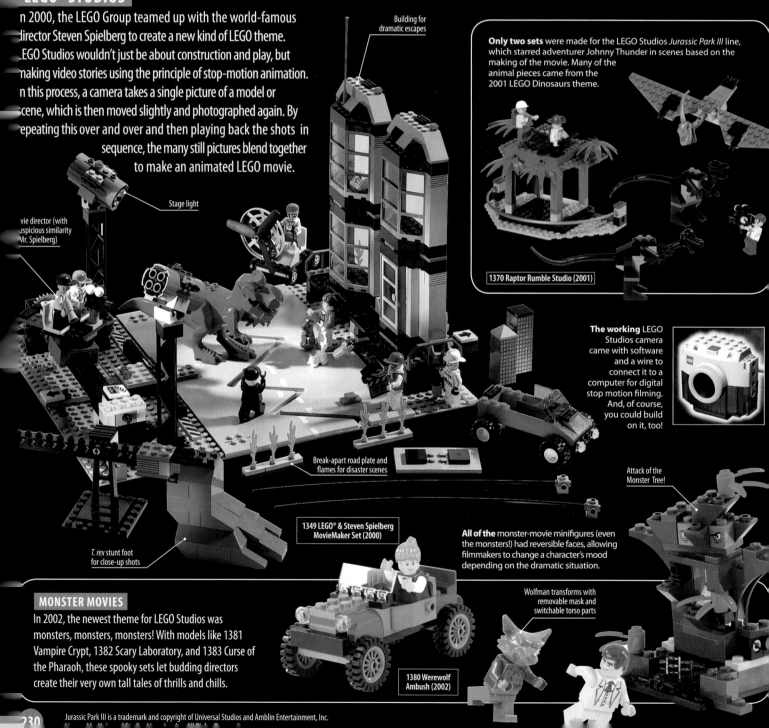

Building for dramatic escapes

Stage light

Movie director (with suspicious similarity to Mr. Spielberg)

Only two sets were made for the LEGO Studios *Jurassic Park III* line, which starred adventurer Johnny Thunder in scenes based on the making of the movie. Many of the animal pieces came from the 2001 LEGO Dinosaurs theme.

1370 Raptor Rumble Studio (2001)

The working LEGO Studios camera came with software and a wire to connect it to a computer for digital stop motion filming. And, of course, you could build on it, too!

Break-apart road plate and flames for disaster scenes

1349 LEGO® & Steven Spielberg MovieMaker Set (2000)

T. rex stunt foot for close-up shots

Attack of the Monster Tree!

All of the monster-movie minifigures (even the monsters!) had reversible faces, allowing filmmakers to change a character's mood depending on the dramatic situation.

Wolfman transforms with removable mask and switchable torso parts

MONSTER MOVIES

In 2002, the newest theme for LEGO Studios was monsters, monsters, monsters! With models like 1381 Vampire Crypt, 1382 Scary Laboratory, and 1383 Curse of the Pharaoh, these spooky sets let budding directors create their very own tall tales of thrills and chills.

1380 Werewolf Ambush (2002)

LEGO MOVIES

On the internet, on television, and on home video, made with old-fashioned stop-motion and cutting-edge computer animation, these movies and mini-movies are all official LEGO films created by and for the LEGO Group!

Go Miniman Go! (2008)

LEGO® Indiana Jones: *Raiders of the Lost Brick™* (2008)

LEGO® Star Wars™: *The Han Solo Affair* (2002)

LEGO® Batman™: *Bricks, Bats & Bad Guys* (2006)

LEGO® Spider-Man™: *The Peril of Doc Ock* (2004)

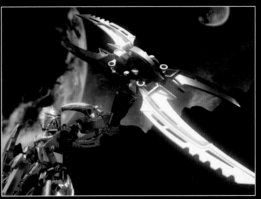

BIONICLE®: *Mask of Light* became the first feature-length LEGO film when it debuted on home video in 2003. Three more movies were released in the series, all of them using computer animation and professional voice actors to bring the heroes, villains, and adventures of the epic BIONICLE saga to life.

BIONICLE®: *The Legend Reborn* (2009)

To celebrate the theatrical release of *Star Wars: Episode III Revenge of the Sith*, this five-minute, computer-animated mini-movie was broadcast on television in May, 2005. Featuring a comedic look at the events of the movie, it ended with the credits rolling over a clone trooper orchestra with Darth Vader as conductor.

LEGO® Star Wars™: *Revenge of the Brick* (2005)

FAN FILMS

Even before LEGO Studios, fans were making their own animations starring LEGO minifigures. Often called Brickfilms, here are just a few examples of the thousands of great LEGO fan films out there!

Jane's Brain, imaginatively animated by Chris Salt to a song by Adam Buxton.

Curt Werline's "Alabama Jones and the Lost Topping of Doom."

Steffen Troeger's "E.A.R.T.H. 2.0," an animated warning about the threat of pollution.

The Fastest and Funniest LEGO Star Wars Story Ever Told was a two-minute stop-motion short that sped through the original movie trilogy at a breakneck pace. Placed online on May the Fourth, 2010, it got over 7 million views and was followed a year later by a prequel edition.

The Adventures of Clutch Powers was the first full-length movie to feature minifigures. Released directly to video in 2010, it starred action hero and explorer Clutch Powers, a character created for the film.

LEGO Ninjago followed a two-episode miniseries in 2011 with an entire season of computer-animated TV adventures in 2012. The story followed the ninja team from trainees to full-fledged heroes.

THE PADAWAN MENACE

Written by Emmy Award-winning writer Michael Price and produced by the Australian visual effects company Animal Logic, LEGO® *Star Wars™: The Padawan Menace* (2011) was a 22-minute feature broadcast around the world in 2011. The DVD and Blu-ray video release included extras like the short film *Bombad Bounty* and a compilation of animations based on *The Clone Wars*.

Created in close collaboration with Lucasfilm, *The Padawan Menace* featured the voice of original actor Anthony Daniels as C-3PO and cameos by Darth Vader and George Lucas himself. The first edition video included an exclusive Young Han Solo minifigure.

3443 LEGO Mosaic (2000)

Sold directly from the LEGO website between 2000 and 2005, LEGO Mosaic let builders use the online Brick-o-Lizer to transform their own photographs into step-by-step instructions for assembling mosaics out of thousands of black, white, and gray LEGO pieces.

Special Edition Sets

THE MODELS on these pages are all special editions, some created for milestone anniversaries, others to thrill the most experienced builders, and some just to look good. If you have any of them in your collection, consider yourself one lucky LEGO® fan ●

Rotating turbine

4999 Vestas Wind Turbine (2008)

This huge working windmill was available only to employees of the Vestas company. More than 26 in (66 cm) high and built from nearly 800 pieces, the authentic reproduction towered over the tiny house and hill below.

21001 John Hancock Tower (2008)

The LEGO Architecture series debuted in 2008 with a series of desktop-sized miniature models of famous buildings from all around the world. Each licensed microscale replica includes a booklet full of facts and information about the history of the real building.

21002 Empire State Building (2009)

21003 Seattle Space Needle (2009)

21000 Willis Tower (2008)

Base with printed building name

21012 Sydney Opera House™ (2012)

Australia's celebrated Sydney Opera House (appropriately conceived by a Danish architect!) was built on a base of tan bricks, with white pieces used to make its interlocking vaulted shells.

21010 Robie™ House (2011)

More than 16.5 in (42 cm) wide and 5 in (13 cm) tall, this model used more than 2,000 small LEGO elements to recreate the landmark Prairie-style house built by Frank Lloyd Wright in Chicago.

9247 Community Workers (2006)

Released in 2005 and revised in 2006 with different pieces and faces, this LEGO Education set contained a whole town's worth of 31 minifigures with accessories, including policemen, firefighters, construction workers, doctors, civilians, and more.

A LEGO Power Functions motor (with a team of Vestas minifigures to keep it maintained) made the windmill spin and turned on lights in the house at its base.

White snow tiles

Street light

The third of the Winter Village sets featured a small-town post office with postal workers, an old-time mail truck with gifts, a pavilion for musicians, and a couple of kids having a snowball fight.

10222 Winter Village Post Office (2011)

Maintenance van

Light-up house

852293 Giant Chess Set (2007)

Brick-built figure bases

Knights' castle tower

Troll fortress

Dwarven mine

Decorative dragon head

Extra weapons and shields

Skeleton dungeon

Packaged in a gigantic book-shaped box, the biggest (and most expensive) LEGO chess set ever made measured 17 in (43 cm) long on each side, was built from 2,481 pieces, and included 33 figures. The board doubled as a playset, with dungeons, armories, and rolling siege-tower rooks to play with in between games.

King

Queen

Knight

Wizard (Bishop)

30029 Pudsey Bear (2011)

Bandage

Pudsey Bear, the mascot of the BBC Children in Need program, was created as a 95-piece LEGO set in 2011, polka-dot bandage and all. All profits from his sale were donated to charity.

5522 LEGO Golden Anniversary Set (2008)

This 2008 creative building set celebrated the 50th anniversary of the LEGO brick with a special-edition golden brick and classic retro-style packaging.

Gold-topped collections like this 1,000-piece tub marked the golden anniversary of the LEGO System of Play in 2005.

4496 50th Anniversary Tub (2005)

LIMITED EDITION

To commemorate the 25th anniversary of the LEGO logo, the company released limited-edition sets in clear, glittery buckets with an exclusive silver brick inside.

Christmas wreath

The first in a series of seasonal exclusive models, the Winter Toy Shop let builders create a snow-covered, old-fashioned toy store with miniature toys in the windows, and a Christmas tree and singing carolers outside.

10199 Winter Toy Shop (2009)

Snowy roof plates

Bakery shop sign

The Winter Village theme continued with a cozy bakery full of treats for a frosty day. It also had a tree-seller's stand and cart, and a frozen pond for ice skaters.

10216 Winter Village Bakery (2010)

Fashion & Style

SOME PEOPLE wear their love of LEGO® bricks and building on their sleeves… and on their wrists, keys, and kitchen tables, too! With so many choices of apparel and accessories, there's something out there to suit every LEGO lifestyle ●

Minifigure head salt and pepper shakers

EXTENDED LINE

Have you ever seen a LEGO lollipop maker? How about salt and pepper shakers shaped like minifigure heads? With key chains, coat racks, children's costumes, and more, these unique Extended Line items were produced for sale at the LEGOLAND® Parks, the LEGO Brand Stores, and the online LEGO Shop (shop.LEGO.com).

Coat rack with building studs and LEGO City minifigures

LEGO brick backpack with zippered stud pockets

Ninjago minifigure keychain

Drinking mug with 3D brick detail

Minifigure-shaped ice pop mold

LEGO Castle children's knight costume

LEGO Friends jewelry box

LICENSED ITEMS

These products were all created by outside companies under licenses from the LEGO Group. They include watches with wristbands that you can make longer or shorter, link by link, colorful pens with LEGO themed beads to build and rearrange, and even light-up minifigure lanterns and brick-styled home electronics for the biggest LEGO fans.

Classic LEGO watch
with multi-piece band

LEGO wallet

LEGO® DUPLO® board book

LEGO Friends
bracelets

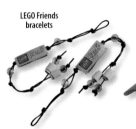

LEGO City
Police cap

LEGO 2x4 brick coin bank

Insulated minifigure lunch bag

LEGO® DUPLO® t-shirt

LEGO City kids' watch

Brick-styled MP3 player

Light-up minifigure lantern

DK BOOKS

The LEGO Group and Dorling Kindersley Publishing have teamed up to create a number of large, high-quality books—in fact, you're holding one in your hands right now! Full of detailed photos and information about LEGO models and minifigures, these best-selling titles and many more have been published in multiple languages and countries around the globe.

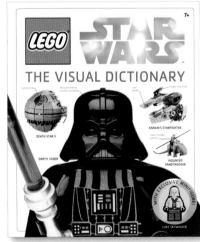

LEGO® Star Wars™: The Visual Dictionary (2009)

The LEGO® Ideas Book (2011)

"50 Years of the LEGO® Brick" book

The LEGO® Club

THE FIRST official LEGO® Club was created by the company's Canadian division in 1966. It was followed the next year by LEGO Sweden. Today, the LEGO Club provides building inspiration and behind-the-scenes information to 4 million club members around the world ●

Membership card mailed to US LEGO Club members in 2007.

INSIDE FEATURES

Games, articles, contests, kids' creations, building steps and more fill the pages of the LEGO Club magazine, with national editions shipping four to six times a year to more than a dozen countries.

The US LEGO Club kicked off in July 1987 with the eight-page, quarterly *Brick Kicks* newsletter.

LEGO UK mailed the first issue of *Bricks 'n Pieces* to collectors in December 1974.

MEET MAX!

Max first appeared as the host of European editions of *LEGO Magazine* in 2007 before becoming the modern mascot of the world-wide LEGO Club. As a minifigure, he has the inside scoop on all the latest company news and upcoming themes. In 2010, Max was slightly redesigned and released as a real figure for the first time!

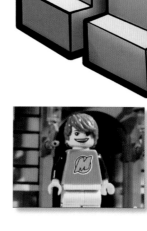

Max appears in stop-motion adventures as part of the LEGO Club Show. The online series features music videos, interviews, and on-the-scene reports from all around the world of LEGO building.

BRICK BUILDMORE

"The Adventures of Brick Buildmore" premiered in the very first issue of *Brick Kicks*. Together with his friend Bridget and faithful dog Comet, Brick solved problems the good old-fashioned way: by building!

The UK LEGO Technic Club's magazine shipped four times a year between 1994 and 2000.

LEGO World Club Magazine was first available by subscription in Germany in 1997.

Illustrated, photographed, and even computer-generated comics are a permanent staple of LEGO Club magazines, offering stories and play ideas to help readers get started on their own adventures.

The bilingual *Innovations* replaced the Canadian club's *LEGO Design News* in 1990.

THE LEGO® MANIAC

Based on a series of live-action television commercials, Jack the LEGO Maniac originally introduced the Summer 1989 issue of *Brick Kicks*. He eventually lost his name and became the host of the newly relaunched *LEGO Mania Magazine*, starring in comics in which his imagination took him on adventures inside of his LEGO sets.

In the US, *LEGO Mania Magazine* took over from *Brick Kicks* at the end of 1994…

… switched to plain *LEGO Magazine* in May of 2002 with a big feature on LEGO® Star Wars™…

… became the unified face of the LEGO Club around the world…

…and was finally retitled *LEGO Club Magazine* in 2008.

LEGO® BRICKMASTER

The US-based BrickMaster program was launched in November 2004 as a premium version of the free LEGO Club. Subscribers paid an annual fee to receive a larger magazine, exclusive LEGO sets, and other rewards for the company's biggest fans. The last issue of *LEGO BrickMaster* shipped in November 2010.

20003 Dinosaur (2008)

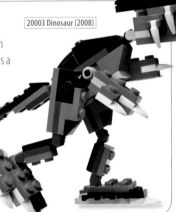

Exclusive T-shirts are given out to club members who attend in-person LEGO Club Meetings at LEGO Brand Stores across the US.

Other versions of *LEGO Club Magazine* include an in-school edition and *Club Jr.* for children under 7.

The official Club website at www.LEGOclub.com is regularly updated with news stories, downloadable building instructions, an online gallery for club members' Cool Creations, an interactive version of the magazine, LEGO Club TV videos, and more.

The introductory homepage is the site's one-stop starting place. Along with information, games, and activities for LEGO fans, it features links to customer service, a company history and timeline, official press releases, and sections for parents and educators.

LEGO.com

WITH THE GOAL of giving fans the ultimate LEGO® experience, the official company website at LEGO.com is one of the most-visited internet sites of any toy manufacturer in the world. With 21 local sites, the award-winning website welcomes visitors that hail from more than 200 countries, from Togo to Tajikistan. At the last count, LEGO.com had more than 14 million unique visitors per month! And yes, the site has a store, too ●

COMIC BUILDER

Have you ever wanted to create a comic? The LEGO.com Comic Builder lets you tell your own story. You can choose a panel layout, drop in backgrounds, and design your own action with a cast of LEGO minifigures and vehicles. It even lets you add dialogue, pose characters, and add special effects just like a real comic book—and then print it out to show your friends your comic creation!

The comic-building fun starts when you click on this big blue button!

SHOPPING FOR BRICKS

LEGO.com/shop, the official LEGO shop, sells the latest sets by mail order to customers from more than 23 countries around the world. Featured items include LEGO Exclusives and Hard-to-Find sets, LEGO Lifestyle and Licensed products like books, stationery, and clothing, and a well-stocked Pick A Brick selection for custom model creation!

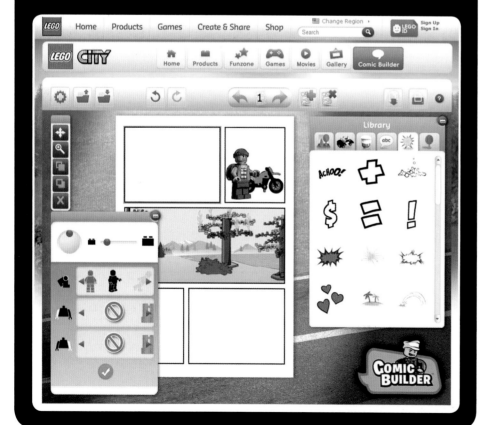

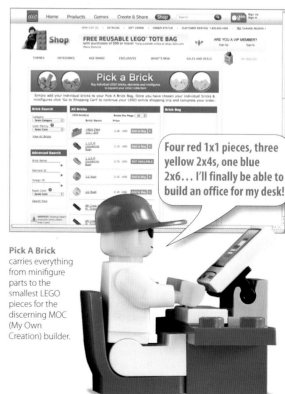

Pick A Brick carries everything from minifigure parts to the smallest LEGO pieces for the discerning MOC (My Own Creation) builder.

GAMES TO PLAY

Whatever your preference, from action and adventure to puzzle-solving, stories, or strategy, the LEGO website likely has a free online game to suit your tastes. The single and multi-player selections are constantly expanded as new themes are released, so there's almost always something new.

In the Ninjago Viper Smash game, players hone their Spinjitzu skills by using game cards and special ninja attacks to battle snake-like Serpentine warriors.

THEME PAGES

Each current LEGO theme has its own section on LEGO.com with characters and stories, online games, and downloadable extras like wallpaper, TV commercials, and videos.

The LEGO® *Star Wars*™ website includes products, games, and computer-animated mini-movies.

There's even a showcase gallery where fans can show off their custom creations.

LEGO.com has preschool games to help even the youngest computer-using builders develop their coordination and pattern-matching skills.

ANIMATIONS & ADVENTURES

From exciting new adventures in a galaxy far, far away to the latest get-rich schemes of the LEGO City crooks, LEGO.com is always packed with stop-motion and computer-animated stories starring models and minifigures from the company's many famous themes.

Computer animation brings the LEGO City Police and other memorable characters from the world of LEGO building to life!

INTERACTION

Ever wanted to talk to other LEGO builders? From the LEGO Club website to moderated message boards, LEGO.com has lots of ways for fans to connect and communicate in an online environment built to be friendly and safe for children of all ages.

KIDS GET ALL THE FUN. I DEMAND MESSAGE BOARDS FOR MINIFIGURES!

LEGO.com/club lets builders upload their Cool Creations and share their masterpieces with the entire world.

The LEGO Message Boards cover topics from favorite LEGO themes to high scores in the site's online games.

LEGO® Education

LEGO Education ABC 123 sets help to develop early mathematical skills and literacy. Mosaic-building kits provide a fun, creative way for young children to start recognizing shapes, colors, letters, and numbers, and the patterns that they can form together.

PLAYFUL LEARNING. It's what LEGO® Education is all about. Established in 1980, and designed in collaboration with education experts, the LEGO Education program offers a wide variety of constructive experiences for teachers, students and children 18 months and older. With guides and activity packs, free early-learning activities available for download at LEGOeducation.com, and a catalogue of products, the program engages creative minds and teaches children the importance of learning by making ●

ROLE PLAY

Filled with pieces that represent familiar people, objects, and locations, LEGO Education Play Theme sets encourage children to act out different scenes from real life. By playing on their own or with friends and family, they learn to understand the needs and feelings of others while improving their own social and emotional skills.

9215 Dolls Family Set (2007)

Sets include illustrated story starter cards to inspire role play ideas.

NOW I GET IT!

Cooperative play helps children explore different situations and learn to respect each others' points of view.

CREATIVE CONSTRUCTION

With enough LEGO pieces at hand, a child can create anything. That's why LEGO Education Creative Construction sets include large collections of colorful bricks and special elements to help stimulate younger children's imaginations, self-expression, and creativity through rules-free building. Products range from boxes of basic bricks, building plates, windows, and wheels to entire DUPLO® town collections and huge, award-winning LEGO SOFT bricks, designed to develop motor skills and spatial awareness in children ages 2 and up.

Kids can make creatures and buildings with tubes of all lengths and shapes using the 9076 Tubes Experiment Set (2007), then roll balls through them to find out what happens.

LEGO SOFT bricks are oversized, durable, and washable pieces that let children create life-sized figures, walls, towers, and anything else that they can think up and build.

9020 LEGO® SOFT Starter Set (1998)

MACHINES & MECHANISMS

These kits and CD-ROM activity packs give students the parts, instructions, and inspiration they need to build both simple and powered machine models with mechanical functions like spinning gears, wheels, and axles. By learning how things work through construction and play, they gain a better understanding of the machines around them every day.

Students use the machines they build to measure time, distance, speed, weight, and more in lesson plans that help them explore energy and how forces affect motion.

This core machine-construction set includes almost 400 LEGO Technic elements and instructions for assembling 14 models with functions that range from studying gearing mechanisms to calibrating and capturing wind. An optional pneumatics set adds even more to build and learn.

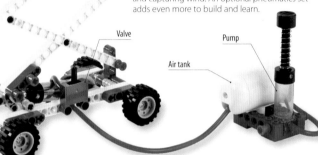

Valve

Pump

Air tank

9686 Simple & Powered Machines Set (2009) with Pneumatics Add-On Set

LEGO® SERIOUS PLAY™

It's not just children who can learn from playing with LEGO bricks. LEGO SERIOUS PLAY is a workshop program in which a certified facilitator helps guide business teams to communicate and work together better by using LEGO construction as a metaphor for their shared strategies and goals. The program has been so successful that a classroom version is being developed as well.

A visual representation of workers at cross-purposes before a Serious Play course.

Everyone on the team contributes and participates in building landscape models, telling stories and playing out possible business scenarios through the medium of LEGO bricks.

ROBOTICS

LEGO® Education WeDo™ kits let elementary school students aged 7 to 11 get a head start on robotics by building models, hooking up computer-controlled sensors and motors, and using a simple programming tool to create behavior and overcome curriculum-based challenges with their robot inventions.

WeDo themes include Amazing Mechanisms, Wild Animals, Play Soccer, and Adventure Stories, covering topics within science, technology, mathematics, and language.

9580 LEGO® Education WeDo™ Construction Set (2009)

USB cable

Power Functions M-Motor

Brick-built LEGO Technic lever arm

Soccer activity goalkeeper

The WeDo Construction Set comes with more than 150 elements, including a motor, motion and tilt sensors, and a LEGO USB hub for connecting the model to a computer.

LEGO® MINDSTORMS®

Students over 8 can learn more complex robotics skills with LEGO® MINDSTORMS® Education sets. Activity packs teach them how to program and control robots built with the NXT Intelligent Brick, test and modify life-like behavior, and analyze their robots' sensor data afterwards.

Developed by Tufts University's Center for Engineering Educational Outreach, the LEGOengineering.com website provides teachers with an online community and resources to help create new classroom activities.

LEGO MINDSTORMS Education activity packs are developed by Carnegie Mellon University's Robotics Academy and include video tutorials, worksheets, and teacher introduction materials.

Ridged grip for leverage

Created in 1988, the LEGO brick separator is a LEGO Master Builder's best friend. This simple, one-piece plastic tool can pop any brick off a model, no matter how tightly wedged-in it may be. A new orange version was released in 2012 that's compatible with LEGO Technic axles, too.

Studs above and tubes below

LEGO® Master Builders

HAVE YOU EVER SEEN a spectacular LEGO® sculpture and wondered who built it? Chances are, it was a team of LEGO Master Builders. Rigorously tested and selected for their creative construction skills, the LEGO Master Builders work at the LEGO model shops, where they assemble an incredible variety of models for in-store use, parks, special projects, and events all around the world ●

The Connecticut, USA, model shop team assembles a 12 ft (3.7 m) long scale model of the newest LEGO factory in Monterrey, Mexico.

LEGO Master Builders can zoom in to make changes to individual bricks. Before digital building, they would have had to take apart the entire model first.

DIGITAL BRICKS

The LEGO Master Builders once used half-scale prototypes to design their giant brick sculptures, but these days they use special computer programs to digitally create models before they start assembling the real thing.

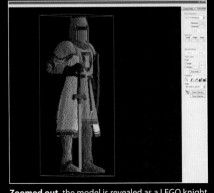

Zoomed out, the model is revealed as a LEGO knight. Purple highlights areas still being worked on.

THE MODEL SHOP

Here's where the LEGO magic happens! With model shops in Denmark, the USA, the Czech Republic, and at the LEGOLAND® Parks, the hard-working LEGO Master Builders are always in the middle of creating something new and amazing. Their workspaces are filled with LEGO models, giant building tables, and racks of bricks in every shape, size, and color imaginable.

LEGO Master Builders love to use specialized pieces in unusual ways. Here, one works on a space monster made out of parts that started as a giant LEGO snake.

A LEGO Master Builder works near the prototype heads for a band of singing robots.

LIGHT, SOUND, & MOVEMENT

This 47,000-piece model of the Hollywood Bowl amphitheater, built over the course of 600 hours for LEGOLAND® California's MINILAND, glows with rainbow-colored electric lights that change to the beat of "The LEGO Symphony." Models with moving and light-up features are a specialty of the LEGO Master Builders.

MASTER DESIGNS

Built at the Kladno model shop in the Czech Republic, this huge statue of an ancient Egyptian pharaoh was designed as a hand-drawn sketch and then constructed brick-by-virtual-brick in full scale on a computer before the first two plastic elements were ever snapped together.

All built and ready for lift-off!

A nose on a minifigure? Built from about 2,400 bricks and standing 2 ½ feet (80 cm) tall, these smiling characters are known as LEGO Friends.

Giant LEGO Friend version of a LEGO Mars Mission astronaut

Mechanized moving jaw

This animatronic *Tyrannosaurus rex* head was built with an articulated, pneumatic metal framework inside that could automatically open and close its toothy jaws.

BUILT TO LAST

Models that will be placed on display outdoors must be sturdy and long-lasting. Some larger models are built hollow with a custom metal frame inside to support the weight of their thousands of bricks. Permanent models are usually glued together to make sure no birds or passers-by make off with stray pieces.

YOU DON'T BECOME a company as enduring and globally-celebrated as the LEGO Group without trying a few experiments, using a lot of imagination, and thinking a little bit outside the box of bricks. What lies ahead for the future of creative construction, and which young stars will rise to become the next generation of building pioneers? Programs like these were developed to answer just those questions—and provide a whole lot of learning and fun along the way ●

21101 Hayabusa (2012)

LEGO® CUUSOO

"Where wishes come true" is the motto of LEGO® CUUSOO, a crowd sourcing experiment devoted to turning fans' dream LEGO projects into reality. The LEGO CUUSOO ("Imagination") website lets builders upload their model ideas and gather support from the online community. When an idea reaches 10,000 votes, the LEGO Group formally considers it for release as an official LEGO set.

Junichiro Kawaguchi, real-life Project Manager for the Hayabusa, was included when it was released as a LEGO CUUSOO set.

The second of two Japan-exclusive CUUSOO sets, the *Hayabusa* ("Falcon") was an unmanned spacecraft launched in 2003. It was designed to travel to an asteroid, collect samples from its surface, and return them to Earth for study.

Sampler

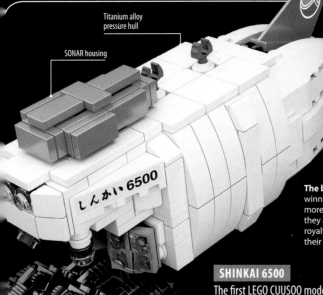

Titanium alloy pressure hull

SONAR housing

しんかい 6500

The builders of winning concepts get more than accolades— they also receive a 1% royalty on the sales of their set.

SHINKAI 6500

The first LEGO CUUSOO model was based on the Shinkai 6500, a real submarine with the greatest depth range of any manned research vehicle in the world. As the first concept to receive the originally required 1,000 votes, it was released as a 412-piece set in a limited edition of 10,000 sold exclusively in Japan

LIFE OF GEORGE

The first interactive Life of George set is designed to work with iOS and Android apps of the same name. Players follow George on his travels around the world as he challenges them to build specific models as fast as they can, then capture their creations with their digital device's camera.

The set includes 144 LEGO bricks and a special play mat to photograph models against.

21200 Life of George (2011)

Builders are graded on time and accuracy, and can compete in two-player mode. You can also create your own album to challenge your friends

High-gain antenna

Solar cell paddle

LEGO® MINECRAFT

Based on the immensely popula
online game, LEGO Minecraf
Micro World was the first ide
submission to earn 10,000 vote
on the new global LEGO CUUSO
website—and it took less tha
three days to do it. The mode
was made up of four cube-like
vignette sections that could be
taken apart and rearranged to
build different landscapes

21102 LEGO® Minecraft Micro World (2012)

The Minecraft model included
buildable "Micro Mobs" of Steve
(the player's avatar in the game)
and a deadly Creeper.

LEGO® MASTER BUILDER ACADEMY

Founded in 2011, "LEGO MBA" is a multi-level program designed to
teach LEGO fans to be better builders by learning the techniques of
the official LEGO Master Builders and model designers. Members
train with a series of themed kits, each containing a handbook and
a collection of bricks. An online site (LEGOmba.com) lets them
upload creations and test their knowledge of new skills.

LEGO® MASTER BUILDER
ACADEMY

20200 LEGO® Master
Builder Academy Kit 1:
Space Designer (2011)

By the time members reach
Level 3, they're experienced
enough to make their own new
story-telling adventure models.

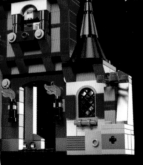

20206 LEGO® Master Builder Academy
Kit 7: The Lost Village (2012)

Each kit includes buildable
accessories for that level's
exclusive LEGO MBA minifigure.

LEVEL 3

LEVEL 2

LEVEL 1

LEGO® Brick Art

SOME ARTISTS paint on canvas. Others carve stone or weld metal. But a special few create art using the unique medium of LEGO® bricks and imagery. The work of these talented "Brick Artists" and others like them is a remarkable visual testament to the creative nature of LEGO building and the unlimited ways that it allows people to express themselves ●

EGO LEONARD

In August 2007, a giant minifigure washed ashore on a beach in the Netherlands. Standing 8 ft (2.5 m) tall and carrying the enigmatic message "NO REAL THAN YOU ARE" on his shirt, the mysterious, ever-smiling Ego Leonard claimed to hail from a virtual world without rules or limitations, and to want to see "all the beautiful things that are there to admire and experience in your world."

Newspapers and internet blogs around the world marveled at "the Giant LEGO Man" and wondered where he had come from.

"Reflection" (right) "is about seeing oneself in brick," Sawaya says. "As an artist, I tend to see the world in little rectangles, a lot like LEGO bricks."

"Reflection"
August 2006

"Red"
August 2005

NATHAN SAWAYA

Brick artist Nathan Sawaya is a full-time freelance builder based in New York. His imaginative life-sized LEGO sculptures and giant mosaic portraits have been featured on television and in a North American touring museum exhibit titled "The Art of the Brick®."

In November 2008, the Dutch artist had an art show in, appropriately enough, the Brick Lane Gallery in London, England.

"Blue"
January 2006

"Yellow"
February 2006

METAMORPHOSIS

Sinking into or emerging from a pile of bricks, opening up to reveal the inner nature, and even putting oneself together piece by piece, Nathan Sawaya's "Red," "Yellow," and "Blue" all represent transitions.

"I create art out of LEGO bricks to show people things they have never seen before, nor will they ever see anywhere else," the artist says.

"The Ant and the Shoe"
February 2009

"The Ant and the Shoe" (left) tells a fairy tale of tough friendship, while "Two Short Orders" spells financial trouble for a cook and an investor.

"Two Short Orders"
October 2008

SEAN KENNEY

Sean Kenney is a full-time artist, officially-licensed LEGO Certified Professional, and self-described "professional kid" who has made LEGO creations for television shows, museums, galleries, celebrities, stores, and companies all over the world. He builds his artwork at a New York City studio containing more than a million LEGO bricks.

"The Walker" 1989

ANDREW LIPSON & DANIEL SHIU

© A. Lipson 2003

Andrew Lipson is a LEGO builder and Technic fan who creates clever working mechanisms and mathematical brick sculptures. Together with fellow builder Daniel Shiu, he designs and constructs 3D recreations of the Dutch graphic artist M.C. Escher's mind-bendingly impossible, physics-defying illustrations, including Escher's "Relativity" in LEGO bricks

MOSAIC ART

Creating artistic mosaics and murals from LEGO bricks is a time-honored hobby for many. Up close, the two-dimensional designs are clearly patterns of solid squares and rectangles, but as you move further away, the shapes and colors become increasingly real. LEGO mosaic artists use everything from scientific graph paper to cross-stitch needlework computer programs to turn photos and paintings into building blueprints.

A LEGO mosaic of the "Mona Lisa," Leonardo da Vinci's famous 16th century masterpiece, was created in 1993 to show how basic brick colors could be combined to create subtle shades.

JØRN RØNNAU

Danish artist Jørn Rønnau grew up playing with the very first LEGO bricks. He describes "The Walker," which is made from 120,000 elements, as "an intuitive self-portrait... partly a robot, built from all kinds of special grey pieces, wheels, antennas, fire hoses, ladders, shovels, etc. He can hardly move his feet... but he is surely trying!"

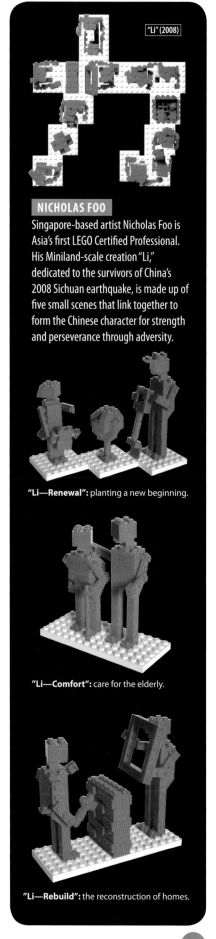

"Li" (2008)

NICHOLAS FOO

Singapore-based artist Nicholas Foo is Asia's first LEGO Certified Professional. His Miniland-scale creation "Li," dedicated to the survivors of China's 2008 Sichuan earthquake, is made up of five small scenes that link together to form the Chinese character for strength and perseverance through adversity.

"Li—Renewal": planting a new beginning.

"Li—Comfort": care for the elderly.

"Li—Rebuild": the reconstruction of homes.

Curved roof design inspired by the builder's own covered cart model

Fan Builders

ALL OVER THE WORLD, grown-ups are rediscovering their childhood love of LEGO® building—except for the ones who never lost it to begin with! With incredible talent and imagination, these AFOLs, or Adult Fans of LEGO, are pioneering new building techniques and detailing, attending fan groups and conventions, and showing off their passion for the LEGO brick every day ●

SOLAR FLARE
Lino Martins, an AFOL from the US, built this bright and sunny classic 1960s station wagon in MINILAND scale for his LEGO car-builder group. It was displayed along with a friend's night-themed car and their Rockabilly band drivers at the Brickcon08 fan convention.

THE BANK
Polish LEGO fan Paweł Michalak was inspired by the official Café Corner set (see p. 172) to create his own model in the Modular Buildings style. "The Bank" was built for the LUGPol (LEGO User Group—Poland) "Klocki Zdrój" diorama.

Nannan Zhang's tiny, high-tech Yamamura Bike was built to race through the streets of a futuristic city.

COLOGNE CATHEDRAL
Here's one dedicated AFOL! It took Jürgen Bramigk two long years to build this 10 ft (3 m) high model of Cologne Cathedral from his native Germany. Assembling it took about 900,000 LEGO bricks in different shades of gray.

Maciej Karwowski based his HD Bobber on the custom stripped-down motorcycles of the 1950s.

DAY AT THE STABLES
Marcin Danielek's model of a two-story country house with an attached horse stable includes details like a pile of chopped firewood, a dog chasing a cat up a tree, and a clever use of LEGO pieces to let a skirt-wearing minifigure sit down.

"CATCH UP!"

A 1955 San Francisco diner purchased by an eccentric billionaire and turned into a motorcycle and moped shop, this whimsical model was built by Jamie Spencer using custom decals and pieces from his LEGO City, LEGO Castle, and LEGO® *Star Wars*™ collections.

Decals on model were custom-made by the builder

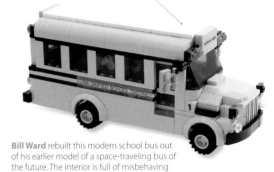

Roof recycled from Luna Unified School District, Bus No. 1

Bill Ward rebuilt this modern school bus out of his earlier model of a space-traveling bus of the future. The interior is full of misbehaving students and one very annoyed driver.

NOPPINGEN

German fan Rainer Kaufmann grew up with the LEGO sets of the 1970s and rediscovered building almost 20 years later. His expansive Noppingen town display started as a one-man project, but has grown to include models made by his fellow builders.

Terrace overhang built from "log wall" pieces

Rainer's Townhouse 3 model includes a sidewalk and section of street in front, and terraces overlooking a small yard at the back.

Lemming lives in the town of Noppingen. He loves walking, riding his bicycle, eating pizza, and showing tourists around his hometown.

Marvelous old houses like these are common in Noppingen. Lemming's was completely renovated and looks like new.

His favorite place is the balcony of his second-floor apartment. From there, he can look around and see the entire town.

PICTURE STORIES

Many AFOLs like to build models that tell stories. Some are single-scene vignettes; others, like Rainer's "Lemming Presents his House" story, are created as a series of changing pictures.

Fan-tasy & Sci-fi

OFFICIAL LEGO® SETS have to contain a fixed number of bricks, but there's no limit to the number of LEGO elements fan builders can use in their custom creations. Fan models can be as huge and as detailed as the builder desires. That really comes in handy when making other-worldly creations like spaceships and monsters ●

THE TOWER OF BROTHERS

Once upon a time in a long-forgotten land, two brothers fought against each other in a crumbling tower. Maciej Karwowski's LEGO Castle fan contest-winning model is filled with spiral staircases, a hanging chandelier, and an intricate use of small bricks to create an age-worn look.

Maciej used lots of small LEGO pieces to make his tower look like the site of an ancient battle.

Uneven stones from LEGO tiles

GOLDFISH BALLOON

Wafting, drifting, swimming in the vast sky… Goldfish Balloon! Japanese builder Sachiko Akinaga has been building for more than 25 years and is known for her beautifully colorful and imaginative LEGO brick creations. Her portfolio of artistic models includes a car with a food-themed town hiding inside, an Earth Park with a motorized escalator and color-changing fountain, and a fortune-telling elephant.

Creeping vines

Ruined road

Membranes made from LEGO glider wings

DRAGON FOREST

Bryce McGlone excels at using LEGO elements to create organic-looking shapes like robots and monsters. His Dragon Forest diorama, displayed at the BrickWorld 2007 LEGO fan convention, incorporates standard bricks with Technic parts to make a fierce mythical beast and rider.

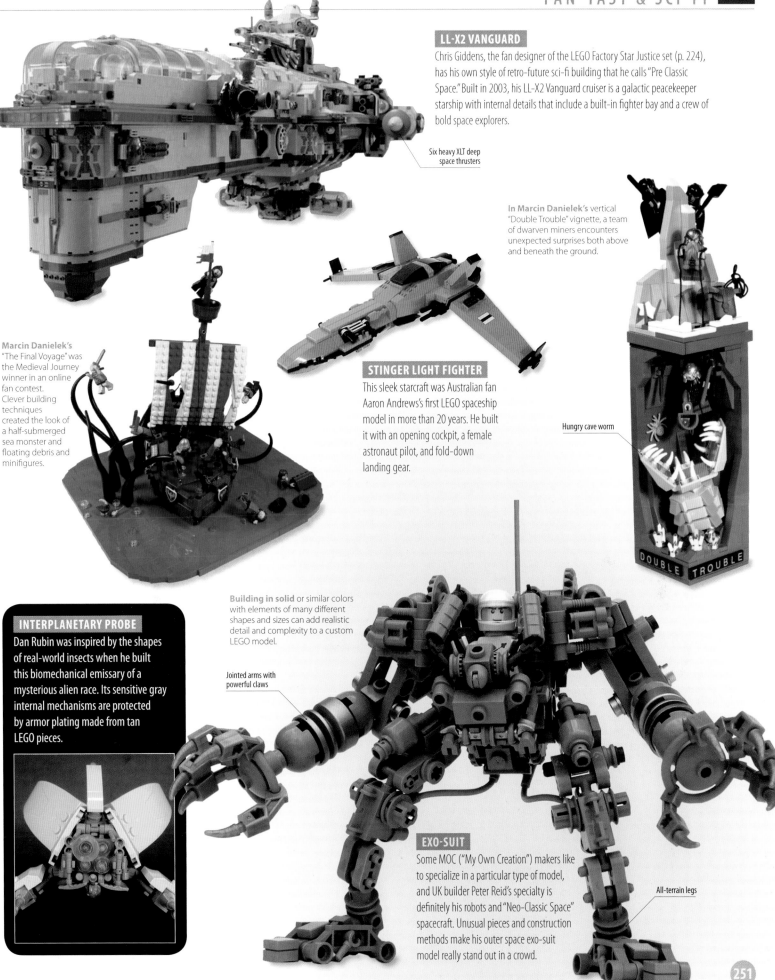

LL-X2 VANGUARD

Chris Giddens, the fan designer of the LEGO Factory Star Justice set (p. 224), has his own style of retro-future sci-fi building that he calls "Pre Classic Space." Built in 2003, his LL-X2 Vanguard cruiser is a galactic peacekeeper starship with internal details that include a built-in fighter bay and a crew of bold space explorers.

Six heavy XLT deep space thrusters

In Marcin Danielek's vertical "Double Trouble" vignette, a team of dwarven miners encounters unexpected surprises both above and beneath the ground.

Marcin Danielek's "The Final Voyage" was the Medieval Journey winner in an online fan contest. Clever building techniques created the look of a half-submerged sea monster and floating debris and minifigures.

Hungry cave worm

STINGER LIGHT FIGHTER

This sleek starcraft was Australian fan Aaron Andrews's first LEGO spaceship model in more than 20 years. He built it with an opening cockpit, a female astronaut pilot, and fold-down landing gear.

DOUBLE TROUBLE

Building in solid or similar colors with elements of many different shapes and sizes can add realistic detail and complexity to a custom LEGO model.

INTERPLANETARY PROBE

Dan Rubin was inspired by the shapes of real-world insects when he built this biomechanical emissary of a mysterious alien race. Its sensitive gray internal mechanisms are protected by armor plating made from tan LEGO pieces.

Jointed arms with powerful claws

EXO-SUIT

Some MOC ("My Own Creation") makers like to specialize in a particular type of model, and UK builder Peter Reid's specialty is definitely his robots and "Neo-Classic Space" spacecraft. Unusual pieces and construction methods make his outer space exo-suit model really stand out in a crowd.

All-terrain legs

Index

A

Action Wheelers 31
Adult Fans of LEGO (AFOLs) 248–51
Adventurers theme 28, 31, 33, 100–101
advertising 24, 28, 30, 130
Aero Booster 113
Aero Nomad 100
Agents theme 32, 33, 109, 119
airports 55, 61, 160
  LEGOLAND Deutschland 211
Alien Conquest 33, 84–85, 87, 103
aliens 39, 80, 81, 84–85, 87, 251
Allianz Arena 216–17
Allied Avenger 86
Alpha Team 31, 108
Amazon 100
Ambulance 149
Andrea's Stage 153
animals 39, 57, 59, 71, 173, 218
  Creator sets 143, 144
  DUPLO 38, 39, 159
  wooden pull-along 12, 13
anniversaries 19, 21, 25, 30, 32, 36, 233
Aqua Raiders 32, 104
Aquazone 28, 104, 119
Architecture series 32, 232
Arctic 31
Armada 93, 97
Armored Drilling Unit 81, 87
art 246–47
Art of LEGO exhibition 24
astrobots 31, 79
Atlantis 33, 85, 105, 119
Avatar: The Last Airbender 31, 199
Avengers, The 194
Axonn 132

B

Baby 24, 30, 162, 163, 201
baseplates 22, 38, 58, 86
Basil the Bat Lord 67, 68
Basketball 30, 124
Batman 31, 190–93, 226, 229, 231
Beach House 143
BELVILLE 28, 39, 150
Ben 10 33
Bendy Caterpillar 162

Bill Starling 31, 79
Billund 12, 16, 17, 20, 21, 22, 24, 42, 210
BILOfix 20
BIONICLE 31, 33, 39, 40, 121, 128–35, 136, 140, 141
  games 227
  movies 30, 31, 231
Black Falcons 24, 68, 74
Black Knights 66, 68
Black Phantom 138, 141
Black Seas Barracuda 90, 96
Blacksmith Attack 71
Blacksmith Shop 71, 73, 75
Blacktron 25, 78, 79, 86
Block-O-Dile 158
boats and ships 23, 56, 57, 62, 233
  Police Boat 149
  Pirates theme 88–97
  pre-school 160, 164
  Viking longboat 68
Bob the Builder 30
Bohrok 130, 131
books 31, 164, 165, 235
Breeze 137, 139
Brickfilms 231
BrickMaster 30, 237
brick separator 242
brick pick-up tools 29, 158
bricks 11, 12, 15, 16, 18, 34–37
  Automatic Binding Bricks 14, 16, 17, 38
  colors 30, 42, 45
  DUPLO 156
  light-bulb 21, 39
  manufacture 42–45, 219
  materials 14, 21
  patent 34–35
  programmable 38, 39, 174–76, 241
  QUATRO 38
  roof-tile 20
  shapes 34, 35
  SOFT 240
  stud and tube system 11, 21, 34, 35
Brok, Eric 172
building instructions 20

C

Camouflaged Outpost 69
Captain America 195
Captain Brickbeard 91, 92, 94
Captain Ironhook 93
Captain Redbeard 90, 92

carousel 171
cars 13, 111, 146, 148, 248
  Action Wheelers 31
  Creator series 142
  custom 224, 225
  DUPLO 160, 161
  Expert Series vintage cars 23
  Friends 153
  licensed themes 205
  Racers 30, 31, 120–23
  small car sets 22
  Super Models 170, 171
  Tiny Turbos 31, 120
  Town and City series 54, 59
  Town Plan sets 14, 18, 19
Cars movie 33, 205
Castle 22, 24, 29, 32, 38, 40, 46, 51, 64–75, 126, 250
  clothing 234
  DUPLO 159, 161
  licensed themes 196, 207
catalogs 26–27
catapults 67, 70, 74, 90
Cedric the Bull 67, 68, 75
Cement Mixer 148
Cherry Picker 149
chess 226, 233
Circus 158
Citadel of Orlan 69, 75
City 30, 32, 46, 52–61, 126, 234
City Police 33, 239
CLIKITS 31, 38, 151
Clone Wars 184–85, 214
clothing & accessories 28, 164, 234–35, 237
Clumsy Hans 12
Coast Guard 56, 61, 149
Comic Builder 238
competitions 24, 29, 31, 33, 224
computer control 24, 174, 175
Cool Cars 142, 148, 153
Core Hunter 139
crafts kits 245
cranes 47, 55, 56, 57, 59, 93, 168–69

Creative Cakes 159
Creator game 226, 227
Creator sets 33, 142–45
Crusaders 24, 68
Crystal Reaper 81
custom designs 32, 63, 224–25, 250–51

D

Dash Justice 108
DC Universe Super Heroes 33, 192–93
Design byMe 32, 33, 224, 225
design process 46–47
Designer Sets 31, 142
Destiny's Bounty 116–17
Digital Designer 224–25
Dino 33, 85, 103, 119
Dino 2010 30, 102, 118
dinosaurs 30, 31, 100, 102, 103, 118, 119, 143, 243
Discovery Centers 32, 33, 218–19
Discovery NASA sets 31
Disney themes 30, 32, 200–05
DUPLO Princess 33, 201
Disney Village, Florida 29
Dr. Inferno 109
Dr. Rodney Rathbone 110
dollhouses and furniture 23, 151, 153
Dolphin Point 60, 150
Dora the Explorer 30, 31, 199
Dragon Fortress 100, 118
Dragon Knights 70, 71
Dragon Masters 67
dragons 38, 66, 67, 75, 115, 144, 159, 218
Droid Developer Kit 175
duck, wooden 10, 12, 16
DUPLO 20, 21, 30, 151, 154–61
  airport 160
  animals 38, 39, 159
  bricks 38, 156
  buckets 24, 25, 159
  buckets & storage 24, 25, 157, 158, 159
  castles 159, 161
  catalogs 26
  Circus 158
  Disney themes 29, 32, 33, 201, 205
  Ferrari 122, 123

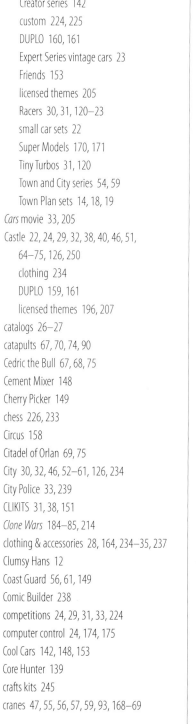

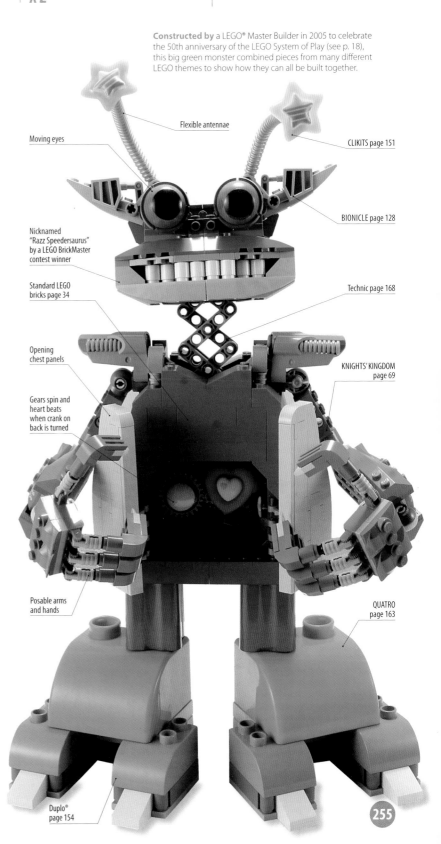

Constructed by a LEGO® Master Builder in 2005 to celebrate the 50th anniversary of the LEGO System of Play (see p. 18), this big green monster combined pieces from many different LEGO themes to show how they can all be built together.

Flexible antennae

Moving eyes

CLIKITS page 151

BIONICLE page 128

Nicknamed "Razz Speedersaurus" by a LEGO BrickMaster contest winner

Standard LEGO bricks page 34

Technic page 168

Opening chest panels

KNIGHTS' KINGDOM page 69

Gears spin and heart beats when crank on back is turned

Posable arms and hands

QUATRO page 163

Duplo® page 154

Acknowledgments

For Nina, John, and Amy

And with special thanks to Jette and Randi!

Picture credits
211 Corbis: Edmund D. Fountain/Zuma Press (far center right)

Special Photography
Tim Trøjborg Matthäi (Billund shoot), Brian Axel (cover).

Additional Photography
Joseph Pellegrino (pp.242–3), Ben Ellermann, Johannes Koehler, Yaron Dori, (pp.66–7, pp.68–9, pp.90–1, pp.92–3),
Daniel Rubin (pp. 78–9), Sarah Ashun (p.35), PHOTO: OOPSFOTOS.NL. (Mount Rushmore, p.22),
Steve Scott (Bilofix image, p.20), Nick Ricks of TT Games (pp. 228–9).

Brick Film Stills
Chris Salt, Curt Werline, Steffen Troeger (with Sandra Abele).

LEGO® Brick Artists
Nathan Sawaya, Jørn Rønnau, Ego Leonard, Andrew Lipson & Daniel Shiu, Sean Kenney, Nicholas Foo.

Adult Fans of LEGO (AFOLs)
Lino Martins, Paweł Michalak, Nannan Zsang, Jürgen Bramigk, Marcin Danielek, Maciej Karwowski,
Jaime Spencer, Rainer Kaufmann, Bill Ward, Sachiko Akinaga, Bryce McGlone, Chris Giddens, Marcin Danielek,
Aaron Andrews, Peter Reid, Dan Rubin.

Dorling Kindersley would like to thank the following for their help with the visual content of this book
Andy Crawford, Erik Andresen, Alexander Pitz, Monica Pedersen, Anders Gaasedal Christensen, Mona B. Petersen, Dale Chasse,
Erik Varszeg, Steve Gerling, Dan Steininger, Paul Chrzan, Mark Roe.

The Author and Dorling Kindersley would like to thank the following for their help in producing this book
Randi Kirsten Sørensen, Jette Orduna, Stephanie Lawrence, Keith Malone, Christina Bro Lund, Mona B. Petersen, Anja Sølvhviid,
Annemarie Kvist, Dawn Stailey, Gregory Farshtey, Haakon Smith-Meyer, Lluis Gilbert, Tobias Roegner, Valerie Barnes, Holger Matthes,
Anders N. Ravnskjær, Flemming Lund Kristensen, Jan Beyer, Richard Stollery, Anders Gaasedal Christensen, Monica Pedersen,
Peter Hobolt Jensen, Kristin Robinson, Hanne Bornstein, Jesper Just Jensen, Matthew James Ashton, Ronald Turcotte,
Benjamin Jackson, Annmarie Lomonaco, Nicholas Ricks, James Hall, Bill Vollbrecht, Valerie Barnes, Mike Pastor, Nicholas Groves,
Heidi Bailey, the entire international LEGO® Club team, Steve Witt, Jordan Schwarz, Jeramy Spurgeon, Daniel Rubin,
Mark Sandlin, Ben Ellermann, John McCormack, Brian Regini, Sanne Østergaard Jacobsen, Kelly McKiernan, Danielle Ezold,
Lisa Chiarella, Yole Anna Russo, Tine Froberg Mortensen, Kristian Hauge, Shawn Curtis, Jason Cosler, Melinda Oakes,
Phillip Ring from TT Games, Erni Marlina, Dawn Stailey, Ali Sayers, Ali Slayton.